N.Y.) Sheltering Arms (New York

Annual Report of the trustees of the Sheltering Arms

1867-1873

N.Y.) Sheltering Arms (New York

Annual Report of the trustees of the Sheltering Arms
1867-1873

ISBN/EAN: 9783741177415

Manufactured in Europe, USA, Canada, Australia, Japa

Cover: Foto ©Andreas Hilbeck / pixelio.de

Manufactured and distributed by brebook publishing software (www.brebook.com)

N.Y.) Sheltering Arms (New York

Annual Report of the trustees of the Sheltering Arms

SHELTERING A]

THIRD ANNUAL REPORT.

NEW-YORK,

1867.

New-York:
F. NESBITT & CO., PRINTERS AND ST:
CORNER OF PEARL AND PINE STREETS.

Trustees of The Sheltering Arms.

President.
Rev. THOMAS M. PETERS, D.D., Address, B'way, cor. 101st St.

Vice-Presidents.
FRED'K S. WINSTON, -	-	Address, 144 Broadway.
WM. ALEX. SMITH, -	- -	" 63 Wall Street.
WM. J. BEEBE,	- - -	" 149 Front Street.

Secretary.
HENRY J. CAMMANN, - - Address, 52 Beaver Street.

Treasurer.
HERMANN C. VON POST, - Address, 68 Broad Street.

BENJ. H. FIELD,	127 Water Street.
JAMES PUNNETT,	Bank of America.
WM. K. KITCHEN.	Park Bank.
WM. A. HAYNES,	374 Broadway.
B. WATSON BULL,	44 Cedar Street.
GIDEON POTT,	61 Wall Street.
REV. ROBERT S. HOWLAND, D. D.,	400 West Twenty-third Street.
D. TILDEN BROWN, M. D.,	Manhattanville.
PETER C. TIEMANN,	Manhattanville.
WM. B. CLERKE,	25 William Street.
CHARLES H. POND,	177 Broadway.
WM. B. ASTEN,	35 Pearl Street.
WM. L. ANDREWS,	72 Gold Street.
FREDERICK HUBBARD,	44 Irving Place.
WM. H. FOGG,	32 Burling Slip.

Visitor.
Rt. Rev. H. POTTER, D. D., D. C. L.

Physician.

ANK A. UTTER, M. D.,   -   Broadway, near 100th Street

Consulting Physician.

B. DALTON, M. D., -   -   -   - 99 Madison Avenue.

ıdies' Association of The Sheltering Arms.

ıs J. VAN HORNE, *Secretary*, 31 Chambers Street.
   E. KEMBLE, *Treasurer*, - 52 West Twenty-fifth Street.
   S. CAMMANN, -   -   Fordham.
   M. CHAUNCEY, - - 53 West Thirty-sixth Street.
   S. E. KITCHEN, - - Park Bank.
ɜ. WM. P. LEE, - - - 326 Fifth Avenue.
ɜs S. B. NEWBY, - - 184 West Twenty-eighth St.
   L. PETERS, - - - Broadway, corner 101st Street.
   J. A. TIEMANN, -   Manhattanville.
   S. E. WHEELER, - - 43 West Twenty-fifth Street.
   A. M. CAMMANN, - 31 West Thirty-third Street.
   S. BOSTWICK, - - 75 East Twenty-second Street.
   L. LAWRENCE, - - Fordham.
   KATE COMSTOCK, - 141 West Twenty-second Street.
   F. A. COOPER, - - 17 Burling Slip.
ɜ. WM. C. GILMAN, - - 19 West Thirty-first Street.

THIRD ANNUAL REPORT

OF THE

Trustees of The Sheltering Arms.

As this Report may fall into the hands of many persons unacquainted with the aim of the Institution, the following sentences, indicating precisely the purpose of the Trustees, are quoted from the Report of the first year:

"The object of this Incorporation is thus stated in the Circular issued last autumn:

"'The Sheltering Arms is intended to furnish a home for various classes of children who, under present rules, cannot be admitted, or are not likely to be sent by their friends to any existing institution.'

"In their desire fully to supply the gap remaining in the public charities of the city, the Trustees announced the intention of taking all children, however young, and without regard to the state of their health, provided they are not ill with contagious diseases.

"Acting upon the advice of persons of long experience in the administration of city charities, the Trustees of The Sheltering Arms have considered that their original intention would be most thoroughly carried out by requiring of the friends of children received, a payment for board. Parents unable, from various reasons, to keep their children at home, and unwilling to give up the control of their own offspring, place them here, subject at any time to withdrawal, and pay, according to their means, a third or a half, or larger proportion of the expenses of their support. Several of our children must be, through life, dependent upon others' aid, being blind or dumb, or permanently crippled. Blind children or deaf mutes are kept only until they reach the age limited for admission into the Blind or Deaf and Dumb Asylums. Incurables and hopeless cripples have from the beginning formed part of our household. These disabled children have generally found friends in some individual or Sunday-school or Church, ready to assume the entire charge of their support.

" The larger part of the children have parents living, and yet either have no home, or none where they would receive proper physical care or moral training. Some are placed here by fathers of small means, with wives invalid, or owing to intemperance or other bad habits unfit to have the care of their children, paying so much as they are able of the cost of maintenance. Mothers deserted by their husbands, or for any cause thrown upon their own exertions for support, in like manner commit their little ones to The Sheltering Arms, going out themselves for day's work or household service, and paying as board for their children part of their earnings or wages. Children once sadly neglected, in some cases, indeed, living in squalidness and filth, are now clean and orderly under the roof of this home, are merry and happy, as they are trained for usefulness in the present life, for heaven in the next."

The original intention has been carried out to the present time, save that infants of a few months are no longer received, both because it was found almost impossible to rear them and also because better provision for that class of children is made at the Infants' Nursery.

The Trustees, in reviewing the record of the past twelve months, find many causes for thankfulness to God and abundant reason for encouragement; nevertheless they cannot altogether repress the regret that they are so far from fulfilling their desire of receiving many more in need of such a home as has been here provided.

They cannot be too thankful that the misgivings with which their weak faith undertook, a year ago, the support of a household more than doubled, increased in one day from forty children to ninety, have proved utterly groundless. He whose are all riches and all souls has sent us new friends and opened to our anxious sight many fresh sources of supply. The same effort upon the part of the Trustees which brought in $6,000 the year previous has met the outlay of $11,000 for the year just closed.

Under the blessing of God, the general health of the many weak and sickly children admitted upon the erection of the new building has greatly improved. Wasted forms have rounded into fulness, and pale cheeks taken on the hue of health. To the self-denying attention of the sisters, having charge of the house, is owing much of this success. Our thanks are due further to Drs. Carmalt and Watts, who, with great inconvenience to themselves, have, during the year, faithfully fulfilled their voluntary task; also to Dr. James Knight, who has kindly given apparatus needed by the crippled children. With all the care bestowed, however, a few sweet little faces, which lighted up at the kind ministrations of gentle hands, smile upon us no more. The perishing scenes of human life have given place to the changeless glory of the eternal world. In the arms of the Good Shepherd they have gained a better shelter. Six little beds have been emptied of their occupants; six little graves in St. Michael's Cemetery cover those loved forms.

The whole number of children in the house during the year was 137. Of these, 38 have been returned to friends, 3 sent to other institutions, 6 have died, and 90 now remain. Six of these are permanent cripples, one is blind, and one of feeble mind.

While recording what has been accomplished, we must not conceal the extent to which we have fallen short. Those for whom there is room form but a small proportion of the needy applicants. Hundreds of children have been refused admission, not a few of them cases of peculiar hardship—denied entrance solely because there was no room.

The attempt in some degree to accommodate beyond our necessarily limited number has caused to some of our friends a disappointment of another kind. The expectation was held out at the beginning of this undertaking that the receipts for board from relatives of the children would meet a third, perhaps one-half, the current expenses. Among the crowd of applicants, however, it was necessary to discriminate. Should it be by admitting those who could pay the most or those in greatest destitution? In the one case the poor children must suffer, in the other the treasury. We chose rather to throw the burden upon the latter, and, accordingly, have taken in the utterly helpless, sending away others whose friends could pay elsewhere for an endurable though not desirable home. Not a few have been received entirely without charge, in order that the slender means of a parent might be devoted to procuring elsewhere for one or two other children a safe and comfortable boarding place. Were it in our power to admit all proper applicants the proportion of our expenses chargeable to the charitable fund would be greatly lessened.

It has often been asked why we do not take the same course with some other institutions, and procure large grants from the City or State. We reply, some of the Trustees have advocated this resort; others have considered that charitable institutions, organized and carried on neither by the City nor the State, should be supported by those especially interested. The President of the Board has never doubted that charity would do this work more thoroughly than any donations of public funds drawn compulsorily by taxation from those who may disapprove our principles and our practice. Such a resource must some day fail us. Our work is, we know, God's work, who will not cease to raise us up friends. Into the hearts of many unknown to us by face has He put the desire to aid us. Our list of contributions tells how many little rills from widely separated fountains have helped to swell our stream of supply. From States near and distant, from among all denominations of Christians, and from the descendants of Abraham, have donations been received. These voluntary gifts of willing hearts and liberal hands are our surest reliance. It was thought by some a rash venture when, entirely without funds, we opened with forty children. It was rather startling to good friends when, after eighteen months of existence, we said, we have ninety children to carry through the next year. Yet the forty were fed and clothed. So were the ninety. In our Fourth Report we hope to say, we count now one hundred and twenty.

And how is this ever-increasing family to be supported? As hitherto, so in the future; one must tell our story to another, with an invitation to visit our house. Parents and teachers must set the children at work in families, and societies, and schools. It is the care of children in need; let them be cared for by the children of plenty. If any Sunday-school or circle of children desire a child to look after, and pay the $10 monthly and clothe their protégé, let some one come and make a selection. If in or about the city, visit us; if at a distance, write. Money is always welcome; so is clothing, new or old. If you meet with any subject for our care, especially if it be a crippled child, make application; perhaps we can take it in.

We must have more room, however, to supply which will be our next great effort. The luxury of New-York has invaded our retired and quiet home. The new drive, or boulevard, as some name it, sweeps away the recently finished building and destroys our grounds. It is, in the opinion of the Trustees, more to the interest of the Institution that the money awarded us by the Commissioners should be used in the purchase of ground on which to erect suitable buildings than to incur any further expense upon our present leased and much diminished premises. After examining various locations, on the island and off, it has been decided to purchase about an acre of ground in Manhattanville, on Tenth Avenue, Lawrence Street and One Hundred and Twenty-ninth Street, and to erect buildings in which the children will be in separate families of twenty-five each. The required accommodations for a family are estimated to cost $5,000. One individual has subscribed $5,000 to build such a cottage. May our Heavenly Father send us many like-minded friends. The cottages thus provided for will be known by the name of the individual or church contributing the funds. There have also been received further subscriptions towards this permanent property to the amount of $3,200. No general application has yet been made, as, until the negotiations for the land were successfully closed, no specific plans could be laid before the public. The Trustees are happy to announce that the bargain for the purchase is at length concluded, and further hereby inform their friends that, in addition to the $11,000 for current expenses, there is wanted $50,000 the present year, for buildings and payment on property. The amount may be deemed large. It is, however, the object of the Trustees to place this Charity on a permanent footing, with ample buildings and no debt. This end reached, the current expenses will be easily met.

As God has been with us in the days which are past, so may He also prosper us in the time to come.

T. M. PETERS,
President.

TREASURER'S REPORT, MAY 1, 1867.

By Balance of last Report		$158 96
Donations and Subscriptions		9,610 04
Board		1,585 67
Loan		5,000 00
		$16,354 67
To Bills paid for completing extension	$2,753 87	
Bills paid for furnishing the same	1,127 71	
Current expenses, viz.:		
Bread	$2,014 14	
Milk	912 84	
Meat	1,710 49	
Groceries and vegetables	1,808 00	
Fuel	607 25	
Gas	301 60	
Wages and labor	1,065 65	
Repairs and alterations	753 72	
Insurance	78 83	
Taxes	184 00	
Household materials	399 37	
Printing and advertising	142 78	
Rent of School-room	150 00	
Sundries	754 06	
		10,882 73
Christmas and Thanksgiving expenses	244 85	
Interest, at six per cent., on Loan	194 41	
Loan of last year paid off	700 00	
		15,903 57
Balance in the Treasury May 1, 1867		$451 10

LIST OF DONATIONS.

Ch. All Angels..	$ 3 00
W. L. Andrews, through Miss S. Cammann................	100 00
D. H. Arnold...	10 00
Anonymous...	5 00
Anthon Memorial Church.................................	167 25
W. Armstrong..	100 00
Abbatt & Moore..	10 00
Articles from Fair.......................................	4 00
Wm. H. Aspinwall..	50 00
Mrs. Aaron Arnold, through Miss A. Cammann...........	25 00
Mr. Alvord...	5 00
Mrs. R. T. Auchmuty.....................................	20 00
Alms Box...	66 22
Miss Anthony...	11 00
Annandale Parish School, older girls and boys..........	18 00
Mrs. Eliza B. Ash..	10 00
Mrs. Beach, through Miss Kitchen	5 00
B. W. Bull..	50 00
W. Boskerck..	2 00
Mrs. James Brooks	5 00
H. J. B...	25 00
Mrs. B. W. Bull..	5 00
Mrs. W. Bradford	50 00
James J. Bricknell, through Miss Louise Lawrence.......	25 00
Cora L. Bull, savings, through Miss Peters..............	50 00
Mrs. N. P. Bailey, through Miss A. Cammann............	25 00
Jas. Bogart...	25 00
Miss Amy Boardman.....................................	5 00
J. B., through Miss Kemble...............................	20 00
Edward A. Bibby...	5 00

Mr. Burrill	$3 00
S. B. Jr.,	10 00
Herm. Bruen	5 00
W. Belden	5 00
W. J. Beebe, for Christmas	15 00
Mrs. Chas. Beebe, for Christmas	25 00
Allie Beebe, for Christmas	1 68
Mrs. Geo. Bliss, Jr., for Christmas	5 00
Mrs. Dr. Brown, for Christmas	5 00
Mrs. Dr. Bumstead, for Christmas	5 00
W. J. Beebe	250 00
Cash	50 00
Church of the Intercession Sunday School	1 00
Cyrus Curtiss	50 00
Columbia Hall, Lebanon Springs, Children's Fair, through Mrs. J. B. Kissam	113 80
Calvary Church collection	75 00
Cash	25 00
Cash	20 00
Cash	5 00
Carlos Cobb	20 00
Cash	5 00
Jay Cooke & Co., through Miss S. Cammann	100 00
W. B. Clerke	25 00
Cash	10 00
Christ Church, Riverdale, Sunday School	20 00
Cash, through Miss Louise Lawrence	85 00
Mrs. Peter Cooper, through Miss Tiemann	100 00
Peter Cooper Golden Wedding Fund	50 00
Church of the Ascension Fair, Mrs. Steers	310 00
Thos. Crane	25 00
Geo. T. Curtis	5 00
Marg. J. Corlies, through J. J. Haydock	5 00
Christ Church, Stratford, Ct., Sunday School Anniversary Offering	15 00

Cassidy & Co	$25 00
Cash	1 00
F. W. Coggill	25 00
Stephen Cambreleng	25 00
Church of the Holy Apostles, through Miss Newby	50 00
Miss M. Collins, through Miss A. Cammann	5 00
Miss Carpenter	10 00
Cash	10 00
Cash	5 00
Cash	3 00
Cash	50
Cash	10 00
Cash	1 00
Children's Charity Box	5 18
H. Colt	10 00
Church of the Holy Trinity collection	496 00
John Caswell, for permanent building	100 00
James W. Coates, for Christmas	5 00
Mrs. and Miss Cammann, for Christmas	14 00
H. B. Claflin & Co., for Christmas	4 45
Church of the Advent Sunday School	25 00
Children's Charity Box	50
Calvary Church collection	150 00
Cash	1 00
Cash	5 00
Cash	50
Cash	5 00
Mrs. W. H. Draper	20 00
Samuel Davis, through Miss A Cammann	10 00
H. E. Davies	5 00
General Davies	5 00
C. F. D.	10 00
Mrs. Frederick de Peyster	100 00
Mrs. Dashwood	10 00
J. E., through Miss Kemble	10 00

Elmira, through Miss Louise Lawrence.......................	$30	00
A Friend in South Orange................................	25	00
A Friend, through Miss Kemble	2	00
A Friend, through Miss Wheeler.........................	10	00
A Friend in China, through S. E. Moran, Jr................	88	77
A Friend..	100	00
Thos. H. Faile...	200	00
C. B. Foote..	2	00
A Friend, through John A. Marsh........................	50	00
Fair of Leila M. Eagle, Louise Joyce, Priscilla Duke, Amelia Duke, Augusta Martin, and Carrie Uhlfelder.............	85	00
D. B. Fayerweather.....................................	100	00
J. H. Falconer...	25	00
Fawcett & Benedict.....................................	50	00
Miss Ferguson...	20	00
A Friend..	3	00
F. R. Fowler...	25	00
A Friend..	2	00
Furnace man, for Christmas..............................		25
Four Friends..	10	00
Grace Church, Cherry Valley............................	8	00
Grace and St. Thomas' Churches, Collections.............	512	30
Rev. E. M. Gushee, through Rev. A. B. Hart.............	20	00
W. H. G...	10	00
Mrs. Gerry..	10	00
Mrs. W. C. Gilman	5	00
Rev. Horace Hills......................................	4	00
Hobart Hall Young Ladies, through Rev. Mr. Elmendorf.....	10	00
Mrs. Adam Hay..	2	06
A. S. Hewitt...	50	00
Mrs. Hayes..	6	56
Mrs. T. H. Hubbard....................................	50	00
Mrs. J. W. Hull..	2	00

R. S. H.	$21 00
Mr. Hollingsworth, through Rev. Samuel Hollingsworth, Port Chester	5 00
M. P. H., Thank-offering, through Miss Kemble	10 00
Mrs. W. H. Hurlbut	50 00
James Hartshorne	10 00
Mr. Hurxthal	5 00
S. Verplanck Hoffmann, through Bishop Neely and Mrs. Lee	25 00
Humbert & Co.	2 00
Frederick Hubbard	150 00
Frederick Hubbard, for Christmas and Uniforms	75 00
F. L. H.	1 25
Mrs. Johnson	8 00
Mrs. Charles Jackson, Westchester	5 00
J. L. Jones	25 00
Shepherd Knapp	5 00
Nora Kinney, through Miss Kitchen	2 00
Mrs. N. G. Kortright	10 00
Charles Kneeland	25 00
J. G. King	5 00
Mrs. Lazarus	5 00
Samuel E. Lyon	5 00
Mrs. Charles C. Leigh, through Miss Tiemann	5 00
Cambridge Livingston	10 00
Robt. J. Livingston	100 00
Cyrus J. Lawrence	10 00
H. T. Livingston	25 00
M. Livingston	15 00
W. Livingston	5 00
Mrs. W. C. Moore	10 00
Mrs. Murray	1 00
E. Matthews	25 00

Dr. Metcalfe...	$25 00
Daniel Morrison...	25 00
Fannie Mortimer, Amy Blatchford, Annie Milford, Fanny and Annie Freeborn, Clara Keyes, Kittie Hayden, Kittie Carter, Minnie Buckmaster, Ida Rowes, Edith Watson..........	1 72
J. Macy & Sons...	25 00
J. F. B. M...	10 00
M. T. Merritt..	5 00
Thos. T. Morris..	5 00
Henry Morgan...	25 00
Miss Bertha Miller, through Miss Kitchen.................	2 80
J. W. Minturn, for a permanent Building..................	100 00
Rev. Dr. Montgomery, for Christmas.......................	5 00
B. C. Morris, Jr., for Christmas.........................	5 00
Mrs. M. McDougal, through Miss Newby.....................	10 00
Mrs N...	5 00
Miss N..	5 00
A. Norrie...	100 00
Rev. Samuel Osgood......................................	25 00
O., for Christmas.......................................	1 00
James Punnett...	50 00
M. Porter...	10 00
W. W. Parkin..	20 00
E D. Peters, through Miss Peters........................	25 00
J. Pickard..	25 00
Penfold, Schuyler & Co..................................	25 00
John Pyne...	15 00
A. Craig Palmer...	25 00
C. H. P...	10 00
C. L. Perkins...	10 00
Penny Savings, for Christmas............................	3 76
Louise Punnett..	9 00
Anna Punnet	5 00

Rev. Sylvanus Reed...	$5 00
J. A. Roosevelt...	50 00
W. Rusch...	5 00
J. Renwick...	10 00
Mrs. C. Renshaw, through Miss Chauncey.....................	5 00
Lewis H. Russell, Stratford, Ct..............................	10 00
T. W. Riley..	20 00
Thomas Robins, Jr...	5 00
W. B. R..	100 00
S. Weir Roosevelt..	25 00
Mrs. Rose..	1,000 00
Mrs. Reeder..	10 00
Mrs. L. A. Rodenstein, through Miss Tiemann................	5 00
St. Andrew's Church Sunday-School, Ann Arbor, Mich.......	7 68
St. Luke's Day-School..	5 49
St. James' Church Sunday School, Infant Class, New London, Ct...	55
W. Alex. Smith...	50 00
St. Ann's Church...	24 00
Rev. James Smith..	10 00
Mrs. Smith...	1 00
Francis P. Sage..	10 00
St. John's Church, Stamford, Ct...............................	25 00
Charles L. Skidmore..	5 00
South Orange Presbyterian Sabbath-School.....................	45 00
W. H. Stewart, through Miss Chauncey.......................	25 00
Mrs. Jane E. Smith..	25 00
St. Mary's Church, Manhattanville............................	57 06
St. Michael's Church Sunday-School...........................	13 00
Mrs. W. Alex. Smith, through Mrs. W. C. Schermerhorn.....	10 00
Miss F. Sabine...	5 00
S. T. Skidmore...	5 00
St. James' Church, New London Sunday-School................	60 00
A. D. Stewart..	20 00
St. Mary's Church Sunday-School, Manhattanville............	25 00

A. D. S.	$5 00
David Stewart	50 00
St. James' Church Sunday-School	10 00
C. Howden Smith	2 00
M. D. Sands	10 00
Mrs. Aug. Schermerhorn	50 00
W. Alex. Smith, for Thanksgiving	5 00
Mrs. W. Alex. Smith, for Thanksgiving	5 00
W. Alex. Smith, for Christmas	6 00
St. Clement's Church, Easter offering	50 20
Little Frankie Schreiber	65
St. John's Church, Stamford, Ct., twenty poor children of Mission School	1 25
Mrs. C. L. Spencer, through Miss A. Cammann	100 00
Mrs. Titus	5 00
Mrs. Titus	10 00
Townsend & Davis	26 71
W. Tracy	25 00
Chas. Tracy	5 00
Lewis G. Timpson	5 00
G. T. Thomas, Jr.	2 00
P. C. Tiemann, for Christmas	20 00
Miss Antoinette Tiemann, for Christmas	5 00
Miss Julia Tiemann, for Christmas	2 00
Trinity Church Children	80 91
Mrs. Thorne	10 00
Unknown, for Burials	18 12
Unknown,	5 00
Unknown, through James Pott	5 00
Unknown, for Thanksgiving	25 00
C. Van Santvoord	10 00
H. C. Von Post	100 00
Verein Sewing Society	10 00
Mrs. J. C. Van Horne	5 00

Wooster Street Union Mission Sunday School	$23 00
W. & W	5 00
D. E. W	10 00
Stephen Williams	5 00
John D. Wolfe, through Miss A. Cammann	100 00
John Wells	20 00
Wells Brothers, through Miss Louis Lawrence	25 00
Wm. Whitlock, Jr	25 00
F. Wigand & Co	25 00
Howard Wainwright	5 00
Mrs. Wissner	5 00
Mrs. Elias Wade, Jr	25 00
Mrs. Edwin White	10 00
Mrs. Sidney Webster, through Miss Kemble	10 00
C. S. Weymann, through Miss A. Cammann	5 00
Mrs. James L. White	10 00
Mrs. Wotherspoon, for Christmas	10 00
Miss Whitlock, for Christmas	5 00
Miss Wisner, for Christmas	1 00
Horace Williams, for Christmas	20 00
Mrs. Dr. Watts, for Christmas	20 00
Mary Louise White	5 00
Freddie Morris White, for Christmas	5 00
Wooster Street Union Mission Sunday School, for Christmas	14 75
Mrs. Walker, for her three children	8 00
Mrs. Westray	5 00
Henry J. Young, for Christmas	10 00
Mrs. Zabriskie	20 00
Mrs. Zabriskie	10 00
Mrs. Zabriskie's Children	6 00

LIST OF ANNUAL SUBSCRIPTIONS.

Mrs. Herman D. Aldrich, through Miss Kemble.............	$10 00
Miss Lucy Boardman......................................	5 00
Miss Lucy Boardman, through Miss Kemble................	5 00
D. B. Bedell...	5 00
Miss Boardman, through Miss C. Willett..................	5 00
Mrs. F. J. Bumstead, through Miss Wisner................	5 00
C...	3 00
Thos. P. Cummings.......................................	10 00
Mrs. Colden, through Miss Kemble........................	5 00
Miss M. Cooke, through Miss Kemble......................	5 00
Herman H. Cammann, through Miss A. Cammann..........	5 00
Miss Cunard...	5 00
Mrs. A. B. Dash, through Miss Kemble....................	5 00
Mrs. James F. De Peyster...............................	25 00
Mrs. W. P. Dixon, through Miss Peters...................	10 00
Mrs. James A. Edgar, through Miss Kemble................	5 00
Mrs. Danl. Edgar, through Miss A. Cammann..............	5 00
Miss Emmet	3 00
A Friend..	10 00
Mrs. Fitzgerald...	10 00
Mrs. Farnsworth...	10 00
Mrs. W. H. Guion, through Miss Kemble..................	10 00
Mrs. Gerry..	5 00
Miss Emily Hollingsworth, Port Chester..................	5 00
Mrs. John C. Hull, through Miss Chauncey	3 00
Chas. W. Hull, through Miss Chauncey....................	5 00
Mrs. Abram S. Hewitt....................................	10 00
Mrs. Watson Dildreth, through Miss Chauncey.............	5 00

W. J. Jenkins..	$10 00
Mary S. Jones...	5 00
Miss E. Kemble...	5 00
Mrs. Cambridge Livingston, through Miss Kemble..........	5 00
Mrs. W. P. Lee, through Mrs. Lee........................	5 00
Rev. Mr. Mowbray.......................................	5 00
Mrs. A. B. Morrell......................................	5 00
Ed. Molineux...	5 00
Mrs. John B. Murray, through Miss Kemble................	5 00
Mrs. John T. Metcalfe...................................	5 00
Mrs. McEvers...	5 00
Mrs. J. P. Nazro, through Mrs. Lee......................	3 00
Miss Newby...	5 00
Samuel Newby, through Miss Newby........................	5 00
Mrs. J. B. Ogden, through Miss A. Cammann...............	5 00
Mrs. John J. Phelps.....................................	10 00
Edward D. Peters.......................................	25 00
Mrs. J. P. Phœnix, through Mrs. Lee.....................	5 00
Mrs. L. A. Rodenstein...................................	5 00
Geo. A. Robbins..	10 00
Mrs. Thos. Rutter, through Miss Chauncey................	3 00
Miss C. L. Renshaw, through Miss Chauncey...............	3 00
Mrs. W. Alex. Smith, through Miss Kemble................	5 00
G. Schwab..	10 00
Mrs. Aug. Schermerhorn..................................	5 00
Mrs. C. L. Spencer, through Miss A. Cammann.............	10 00
Miss Catherine P. Tracey, through Mrs. Lee..............	5 00
Miss Tunis' Infant School, through Miss Chauncey........	1 50

Miss C. Van Wyck, Manhattanville........................	$5 00
Mrs. Von Post..	5 00
Mrs. W. H. Wisner.....................................	10 00
Miss A. Wilkes, through Miss Kemble	5 00
Miss G. Wilkes, through Miss Kemble....................	5 00
Miss A. K. Wilkes, through Miss Kemble.................	5 00
Mrs. Robert Winthrop, through Miss Kemble..............	5 00
Mrs. Dr. Ward, through Miss A. Cammann................	3 00
Mrs. Hannah D. Weyman, through Miss Kemble...........	10 00
Mrs. Samuel Wetmore, through Miss Kemble..............	5 00
Hamilton F. Webster, through Miss Kemble...............	5 00
Mrs. Samuel H. Whitlock...............................	5 00

BOARD PAID BY PATRONS AND SUNDAY SCHOOLS.

Mrs. W. J. Beebe.....................................	80 00
Mrs. Ogden Hoffman..................................	80 00
Miss Hoffman...	60 00
Rev. Dr. Hallam......................................	60 00
St. Ann's Church Sunday School........................	132 00

H. C. VON POST,
Treasurer.

DONATIONS IN CLOTHING, PROVISIONS, Etc.

Miss Anthony, Clothing.
Miss Anthony's Sunday School Class, 12 new Garments.
Mr. Andrews, 1 bbl. Apples, Toys and Books.

Mrs. Dr. Brown, Clothing, 6 new Garments.
Mrs. Bacon, South Orange, Clothing.
Mrs. Charles E. Beebe, Clothing.
Miss S. Bostwick, 6 new Garments and 24 Handkerchiefs.
C. H. Bowman, 1 piece Linen Check.
N. A. Baldwin, 10 cases Straw Hats.
H. C. Baldwin, 1 case Felt.
W. H. Beebe, 100 Oranges.
W. J. Beebe, 1 chest Tea.
Mrs. Bliss, 2 Pictures.
Mrs. Bull, Toys.
Mrs. W. J. Beebe, Clothing for one child.

Mr. Claflin, Fordham, 4 bbls. Apples.
Miss Chew, New London, Ct., Clothing.
Mrs. M. H. Caswell, 48 new Garments.
Miss Belle Cooper, 1 Child's Chair.
Mr. J. W. Coates, 2 days' Painting.
Samuel Colgate, 9 doz. cakes Toilet Soap.
Misses Cammann, Toys, Books and Dolls.
Mr. H. J. Cammann, Vegetables, India-Rubber Balls, Candles and Christmas Ornaments.
Church of the Incarnation Fair, a Charity Box.
Church of the Ascension, Miss Steer's Fair, large box of Toys.

Mr. U. H. Dudley, 1 sack Nuts.
Rev. Mr. De Costa, Toys.

Henry Evans, Brooklyn, remnants of new Cloth.
C. Eddy, half bbl. White Sugar.
Rev. Mr. Elmendorf, Illuminated Texts.
Mrs. Wm. Everts, 1 Child's Carriage.

Mrs. James Filor, Clothing.
Mrs. B. H. Field, 41 new Garments and New Material.
A Friend, 5 new Garments.
A Friend, 14 new Garments.
Miss Ferguson, 9 new Garments and 20 pair Stockings.
A Friend, 5 pair Stockings.
Mr. Sands W. Fish, 8 doz. Handkerchiefs.
A Friend, Medicines for the year.

Mrs. Gillespie, 12 new Garments.
Mrs. Glover, 6 new Garments.

Mrs. Edward Haight, Clothing.
Miss Phebe Hewlet, 12 new Garments.
Mrs. Ogden Hoffman, Clothing for 1 Child.
Miss Hoffman, Clothing for 1 Child.

Ladies in Milford, Ct., bbl. of Clothing.
Mrs. W. P. Lee, 11 new Garments.
Ladies' Sewing Society, West Point, 54 new Garments.
Ladies of Church of the Incarnation, making up boys' Uniforms.
Mrs. M. H. Lewis's Sewing-Class, New London, Ct., 8 new Garments and 7 Bibs.
Mrs. W. P. Lee, Clothing, 10 new Garments, Candies and Bon-bons.
Mrs. Lalor, Clothing for one child.
Ladies in New London, Ct., Clothing for two children.

Mrs. E. S. Munroe, Clothing and 14 new Garments.
Mrs Morton, Clothing and Cakes.
A Bereaved Mother, Clothing.
Fanny Milford and others, eleven little girls, 26 new Garments.
Edward Molineux, Illuminated Texts.

Mrs. James N. Paulding, Clothing.
Mrs. Peters, Clothing and Vegetables.
Mr. Prior, Christmas Cake.
Mrs. Pomeroy, Clothing, Pickles, Crackers and Fruit.
Mrs. Philips, Cross Buns.
Popham & Claxton, 25 lbs. Lard.
Mrs. Robertson, Clothing.
Reading Circle, Milford, Ct., 20 new Garments.
Mrs. Rodenstein, Illuminated Texts.
Miss Russell, 2 Pictures.

St. James' Church Sunday-School, New-London, Ct., Clothing.
Mrs. W. Alex. Smith, 2 Illuminations, 10 new Garments, Pickles and Jellies.
St. Barnabas' Society, 32 new Garments, 8 pr. Stockings, 2 pcs. Calico.
Mrs. A. Suydam, 2 new Garments, 7 pr. Stockings.
Miss Schermerhorn, Candies, Clothing.
St. John's Church, Stamford, Ct., twenty poor children of Mission School, through Miss Williams, 26 new Garments.
St. Ann's Church, Miss Comstock's S. S. Class, assisted by Miss Holmes, Miss Jones, Miss Ottiwell and Miss Trumbull, 102 new Garments.
Mrs. J. Newton Sears, 6 pcs. Dress Goods, 2 pcs. Muslin, (value, $97,) and quantity of linen Thread.
Smith & Jewett, 2 bbls. Flour.
Mrs. Schermerhorn, Candies.
Mrs. Wilfred Smith, Toys and Books.
Miss Steers, large box Toys from fair.

Trinity Chapel Employment Society, through Mrs. Caswell, Mrs. Curtiss and Miss Haight, 18 new Garments and 29 Towels.
Mary Turnure, 28 Check Aprons.
Mrs. Daniel F. Tiemann, 9 pr. Winter Gloves, Toys.
Mr. Tiemann, 2 kegs Zinc Paint, 1 can Boiled Oil, 2 bottles Turpentine, 1 Paint Brush.
Mr. Twine, Vegetables.
Miss Tiemann, Clothing for one child.

Mrs. Van Horne, Clothing and 20 pr. new Shoes.
The Verein Sewing Society, through Mrs. W. C. Gilman, 34 new Garments.
Miss Van Horne, a number of Dressed Dolls' Clothing.
Mrs. J. C. Varick, 9 new Garments.
Mrs. Von Post, Toys and Books.

Mrs. Dr. Watts, Clothing and 24 new Garments, Candies for Christmas Tree.
Miss Wisner, Clothing.
Mrs. Elias Wade, Jr., 1 Quilt.
Mrs. Wood, Toys and Books.
Mrs. Wotherspoon, Toys and Books.

Mrs. Zabriskie, Fruit and Cakes.

ADDRESS

DELIVERED BY THE SECRETARY

AT THE

Third Anniversary of "The Sheltering Arms."

(PUBLISHED BY ORDER OF THE EXECUTIVE COMMITTEE.)

I can scarcely realize that more than a year has passed, since I came here on the occasion of our second anniversary at the request of the Board of Trustees, to plead, in the name of charity for this Home for little children; and now again, in answer to the same request, I come before you to renew that appeal, to ask you to aid us in our work—to encourage us by your sympathy—to strengthen us by your prayers—to make provision for our daily necessities.

It is not my intention to draw for you any fancy sketch of poverty and want, or to work upon your feelings by relating painful histories of those poor victims of debauchery and sin, whose very lives are terrible even to contemplate, but I intend simply to present for your consideration, *Facts, plain, stubborn Facts;* and my strongest arguments must be the innocent faces of these children of the poor, in whose behalf, in the name of Christ, I am to plead.

I am free to acknowledge that I have undertaken this to-day with some reluctance—not that I am weary of begging for this Institution or of urging its claims—but I would have preferred that one more competent than myself had been chosen to tell you of our wants and to enlist you as co-workers with us in this endeavor to follow our great Leader in going about and doing good—I would that an abler pen than mine had undertaken the simple story of this charity. However, having accepted the task, I can only assure you that it is my intention to call upon you for assistance to the utmost of my ability, and do not think that I shall feel any reluctance or timidity in presenting our cause—I shall plead in full confidence of success, because I plead for children—for those whose hearts still beat responsive to the promptings of virtue—for those whose lips have not yet touched the sweetened cup of vice—for those whose youthful steps may be easily trained to tread the paths of honesty, and whose hands may still be kept from touching that which is unholy and unclean—*my words* may indeed fail to convince you of the great importance of this work, but the sight of these little ones, in this, their cheerful, happy Home, must surely aid me in calling forth from every heart, the firm resolution to do something in their behalf—something for His sake, who has promised that a cup of cold water only given in His name shall not lose its reward.

I shall ask you, then, to listen patiently to me whilst I trace for you the history of *"The Sheltering Arms:" the Past*, with all its experiences and results—*the Present*, with its encouragements and success—*the Future*, with its hopes and fears; this is to be my theme, and may He, who has already blessed us abundantly in our labors, create in your hearts a true sympathy for these His unfortunate children, who have been committed to our care; so that to our appeal for aid, such a response may come, as shall enable us to open still wider our doors and welcome to this Home of charity, Christ's poor—the halt, the maimed, the blind.

But before entering upon this part of the subject, let me, in a few words, propose to you a question, which has frequently arisen in my own mind, and to which I think I have at last found a satisfactory solution: I have given this subject much thought and study and gladly take this opportunity of bringing it to your notice.

The question is a very important one, and deserves serious attention: "*Why is it that our Charitable Institutions are obliged so frequently to urge their claims upon the public and to resort to so many ways to obtain the necessary means to carry them on?*" Is it because human nature has gradually been growing more and more indifferent to the cry of the poor and needy, requiring such strong appeals to arouse its sympathy, that few are able to awaken it? Is it because the world has been growing more and more peremptory in its demands—its shrines of fashion and pleasure more and more attractive—its seductions so strong that its votaries dare not for a moment look upon the dark side of life, lest it should cast an unwelcome shadow on their own bright path? Is it because the boasted civilization of this nineteenth century would deny the poor, the sick, the unfortunate, the recognition they deserve from those to whom God has entrusted the wealth of the world? lest Dives should feel less refined or cultivated if asked to minister to the troubles of Lazarus! or, is it because Charity accomplishes so little good—supplies so few of the wants of the poor—arrests so small a number of those streams of dissipation and vice which mar in their turbid flow the beauty of the earth—gives bread to so few of the hungry or wipes away so few tears from the face of suffering humanity—in proportion to the amount of means annually poured into her treasury? Are these, all or any of them, satisfactory answers to our question? To my mind, they are not. I tell you that the world has not yet succeeded in destroying that better part of our nature which believes in the Bible teaching, that it is indeed more blessed to give than to receive; and so long as the Gospel shall be faithfully preached in this land, so long shall the charities of America be the boast of her greatness and her enlightenment—as I stated once before, on a similar occasion to the present, so I repeat it now, that there is no city in the world where the people, as a general thing, give more willingly, more unsparingly to charity than in this which we all love so well. Where then must we seek our answer—*if all I have stated be true, why do our Charitable Institutions languish?*

We must seek the true answer, I think, nearer home, and I fear no contradiction when I affirm that the trouble lies chiefly with those who constitute what is usually known as the "Board of Trustees"—those who have the management of our asylums, our homes, our hospitals. It is not a pleasant thing, I know, to take upon ourselves the blame, but truth requires it, and we cannot deny her claims. Let me give you the results of my own investigation of the subject, and you shall answer if I am not correct in my conclusions.

I believe that the correct answer is to be found in the fact that, too frequently, those who give their time and attention to our charitable institutions undertake to accomplish too much. They send forth their influence and energies in too many different channels—they do not concentrate their labors to a sufficient degree on one object. Take, for instance, any one of our charities having a board of trustees of fifteen or twenty members, and you will almost invariably find that those who make up the board are interested not only in that one, but, at the same time, in several other benevolent undertakings. True, they are very active in the cause— *constantly* working, *constantly* begging, *constantly* giving; but, as their labor is wide-spread, so is the result diffused over too large a surface. Do not let me be misunderstood. I seek not to disparage the claims of any of the manifold objects we are so frequently called upon to support; but what I do assert is this, that if those of us who are willing to obey the calls of charity were to confine ourselves to *one*, or, *at the most, two* institutions, we would accomplish much more than by dividing our forces and undertaking more than we can faithfully perform. To this charge I must plead guilty myself, and therefore I may speak the more plainly on the subject. I firmly believe that we shall see our institutions flourish in exactly the same proportion as we shall give our entire attention to that special object in which we may be the most interested. I have often heard the officers of some of our charities complain that they could not perform their duties satisfactorily, because they had so many different claims upon their time, and for that reason they had often determined to resign from all. THE TRUTH IS, that we all feel a secret pride in seeing our names attached to a number of worthy undertakings, but are not so willing to allow that we are personally responsible for a full share of the work in every one of them. There are in this city men and women enough who are willing to work in behalf of the poor, and there is certainly enough for all to do; but it is not right to impose upon one person because he or she may be willing, in their desire to do all they can, to assume the labor, what should properly be the work of *three* or *four*. As far then as regards The Sheltering Arms, I trust the day is not far distant when those of us who are specially interested in its success will determine to devote ourselves more exclusively to the work in hand, and with the united, concentrated efforts of such a Board as we now have, aided by those who are co-workers with us, what may we not reasonably hope to accomplish? I do not deny that it is very praiseworthy in any man to be anxious to aid every one who calls upon him for assistance, but is it not the part of prudence rather to help one poor unfortunate fellow-being to stand upon his feet and walk than to stretch forth our hand at one time to so many that we only become in the end an impediment, when, by a little judgment, we might have been the means of doing so much good? The temptation, to one who is truly interested in this work, to respond to the call when some new charity asks for his assistance, I confess, *is great*, but we have only to give up to the temptation to learn in a short time that it is as true of us as of all others, that one cannot well do the work of five, be his spirit never so willing.

I may seem, to some persons, to be too positive in my assertions: but, I tell you, it is NO CHILD'S PLAY this caring for the poor, the sick, the needy; and when we join the ranks of those who carry on this work it must be as *earnest, persevering workers*, intent upon that which our hand findeth to do, or we cannot expect to have our efforts crowned with success.

I must, however, leave this subject here, and return to the consideration of that for which we have met together, namely, the claims of this noble charity, which I love so well to urge upon those who feel any interest in the temporal and spiritual welfare of the lower classes of our population—those little waifs of society whom we find growing up on every hand as future candidates for our work-houses, our asylums, or, it may be, our prisons. Such are the little ones for whom we plead—such the applicants we find daily at our doors. The work, we admit, is, on many accounts, a difficult one, but it has its lights as well as shadows, and it will surely have its rewards. It is also, necessarily, rather an expensive work, but, believe me, it does not cost as much to care for the young before they become steeped in vice and wretchedness as it does to bring to punishment those who have brought the full strength of manhood to bear upon society in breaking the laws of God and man. Of the two expenses the balance is certainly in favor of the young. Educate them properly, and you will find in the future less need of your Tombs, your prisons and your almshouses.

"*The Sheltering Arms*" commenced its operations on the sixth of October, 1864. It originated in a simple desire to help and comfort a class of sufferers whose necessities and distresses have hitherto found no institution especially adapted to their relief, and the urgent necessity of such an establishment has been sufficiently proved by the fact that we are constantly obliged to refuse admission to applicants, whom we have to turn unwillingly from our doors, for want of room. The class we especially seek to relieve is composed of those who, under present rules, cannot be admitted, or are not likely to be sent by their friends to any other institution. We have endeavored, as we advanced step by step, to practise the utmost economy in every department, and yet, for some time back, we have been scarcely able to meet our daily expenses. During the past year the building we occupy has been enlarged and furnished, enabling us to increase the number of children from forty to ninety; and from many sources we have received various supplies where we little thought the Institution had even been heard of. Thus, as we stand to-day and review the past, we find many reasons why we should take courage and proceed with thankful hearts in our work, for God has truly caused His face to shine upon us.

But, as I look back upon the road along which we have travelled, I cannot avoid noticing that the brightness has been dimmed at times by that dark shadow which must so surely fall upon the life of every one of us: here and there, a small stone marks the spot where we have committed to the ground some little one, who has been called away when, as yet, its career was scarcely begun—removed from "The Sheltering Arms" on earth to the arms of Him who dwells in heaven, where charity's gifts shall never more be needed. The marks of those little graves we would not have effaced, for, whilst we devote all our care and attention to the living, we would not neglect our dead. We love to think of them as of those who have been kindly taken by the "Unseen Friend" from the boisterous waves of life only to be anchored safe in some friendly, sheltered nook, until the Master himself shall come and call them forth. It is one sad feature of every institution of this kind, that on the pages of its Past there must always be such frequent marks of the hand of death—so many proofs that even the young must supply their quota towards filling up the ranks of the vast army of the tomb.

But, do yonder turf-mounds mark alone the graves of children—has death only taken from us those whom we were wont to watch over and care for? Are the watchers themselves all with us to-day, as when at the first we banded ourselves together for the work? Let us, for a moment, linger round this grave, which is larger and newer than the others, and listen to the lesson it shall teach us. It will remind us that, since we last met together, a familiar voice has been forever hushed—a familiar form forever taken from our midst—and when that grave was made ready for its occupant, when by loving hands the words, "Sacred to the memory of Simeon Draper," were engraved upon the stone that marks his silent tomb, it was the first time that our Board of Trustees had lost one of their members by death. It is not asserting too much, when I tell you that it was he who first proposed the necessity of "The Sheltering Arms" to our President, and to his advice we are largely indebted for much of our success. He was, indeed, a true friend to the poor, and especially interested in all efforts calculated to rescue the young from their peculiar temptations and sufferings; he fully appreciated the great importance of endeavoring to eradicate error by educating the youth, rather than by punishing those who had grown old and hardened in the practice of their crimes. Whatever else we may find to admire in his character, this one great lesson he has taught us, that it is the duty, as it should be the delight, of every one of us to give up a portion of our time and talents in endeavoring to help the unfortunate—to feed the hungry—to minister to the sick.

Thus has the past been diversified by light and shadow, but, viewing it all, as not only allowed but also directed, in all its phases, by Him who doeth all things well, we are enabled to close its page with praises to His most holy name and turn with thankful hearts to the examination of the present.

We have invited you here to-day to judge for yourselves as to what has been accomplished. You will find, we trust, everything in most excellent and satisfactory order. The ladies in charge of the House have been untiring in their attention to the children, and would thankfully acknowledge the assistance they have received, in many ways, from those interested in this work. We have turned to good account all the room we had at our disposal, but have been obliged to turn away many of those who asked to come in lest we should over-crowd our wards. There is one thing, just now, causing us considerable anxiety, and to which we must ask you to give your serious attention—it is the debt which we have been obliged to incur, and which we would ask you this day to help us liquidate. We are thankful to say that it was not brought upon us through any extravagance on our part, nor was it created by pushing on the work too fast—it was simply the result of necessity. When we had nearly completed the new addition to our House, we found that the Boulevard now being laid out on this side of the island, would pass directly through our grounds, taking away a great portion of the new building, and we were advised to push on the work as fast as possible, so as to occupy it before a certain date, that we might make our claim for damages when the new drive should force us away. To accomplish this, we were obliged to go into debt, and, although we shall eventually receive it all back again, still, the amount being small, we beg you to help us in paying it off. If this were done, we could apply all the money we receive to our daily expenses.

Consider for a moment the class we seek to relieve, and tell me, can there be any stronger claim presented to us than that of helpless infancy? Is there anything on earth more calculated to arouse our sympathies than the sad cry of a weak suffering child? Examine the list of those who have been under our care, and let that plead with you. Here, for example, is one who has been with us from the first. She who should have been this little girl's best and most watchful friend—she who should have guarded her offspring from all harm—was the cause of all her present misfortune. *Through her own mother's neglect*, the eyes of this child were for ever closed to the light of day and she was sent forth dependent upon the charity of strangers. But He who can restore even sight to the blind led her to our door, and you will find to-day little Blind Minnie one of the most cheerful and happy of the group. *This little boy*, a poor helpless cripple, whose father was unable to give him the comforts of a home and tried in vain to find some asylum where the little sufferer might be cared for, as he could neither be cured nor helped by medical treatment, was brought at last to us, and was soon made as comfortable as his unfortunate condition would allow. *Two little girls* were one day brought to us whose history was indeed a sad one. Their father had been induced to bring his family to America in the hope of bettering their condition. He landed at Castle Garden only to find that the tickets he had bought with his small savings to take him and his family to the far West were useless, as he had been cheated by the party from whom he had purchased them. The Commissioners of Emigration sent him and his family to Ward's Island, and there all were taken sick. First his youngest child died, then his wife, and at last the poor man himself was so broken down by sickness that he could not care for the others, and begged that they might be sent to some Christian Asylum until he could provide them once more a home. *A young boy* was, at one time sent to us, who was said to be dumb, and appeared almost idiotic. His parents were both deaf mutes and not able to take care of him. For a long time he did not seem to improve, but at length those who had him in charge perceived a decided change for the better, and he is now able to speak, and he is learning also to read. Had he been left to his parents is it at all probable that he would not have been to-day dumb, at least, if not worse?

But I would not weary you with the recital of the many sad cases we have constantly brought to our notice. Those already quoted tell the story and are sufficient to prove to you that " The Sheltering Arms " is doing a noble work. It should, indeed, be esteemed a privilege to provide anything pleasant for such little sufferers—to make the world easy and cheerful to them now, for *theirs is a short spring.* When your children are just beginning to gather the bright flowers scattered by the hand of love and affection in their path, these children of the poor must begin to work and toil.

Let us now look upon the Future and we will show you what we hope soon to accomplish. Our first and great desire is to secure some land on which to erect permanent buildings, capable of accommodating at least 400 children. The best plan we have now before us is one similar to that adopted to a great extent in Germany, where this subject has been, perhaps, better developed than in any other country. *There*, they frequently build several cottages in the place of one large institution, so that the children are banded together in groups or families, instead of all being under one roof, each cottage having its own play-ground, &c. What a noble gift it would be for one person to provide the means to erect one house of this kind, to be known, if so allowed, by the name of the donor. The land we now have in view would be adapted to four such cottages, and we could soon find occupants for them. During the past few weeks we have been greatly encouraged in the prosecution of this plan by the gift of a sufficient sum to erect the first division of a cottage from one who has always been a good friend to The Sheltering Arms, and who has often before made it the recipient of his liberality.

But that you may the better appreciate the benefits we believe would arise from such an arrangement of our buildings, come with me in imagination and let me take you through one of these cottages as we would propose to build them.

You will observe, in the first place, that there are five distinct houses, two stories high, under one roof. The centre building is used partly as a kitchen and laundry for the other four, all of which are occupied by the children and those persons who have charge of this portion of the institution. Entering this centre house you will find it arranged on the first floor—one-half for a large kitchen, the other for a laundry—having no communication with the other parts of the cottage, except in the rear, where a flight of stairs leads to the second story. Ascending these you will come into a large, airy and cheerful dining-room, communicating with the houses on either side by doors. In this room all the occupants of the cottage meet at their meals, and at morning and evening prayer. Leaving this room at the rear door you enter upon the gallery or piazza, which runs the whole length of the cottage, communicating with each house by side doors, and four flights of steps lead from here again to the play-ground, which is fenced in and used only by the inmates of this particular cottage. Our present plan is to make each house capable of accommodating twenty-five children, so that one cottage would constitute by itself a family of one hundred children, besides the ladies in charge and servants, and would cost about $25,000. Now, let us enter one of the four buildings, which is the exact counterpart of the other three. Entering from the play-ground we find ourselves upon the ground floor, which is divided into one large and two small rooms, so arranged for school-rooms that the largest one may also be used in rainy weather as a play-room. This floor has two entrances—one from the front and one from the rear—and communicates also with the second floor by a flight of stairs. Ascending these, we enter the second floor, which is used for dormitories and wash rooms. You will observe that the painting and general finish of the house is all perfectly plain, but so arranged as to give a pleasant, home-like appearance: our endeavor being to surround the children with such things as we all know by experience go very far in making us of a cheerful and contented temperament. This floor opens on the covered gallery, which we have already seen, so that the children from each of the four houses can pass in regular order directly to the dining-room or the play-ground. Let us now follow this gallery and enter once more the large room in the centre house.

It is now about the close of the day, and we find the play-ground deserted, and all around and in the cottage a welcome stillness, which is in striking harmony with the evening hour; but where are all the little occupants of the cottage? Surely one hundred children cannot be anywhere near us, and yet such silence reigns. Let us seek them and see how they are employed. Gathered around the tables, on which is spread their simple evening meal, we will find them engaged in prayer. They have already finished the hymn, and now, with folded hands, and, we trust, with earnest hearts, they bend before the throne of God in supplication and praise; they are imploring forgiveness for the sins of the past day, safety during the silent watches of the coming night, and now we hear them unite in an earnest petition to our common Father that He would bless with many blessings those whose hearts and hands have gone forth together to provide for the orphan and the destitute: those stewards, who, blessed with wealth and time, have freely given both to smooth the rugged pathway of the poor, causing them, it may be, to rejoice in the welcome provision of "The Sheltering Arms;" and, as we pass out, the last sounds we shall hear will be that most welcome of all sounds, the invocation of God's blessing from children's lips upon those who, for Christ's sake, have gone forth and ministered unto them.

Such is the picture of the future as we are wont to draw it, as we hope to make it, and we now ask you to aid us in doing so. The field is ready—it needs but the laborers to enter in and possess it. But it is not necessary for me to dwell any longer upon the importance of the work. It is now no experiment; the past two years have proved it a success. Were I addressing those whom I believed had never taken any interest in the holy work of charity, I would have followed a very different line of argument, but I came not here to teach you your duty—I came to plead for "The Sheltering Arms," and I must now leave the result in your hands. We all recognize the great law of the Almighty Ruler of the Universe, that we must always have the poor in our midst, and that it is the bounden duty of every man, as God has prospered him, so to minister to their necessities. It is not for me to question, for one moment, as to the manner in which any one now before me obeys that law; my aim has been simply to have presented the claims of that class of the poor for whom this Home was established. And, in conclusion, I ask you, one and all, in the name and for the sake of Him who is the Saviour of the rich and poor alike—in the name and for the sake of suffering humanity—by the remembrances of your own sad hours and your own happy days of the past—by the bright hopes with which the Cross crowns the Christian's future in that land where the sad cry of the poor shall never more be heard—to strengthen and encourage us in this endeavor to shield these little children from some of the many hardships and sufferings peculiar to their walk in life ; and of this one thing I am certain, if you cannot contribute towards the support of the Institution we represent, you can and will unite with us, in the earnest prayer, that "He who has taught us in His holy word that all our doings without charity are nothing worth, will pour into the hearts of all His people that most excellent gift of charity, the very bond of peace and of all virtues, without which whosoever liveth is counted as dead before Him, and that He will grant this for the sake of His only Son, our Saviour, Jesus Christ." Amen.

PRAYERS

TO BE USED BY THE FRIENDS OF

"The Sheltering Arms."

ALMIGHTY and most merciful Father, whose well beloved Son, our Saviour, did welcome the young children to his arms and bless them, look with pity, we beseech Thee, upon these little ones committed to our care, that, being shielded from temptation and delivered from evil, they may glorify Thy holy name, and finally, by Thy mercy, obtain everlasting life, through Jesus Christ our Lord. *Amen.*

OH, Lord God and Heavenly Father! infinite in love and full of mercy, send down thine Holy Spirit, as upon all friendless children and orphans, so especially upon these little ones, whom Thou hast given into our keeping, grant that the old Adam in these children may be so buried, that the new man may be raised up in them.

Grant that all sinful affections may die in them, and that all things belonging to the Spirit may live and grow in them.

Grant that they may have power and strength to have victory, and to triumph against the devil, the world, and the flesh.

Grant that, being dedicated to Thee, they may also be endued with heavenly virtues, and everlastingly rewarded, through Thy mercy, O blessed Lord God, who dost live and govern all things, world without end. *Amen.*

"THE SHELTERING ARMS."

FOURTH ANNUAL REPORT.

NEW-YORK.

1868.

New-York:
GEORGE F. NESBITT & CO., PRINTERS & STATIONERS,
CORNER OF PEARL AND PINE STREETS.
1868.

Trustees of the Sheltering Arms.

President.

Rev. THOMAS M. PETERS, D.D., Address, B'way & 101st St.

Vice-Presidents.

FRED. S. WINSTON, - - Address, 144 Broadway.
WM. ALEX. SMITH, - - - " 63 Wall Street.
WM. J. BEEBE, - - - " 149 Front Street.

Secretary.

HENRY J. CAMMANN, - - Address, 28 Old Slip.

HERMANN C. VON POST, - - 68 Broad Street.
D. TILDEN BROWN, M.D., - - - Manhattanville.
B. WATSON BULL, - - - - 44 Cedar Street.
WM. D. CLERKE, - - - - 22 Broad Street.
BENJ. H. FIELD, - - - - 127 Water Street.
Rev. ROBERT S. HOWLAND, D.D., - 409 West Twenty-third Street.
WM. K. KITCHEN, - - - - Park Bank.
JAMES PUNNETT, - - - - Bank of America.
PETER C. TIEMANN, - - - Manhattanville.
FREDERICK HUBBARD, - - - 40 Irving Place.
WM. H. FOGG, - - - - 32 Burling Slip.
JOHN B. CHURCH, - - - Manhattanville.
THOMAS WATT, - - - Harlem.
WM. P. LEE, - - - - 59 Wall Street.
WM. M. KINGSLAND, - - 55 Broad Street.

Visitor.

Rt. Rev. H. POTTER, D.D., D.C.L.

Treasurer and Financial Agent.

JAS. S. BREATH, - - - - 306 Mulberry Street.

Physician.
FRANK A. UTTER, M. D., - Broadway, near 100th Street.

Consulting Physician.
E. B. DALTON, M. D., - - - - 90 Madison Avenue.

Ladies' Association of The Sheltering Arms.

Miss J. VAN HORNE, *Secretary*, 31 Chambers Street.
" E. KEMBLE, *Treasurer*, - 52 West Twenty-fifth Street.
" S. CAMMANN, - - Fordham.
" M. CHAUNCEY, - - 53 West Thirty-sixth Street.
" S. E. KITCHEN, - - Park Bank.
Mrs. WM. P. LEE, - - - 326 Fifth Avenue.
Miss S. B. NEWBY, - - 184 West Twenty-eighth St.
" L. PETERS, - - - Broadway, corner 101st Street.
" J. A. TIEMANN, - - Manhattanville.
" S. E. WHEELER, - - 43 West Twenty-fifth Street.
" A. M. CAMMANN, - 31 West Thirty-third Street.
" S. BOSTWICK, - - 75 East Twenty-second Street.
" KATE COMSTOCK, - 141 West Twenty-second Street.
" F. A. COOPER, - - 17 Burling Slip.
Mrs. WM. C. GILMAN, - 19 West Thirty-first Street.
" R. W. ADORN, - - 43 West Thirty-ninth Street.
Miss LILLIE C. HALL, - 228 West Fortieth Street.
" S. E. PIERSON, - - 24 Broadway.
" LIZZIE HOLMES, - 123 Fifth Avenue.
" NATHALIE M. JONES, 71 West Twenty-third Street.

The Sheltering Arms is reached by taking the Eighth Avenue cars to One Hundredth street, thence following the road westward to Broadway.

The building stands on Broadway, between One Hundredth and One Hundred and First streets.

FOURTH ANNUAL REPORT

OF THE

Trustees of the Sheltering Arms.

ANOTHER year of care and pleasant toil has brought us to our fourth Anniversary. We thankfully report the fact that the current expenses, about eleven thousand dollars, have been met by the donations, leaving us, however, with small store for the maintenance of ninety-three children during the long summer, when friends are absent and gifts in general scanty.

We cannot report our land paid for and new building erected, but have made provision to meet about one-half of the estimated cost. Two subscriptions of five thousand dollars each are for the erection of cottages to contain thirty children.

The Ladies' Association have also collected between one and two thousand dollars for their cottage. With fifty thousand dollars in hand, we could accomplish, without debt, all that we last year proposed—namely, to put up buildings for 120 inmates. The plan suggested contemplates, when our means allow, an addition of six more houses, to accommodate, with those soon we hope to be commenced, three hundred children.

During the year there have been one hundred and nineteen inmates of the house, of whom twenty-three have been returned to friends, three have died, and ninety-three remain. Of the three who died, one, paralyzed and bed ridden, was brought that she might receive here the constant care which it was impossible for friends to give at home. A second was a very young child, who, to the physician's eye, bore, at her admission, the tokens of early death. The third, also a girl, was stricken down with a short and acute disease, which soon closed her earthly history. Their bodies rest in St. Michael's church-yard, Astoria, beside the little ones who had gone out before. The health of the house has been unusually good, for which, under God's providence, great praise is due to the watchful supervision of the Sisters in charge of the house, seconded by the prompt attendance, when summoned, of the physician, Dr. F. A. Utter.

To all our known and to all our unseen friends who have helped us we are, as ever, grateful. Especially have we been cheered by the many remembrances from Sunday-schools and Church societies in city and country. We notice and thank them more fully in our little monthly paper, "THE SHELTERING ARMS."

During the past year the question has presented itself in the Board of Trustees as to whether it was expedient that the Institution should continue under its original management—that is, of the Sisters of St. Mary's, or that, according to the usual custom, a hired Matron should be engaged. The Trustees considered it their duty to take into account only the best interests, temporal and spiritual, of the children whom the house shelters. Many of the Trustees have had long experience in public institutions under various managements, and are satisfied that, in all respects, "The Sheltering Arms" has ranked among the first for its physical training, and also for its softening influences upon children, many of whom, at their entrance, are rough casts of uncultivated humanity. The growth among them of religious feeling has been like to that in a well-ordered Christian family, which in public institutions is rarely the case. It was once remarked of an asylum for children, conducted for many years under the common system, that, of the many hundreds who had gone out from it, none had left it thoughtful, pious Christians. We may be over sanguine and deceived, but we trust that many of our elder children have already given their young hearts to Christ. Under these circumstances, the Trustees could arrive at no other decision than that it is expedient and their duty to continue in a course into which, under God's guidance, they have been led, and which hitherto has proved so advantageous for the children, as well as economical in its administration of the finances.

According to the original intention of the founders, the children attend worship at the Episcopal Church, and are under the pastoral care and religious training of one of its clergy.

In conclusion, the Trustees would invite all readers of this Report to visit the House. They will not find heaven here, and yet will, we trust, go away believing that Christ is taught and honored, and, if from afar, yet followed. If the little ones are better off here than in temptation and sin, give us your support. That which the good Lord provides, we shall use according to the best of our ability, and there our responsibilities end.

TREASURER'S REPORT, MAY 1, 1868.

By Balance per last Report............................		$451 10
Donations and Subscriptions........................		14,802 39
Board received......................................		1,908 11
		$17,161 60
To current expenses, viz.:		
Bread.......................	$2,127 15	
Meat........................	1,779 03	
Milk........................	939 25	
Groceries and Vegetables.....	1,928 41	
Fuel........................	523 50	
Gas.........................	340 40	
Wages and labor.............	1,263 50	
Repairs and alterations.......	493 08	
Insurance...................	162 36	
Taxes, 1867.................	242 97	
Household material..........	401 41	
Printing and advertising......	400 76	
Rent of School-room.........	150 00	
Sundries....................	901 00	
		$11,713 74
Christmas Dinner and Festival..............	125 00	
Paid Loan of $5,000 and Interest...........	5,289 83	
Balance.....................	33 03	
		$17,161 60

LIST OF DONATIONS.

Alms Box at the Institution	$54 87
John Alstyne	50 00
A Member of St. Ann's Church	10 00
A Lady, through Mrs. Malone	10 00
All Angels' Church, Rev. C. E. Phelps	6 00
Alpha	5 00
Annandale Children	1 50
Anonymous	1 00
Loring Andrews—D. F.	500 00
W. L. Andrews—B. F.	500 00
Mrs. Aaron Arnold, Miss Kemble	25 00
Appropriated by Legislature	786 24
Miss Burr	15 00
Miss Breath	5 00
Mrs. S. C. Baring	100 00
Board Received	1,008 11
Photograph of the House	0 20
W. J. Beebe	250 00
Minnie's Pictures	0 04
Mrs. Breath, per Miss Tiemann	2 00
Mr. Thomas Barron, through H. J. Cammann	50 00
Sale of Books	2 00
Stewart Brown	100 00
James L. Bogart	25 00
Mrs. D. T. Brown	5 00
T. W. Brathwaite	3 75
Bertha Brown	1 00
Mrs. N. P. Bailey	25 00
Miss Bailey	3 50

Mrs. Charles Beebe.	$25 00
Allie Beebe's Savings.	1 83
Miss B——, Elmstead, England.	10 00
Comptroller of the State.	438 91
Christ's Church, Rev. F. C. Ewer.	44 00
Commissioners of Charities and Corrections.	500 00
Cash.	1 00
C.	5 00
Mrs. Chas. P. Cummings, through H. J. Cammann.	25 00
Children of Calvary Chapel, Easter Offerings.	62 32
Lyman Cobb, Jr., Yonkers.	2 00
Cash, through Rev. Mr. Webb.	10 00
Jay Cooke & Co.	50 00
John Caswell, Rev. Mr. Crowe.	50 00
Collection in Christ Church.	42 66
Children Church of the Annunciation, Miss Kemble.	15 36
Peter Cooper, Golden Wedding Fund.	50 00
Children of Sunday School of Grace Church, Hamden, Conn.	4 00
Church of the Transfiguration.—B. F.	350 00
Calvary Church Sunday School.	158 00
W. B. Clerke.	25 00
Jay Cooke (Miss Kitchen).	50 00
Cash, W. P.	10 00
Cash $2 ; Cash $1.	3 00
Collected at Annual Meeting.	18 90
Proceeds of the Concert at Dr. Ward's, through Mrs. Lee—B. F.	1013 75
Calvary Church Collection.	50 70
Members of the Church of the Transfiguration, through Mrs. W. C. Gilman.	198 00
Theodore Clayton.	1 00
H. J. Cammann.	25 00
Miss Josepha J. Case.	3 00
Cottage Hill Seminary, Poughkeepsie, Rev. G. T. Rider, Rector.	30 00
Miss Cooper, Lent Savings.	2 50

Charles Downes, per B. W. Bull	$10 00
Mr. Dawson	5 00
Jno. H. Draper, through H. J. Cammann	25 00
Miss Delaplaine, through Mr. Schieffelin	10 00
James F. De Peyster	25 00
Donation	2 00
Daughters of the Temple, St. Mark's Church, Augusta, Me	5 00
Mrs. Frederick De Peyster	100 00
Leila Eagle, Savings	5 00
Easter Offerings from the Classes of the Good Shepherd and St. Andrew's Sunday Schools, Stamford, Conn., Rev. F. W. Brathwaite	15 20
St. Andrew's Sunday School Sewing Class	5 00
Easter Offerings, from Sunday School of St. Paul's Church, Franklin, N. Y.	13 81
Ella, Gracie, Willie & Nettie Whitlock	5 00
A Friend	10 00
Benjamin H. Field	125 00
A Friend, through Mrs. Ogden Hoffman	56 80
Thomas H. Faile	200 00
Miss Ferguson	20 00
A Friend	5 00
J. D. Fish, through W. J. Beebe	50 00
D. B. Fayerweather, through Mr. Andrews	75 00
A Friend $10, a Friend $5	15 00
W. O. Fitzgerald	1 50
A Friend	10 00
Geo. W. Gibson, through Rev. W. R. Johnson	5 00
Thank Offering for Gracie	50 00
Wardner, Mary and Hattie Harrington, Savings	5 05
Rev. Mr. Halsey	5 00

W. A. Haines...	$50 00
Rev. E. A. Hoffman, D. D.............................	25 00
Mrs. Thomas H. Hubbard	50 00
Mr. Abraham S. Hewitt................................	50 00
Mr. Frederick Hubbard...............................	1000 00
Mrs. W. H. Harlbut, through W. L. Andrews.............	25 00
Geo. A. Hearn, through D. S. Jackson, Jr	25 00
Rev. Horace Hills......................................	10 00
Mrs. Stephen Hyatt, through Mrs. Gilman.—B. F........	15 00
J. and J. J. D., through H. J. Cammann................	25 00
Mrs. Johnson...	1 00
Edward Jones, through Dr. Peters......................	200 00
Mrs. Kimball...	1 00
Miss Julia A. Low.....................................	25 00
R. J. Livingston.......................................	25 00
B. C. Morris, Jr., through H. J. Cammann..............	5 00
Blind Minnie's pennies, from Daisie and Katie..........	0 85
Mrs. George Moke, through Miss Kemble................	50 00
Mrs. H. Meigs, Jr......................................	5 00
Member of St. Ann's..................................	5 00
J. L. Northam...	10 50
Adam Norrie...	100 00
New-York Stock Exchange, per W. Alex. Smith........	250 00
Right Rev. Dr. Neely..................................	2 00
Mabel G. Osgood......................................	22 00
A. Craig Palmer.......................................	25 00
Mrs. Power...	1 00
Mr. W. W. Parkin.....................................	20 00

Parish School of Church of Holy Innocents, Annandale, Rev.
R. D. Fairbairn, D. D. $32 78
James Punnett... 1,000 00
R. Prior... 20 00

Alice Quintard, 1 week old................................ 2 00

D. H. Riker, through Miss Comstock.................... 40 00
George A. Robins, through Miss Kemble............... 20 00
Miss Sarah Richmond..................................... 1 00

St. Ann's Church, found in plate......................... 10 00
Sunday School, Church of the Mediator, Kingsbridge, Rev.
W. T. Wilson... 39 00
Church of Holy Communion, Collection................. 54 16
Mrs. C. L. Spencer, through Miss A. Cammann....... 100 00
A Memorial Offering of a Beloved Christian Child, Rev. Dr.
Montgomery.. 100 00
Sunday School, St. James' Church, Hyde Park, New-York.... 17 00
Sunday School, Calvary Church.......................... 196 00
St. Luke's Day School, New-York........................ 7 00
St. Michael's Church....................................... 1,000 00
The Tithe System... 100 00
Sunday School, St. John's Church, Stamford, Connecticut,
Rev. W. Tatlock... 3 70
Wm. Alex. Smith.. 150 00
A Southern Lady.. 7 13
St. Peter's Church Collection, Rev. Dr. Beach.......... 65 00
St Michael's Church Sunday School..................... 16 23
St. James' Church Sunday School, Fordham, through H. J.
Cammann.. 8 34
Sundry Receipts at Lecture................................ 66 00
St. Mary's Church Sunday School, Manhattan, Rev. C. C. Adams. 20 00
Savings of 5 Little Children............................... 2 20
St. James' Sunday School, Hyde Park.................... 15 00

S. T. Skidmore, through Mrs. Lee............................	$10 00
Mortle Schuyler...	1 00
Alex. T. Stewart...	20 00
Subscriptions to Paper...	72 00
Miss Carrie Swan...	1 00
St. Ann's Offertory...	5 00
Sunday School, St. John's Church, Stamford, Connecticut....	36 39
Sunday School, Christ Church, Poughkeepsie, Rev. P. K. Cady	2 20
St. Clement's Sunday School Easter Offering, Rev. T. A. Eaton	58 00
St. James' Sunday School, Great Barrington, Rev. H. Olmsted, Easter Offering..	50 05
A Tradesman, through Miss Woodham.....................	1 00
Trinity Chapel, through Miss Kemble........................	5 00
Peter C. Tiemann...	50 00
Townsend & Davis..	10 00
Trinity Chapel Offertory..	5 00
Mrs. Jno. Van Vleeck	50 00
H. C. Von Post..	100 00
H. O. Von Post, Building Fund, B. F.	500 00
Fair of Miss Van Ingen's Class in Sunday School of St. James' Church, Hyde Park, N. Y...............................	5 00
William Voorhees...	3 00
Jno. D. Wolfe, through American Church Missionary Society.	450 00
Wooster Street Mission School.................................	10 00
Rev. Geo. Worthington, Balston Spa.........................	42 50
Miss Wing..	1 00
Mrs. Mary Watt, through Dr. Peters.........................	100 00
W. B., through Dr. Peters	100 00
W. T. Wilson, through Mr. Cammann........................	34 75
Widow's Mite..	2 00
Mrs. Laura L. Wallen...	200 00
Robt. Winthrop..	50 00

ANNUAL SUBSCRIBERS.

Mrs. H. D. Aldrich	$10
" R. W. Aborn, through Mrs. Lee	5
" Ballou, through Mrs. Gilmore	10
Mr. D. B. Bedell, through Miss Tiemann	5
Miss Amy Boardman	5
Mrs. F. J. Bumstead	5
" J. L. Cammann, through Miss Cammann	10
Mr. Geo. E. Cooper, through Miss Cooper	5
" Wm. Cooper, " "	10
" Henry L. Cammann, through Miss S. Cammann	5
Mrs. Colden, through Miss Kemble	5
Mr. H. H. Cammann, through Miss A. Cammann	5
Mrs. Mary J. Corlies	5
Miss Mary Cook, through Miss Kemble	5
Mrs. R. D. Cutting	5
Miss R. Cotheal	3
Mrs. H. Cram, through Miss Punnett	5
Miss Kate L. Cammann	3
" Mary Cunard	5
Mrs. George Cornwall	10
Mr. T. P. Cummings	10
Mrs. J. Coddington	5
Mr. F. W. Coggill	10
Mrs. D. B. Dash, through Miss Kemble	5
" Dehon	10
Mr. James C. Day	5
Mrs. Jas. F. De Peyster	25
" David Dows	5
" W. P. Dixon, through Miss Peters	10
" James A. Edgar, through Miss Kemble	5
" D. M. Edgar, through Miss A. Cammann	5
Miss Emmet	3

Mrs. Fitzgerald...	$10
Miss J. E. Faitoute, Miss Comstock.....................	10
Mrs. J. Faitoute..	10
" Saml. Gore...	10
" J. T. Graham...	5
" H. T. Gerry, through Miss Kemble.............	5
" Grafton, " "...........................	10
" Wm. H. Guion, Mrs. Gilman......................	10
Miss M. Glover, through Miss Comstock...............	5
" Mary M. Gandy, through Miss Kemble........	5
" Mary E. Horner, through Miss Wisner........	10
" Emily Hollingsworth, Portchester...............	5
Mrs. Hollingsworth...	5
Miss M. E. Hamilton, through Miss Pierson............	3
Mrs. J. C. Hamilton...	5
" P. R. Hoffman, through Miss Kemble.........	10
" Chas. W. Hall..	5
Miss Rosalie M. Heiser.......................................	3
Mrs. J. C. Hull...	3
" Abrm. S. Hewitt.....................................	10
" Watson Hildreth, through Miss Chauncey....	5
" Heywood..	5
Mr. W. L. Jenkins...	10
" Meyer Isaacs..	5
Miss M. S. Jones, through Miss Kemble.................	5
" C. H. Isham, through Miss Pierson............	5
M. S. Isaacs..	5
Miss Jessie Kestor...	5
" E. Kemble..	5
Mrs. Hugh Laing...	5
" Walter H. Lewis, through Miss Kemble......	5
" G. L. Lee...	5
" C. Livingston, through Miss Kemble.........	5

Miss Louisa Lawrence, through Miss Kemble	$5
Mrs. Laidley	5
Through Mrs. Lee	5
Miss Julia A. Low	5
Mrs. Wm. P. Lee	5
Mr. E. L. Molineux, through Miss Tiemann	5
Mrs. J. B. Murray, through Miss Kemble	5
" Isaiah Mankin	5
Mr. Nelson Merrill	5
Mrs. J. T. Metcalfe	10
" A. D. Morrell	5
" Bache McEvers	5
" H. Meigs, Jr.	5
Miss North	5
Mrs. J. P. Nazro	3
Miss Newby	5
Mr. S. Newby	5
Mrs. Geo. P. Ogden	5
" J. J. Phelps	10
" Pomeroy	10
Mr. Ed. D. Peters	20
Miss S. F. Pierson	5
Mr. H. L. Pierson, Jr.	5
Mrs. J. P. Phoenix	5
Mr. James Pott	5
" Sylvanus Reed	5
Misses Renshaw, through Miss Chauncey	10
Mrs. Thomas Rutter	5
" George Redding	2
" L. A. Rodenstein	5
" Edwin Stoughton	5
" G. R. Schieffelin	5

Mrs. Shedden, through Miss Comstock	$5
" Wm. A. Smith, through Miss Kemble	5
" P. A. Schermerhorn	5
" Simmens	5
" Augusta Schermerhorn	5
" A. T. Sackett	10
" C. L. Spence	10
Mr. Edward Schell	10
" Gustav Schwab	10
Mrs. D. F. Tiemann	5
" Theodore Timpson, through Mrs. Lee	5
" Francis Tomes, Jr	5
" Catharine Tracey, through Mrs. Lee	5
" A. J. Vanderpool	5
" H. C. Von Post	10
Miss Cornelia Van Wyck	5
Mrs. Genl. Wallene	5
Mr. H. F. Webster, through Miss Kemble	5
Mrs. J. Williams	5
Chas. S. Weyman, Miss Camman	5
Miss A. Wilkes, through Miss Kemble	5
" H. K. Wilkes, " "	5
" J. Wilkes, " "	5
Mrs. Chas. W. Whiley	10
" Wm. H. Wisner, Miss Comstock	10
" H. D. Wyman, Miss Kemble	10
" S. Wetmore, "	5
Mr. J. H. Wainwright	10
Mrs. T. Wane	8
" G. H. Warren, through Mrs Lee	10
Wm Whitlock, Jr	10
Mrs. E. Wade	25
" Saml. H. Whitlock	5
" Zabriski	10

BOARD PAID BY PATRONS AND SUNDAY SCHOOLS.

Mrs. J. N. Sears	$40 00
" W. J. Beebe	112 00
St. Ann's Sunday School	156 00
St. James's Church, New London, Rev. R. A. Hallum, D.D.	80 00

DONATIONS IN CLOTHING, PROVISIONS, &c.

MAY, 1867.
- Mrs. Johnson, 3 Garments.
- Mrs. Van Horn, Clothing.
- The Old Ladies' Benevolent Society of St. Luke's Home, Hudson street, 43 Aprons and 3 Skirts.
- Mrs. Lucy E. Lee, Clothing.
- Mrs. Newton, South Orange, Clothing.
- Mrs. D. T. Brown, Clothing.

JUNE.
- Mrs. Orr, 3 pr. Socks.
- Mrs. H. Von Post, 32 pr. Socks.
- The "Verein" Church of the Transfiguration, through Mrs. William Gilman, 4 Dresses, 2 pr. Drawers, 1 Chemise.
- Mrs. Harrington, Westchester, Clothing and Strawberries.

JULY.
- St. James' Sewing-School, Roxbury, Mass., 50 new Garments.
- St. James' S. School, Fordham, N. Y., box of Fire Crackers and Torpedoes.
- Mrs. J. W. Fowler and Mrs. Nathan Baldwin, of Milford, Ct., 1 bbl. Clothing.
- Mrs. Pomeroy, boys' Clothing, nearly new.

AUGUST.
- Charles W. Whiley, Fruit.
- House of Mercy, Vegetables.

SEPTEMBER.

Friends from South Brooklyn, Clothing.
Mrs. W. C. Gilman, Clothing.
Mrs. D. F. Tiemann, Fruit.
Mrs. Ferguson, through Rev. G. Hepburn, Clothing.
Mrs. W. M. Chamberlain, Clothing.
Mrs. E. L. Gookin, Clothing.
Mrs. E. C. Bogert, through Mrs. Gilman, Shoes.
Dr. Knight, Apparatus for two children.
Mr. Frederick Hubbard, a Microscope and Magnet.

OCTOBER.

Old Ladies of St. Luke's Home, 15 pr. knitted Stockings.
C. H. Bowman, 1 pc. Towelling and 2 pcs. Cloth for cloaks.
Mrs. W. H. Draper, Clothing.
Miss Tiemann, Clothes for Maggie Hill.
Mrs. Lalor, Clothes for Jeannette Paine.
Mrs. Tiemann, 4 pr. Stockings.
Mr. Bedford, Combs.
Mr. Wm. T. Furniss, 10 tons Coal.

NOVEMBER.

Mrs. William Reed, Clothing.
Mrs. W. C. Gilman, Clothing.
Mrs. Graham, 18 Spelling-Books.
Mrs. A. Suydam, 6 pr. knitted Stockings and Clothing.
Mrs. Breese, child's Bedstead and Clothing.
Mrs. Orr, 3 pr. knitted woollen Stockings.
Mrs. W. C. Gilman, from "Verein Society," 17 new Garments.
Mr. Robert Watts, large package Clothing.
Mrs. Craver, Fifth Avenue, large package Clothing.
Mrs. Dater, Clothing.
Mrs. W. A. Smith, 5 new Garments and other articles.
Adolphus Baldwin, 5 pr. knitted Stockings.
American Condensed Milk Company, 12 quarts Condensed Milk.
Young Ladies of Hobart Hall, 40 Collars, 13 Bibs, 4 winter Dresses.

DECEMBER.
    Mrs. W. J. Beebe, Cakes and Toys.
    A Lady from St. Paul's, Eastchester, 7 pr. knitted Stockings and Clothing.
    "Anonymous," 10 new Garments.
    Mr. C. H. Bowman, 8½ doz. Dolls.
    Mrs. Bogarth, Clothing.
    Mrs. Thompson, Clothing.
    Mrs. Tweddle, Clothing.
    Mrs. Chester, Clothing.
    Mrs. Godkin, Clothing.
    Mrs. H. W. Guion, Toys.
    Young Ladies of Hobart Hall, 2 doz. dressed Dolls.
    Mr. James Bridge, Candies.
    Mr. William Taylor, through Mrs. Tiemann, Christmas Toys.
    Mrs. C. A. Cammann, 10 dressed Dolls and other toys.
    Miss Anna M. Cammann, 1 doz. Drawing-Slates, Pencils and Picture Books.
    Mrs. Ogden Hoffman, 1 pc. Muslin and 2 Dresses.
    John D. Wolfe, 50 Pies.
    Mrs. Sydney Harris, Toys and Books.
    Mr. Prior, a quantity of New-Year Cakes.
    Mrs. D. F. Tiemann, New-Year Cakes, dressed Dolls and Toys, &c.
    Mrs. J. C. Vark, 12 new Garments.
    Sewing Society of St. Ann's Church, through Miss Comstock, 60 new Garments, 6 pr. Shoes.
    William L. Sanford, Christmas Greens, $5.
    John Sullivan, Labor and Material, $10.70.
    Townsend & Davis, Labor and Material, $8.50.
    Ladies of Milford Church, 1 barrel Clothing.

JANUARY, 1866.
    Mrs. Michean, 8 new Garments.
    Mrs. Dr. Morgan, Clothing.
    Miss Ferguson, 6 pr. knitted woolen Stockings, 2 pr. cotton ditto, 41 new Garments.

Ladies' Charitable Association of Christ Church, 17 grey flannel Skirts.
Mrs. Orr, 3 Aprons.
Mrs. W. C. Moore, 4 pr. cloth Slippers.
Rev. J. S. Clark, Madalin, N. Y., 60 new Garments and Candies.
Mrs. G. Schieffelin, 13 yards material for Dresses.
Old Ladies of St. Luke's Home, 5 pr. of knitted Stockings, and making 4 doz. Pillow Cases.
Mrs. Wm. H. Lindsley, 6 pr. of knitted woolen Stockings.
The "Verein," through Mrs. James Heeney, 44 new Garments.
The Earnest Workers of Mrs. Williams' School, 48 new Garments.
Mrs. Williams, 26 West 39th street, 6 Hoods and other Articles.
The "Verein," through Mrs. W. C. Gilman, 19 new Garments.
Mrs. W. C. Gilman, 7 pr. half-worn Shoes.
John Draper & Co., 200 cans of Beef Stock.
Rev. Dr. Irving, 6 copies of Young Christian Soldier, for the year.

FEBRUARY.

Through Rev. J. S. Clark, Madalin, N. Y., 14 new calico Dresses.
Rev. Dr. T. M. Peters, 2 Pictures.
The "Verein," 22 new Garments.
Mrs. W. H. Lindsley, 6 pair knitted woolen Stockings.
" Tweddle, Clothing.
" Wm. C. Gilman, Clothing.
" James Filor, large amount of Clothing and Hair for Pillows.
Ladies of St. Paul's Church, Englewood, N. J., 37 new Garments and Clothing, half-worn, value $35, through Mrs. Rider.
The Ladies' Church Aid Society, Goshen, through Mrs. Murray, 15 calico Dresses and 15 Aprons (*new*).

MARCH.

Ladies of Great Barrington, Mass., 9 new Garments and half-worn Clothing.
Three Young Friends, Cakes and Candies.
St. Ann's Sunday School Sewing Society, through Miss Comstock, 20 new Aprons.
Miss Alice Watts, a barrel and box Clothing, Toys and Books.

APRIL.

Mrs. Lucy Stephens, Clothing.
Mrs. G. Schieffelin, Toys and Candies for 42 children.
Miss Brewster, Candies for Easter.
Easter Flowers from the Children of St. John's Sunday School, Stamford, Connecticut.
Mrs. Samuel Gore, 1 pr. knitted woolen Stockings.
St. Andrew's Sewing Class, Stamford, Connecticut, 28 new Garments.
Through Mrs. W. C. Gilman and Mrs. E. C. Bogert, 1 piece Dress Goods, value $14.
From Julia Peters and her little friends Louise and Alice Leavitt Emma and Julia Leavitt, and Fannie and Ella Avery, 7 Undergarments.
The "Verein," 19 Garments.
Mrs. C. S. Bodley, Toys, Sleds, Child's Chair.
Miss Tiemann, 1 doz. Towels.
Ladies of Trinity Chapel, 60 new Garments.
Mrs. W. C. Moore, St. Luke's, N. Y., 27 new Garments.
Mrs. H. D. Aldrich's Bible Class, Calvary Church, 16 new Garments.
Bible Class of St. John's, Stamford, Connecticut, 18 new Aprons.
The Lent Work of the Children of Emanuel Church, Stamford, Connecticut, 13 new Garments.
Mrs. D. F Tiemann, 1 doz. Towels.
Mrs. Orr, 1 Apron.
St. Ann's Sunday School Sewing Society, through Miss Comstock, 7 Aprons and 3 Drawers.
Mrs. Philips, Flowers for the Annual Festival.
" William H. Lindsley, 40 yards Calico.
" G. R. Schieffelin, 2 new Dresses.
Miss C. L. Gardiner and Miss R. T. Vose, 28 new Garments and 4 pair knitted wool Stockings.
Miss E. H. Gardiner, Gardiner, Maine, Slates, Pencils and Thimbles for the nursery children.

PRAYERS

TO BE USED BY THE FRIENDS OF

"The Sheltering Arms."

ALMIGHTY and most merciful Father, whose well beloved Son, our Saviour, did welcome the young children to his arms and bless them, look with pity, we beseech Thee, upon these little ones committed to our care, that, being shielded from temptation and delivered from evil, they may glorify Thy holy name, and finally, by Thy mercy, obtain everlasting life, through Jesus Christ our Lord. *Amen.*

On, Lord God and Heavenly Father! infinite in love and full of mercy, send down thine Holy Spirit, as upon all friendless children and orphans, so especially upon these little ones, whom Thou hast given into our keeping, grant that the old Adam in these children may be so buried, that the new man may be raised up in them.

Grant that all sinful affections may die in them, and that all things belonging to the Spirit may live and grow in them.

Grant that they may have power and strength to have victory, and to triumph against the devil, the world, and the flesh.

Grant that, being dedicated to Thee, they may also be endued with heavenly virtues, and everlastingly rewarded, through Thy mercy, O blessed Lord God, who dost live and govern all things, world without end. *Amen.*

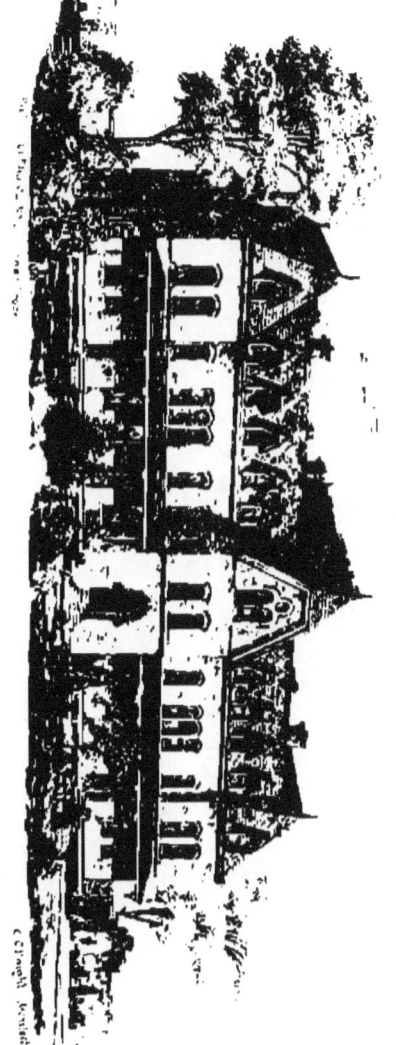

THE SHELTERING ARMS.

"THE SHELTERING ARMS."

FIFTH ANNUAL REPORT.

NEW YORK.

1869.

NEW YORK:
W. C. ROGERS & CO., STATIONERS AND PRINTERS,
26 JOHN STREET.

1869.

Trustees of the Sheltering Arms.

President.

Rev. THOMAS M. PETERS, D.D., Address, B'way & 101st St.

Vice-President.

FRED. S. WINSTON,	- Address,	144 Broadway.
WM. ALEX. SMITH,	- "	40 Wall Street.
WM. J. BEEBE,	- - "	149 Front Street.

Secretary.

HENRY J. CAMMANN, - - Address, 8 Wall Street.

HERMANN C. VON POST,	68 Broad Street.
D. TILDEN BROWN, M.D.,	Manhattanville.
B. WATSON BULL,	44 Cedar Street.
WM. B. CLERKE,	25 Broad Street.
BENJ. H. FIELD,	127 Water Street.
JAMES PUNNETT,	Bank of America.
PETER C. TIEMANN,	Manhattanville.
FREDERICK HUBBARD,	33 Broadway.
WM. H. FOGG,	32 Burling Slip.
JOHN B. CHURCH, Jr.,	Manhattanville.
THOMAS WATT,	Harlem.
WM. P. LEE,	50 Wall Street.
WM. M. KINGSLAND,	110 Fifth Avenue.
Rev. H. E. MONTGOMERY, D.D.,	Madison Av. & 35th St.
FRANKLIN EDSON,	19 Whitehall Street.

Treasurer.

JAS. S. BREATH, - 306 Mulberry Street.

Physician.

FRANK A. UTTER, M.D. . . Broadway, near 100th Street.

Consulting Physician.

E. B. DALTON, M.D., - - 99 Madison Avenue.

Ladies Association of The Sheltering Arms.

Miss J. VAN HORNE, Secretary, 31 Chambers Street.
" E. KEMBLE, Treasurer, 52 West Twenty-fifth St.
" M. CHAUNCEY, - - 53 West Thirty-sixth St.
" S. E. KITCHEN, - - Park Bank.
Mrs. WM. P. LEE, - . 326 Fifth Avenue.
Miss S. B. NEWBY, - - - 314 West Twenty-eight St.
" L. PETERS, . - - Broadway, corner 101st St.
" J. A. TIEMANN, - - Manhattanville.
" S. E. WHEELER, - 48 West Twenty-fifth St.
" A. M. CAMMANN, - - 31 West Thirty-third St.
" KATE COMSTOCK, - 204 Lexington Avenue.
" M. A. COOPER, - - Bushwick, L. I.
Mrs. WM. C. GILMAN, - - 31 West Thirty-Sixth St.
" R W. ABORN, - 48 West Thirty-ninth St.
Miss LILLIE C. HALL, - - 228 West Fortieth Street.
" S. E. PIERSON, - - 24 Broadway.
" LIZZIE HOLMES, - - 128 Fifth Avenue.
Mrs. ROBERT WEIR, - 29 West Tenth Street.

REPORT

OF THE

Board of Trustees,

ADOPTED AT THE ANNUAL MEETING,

MAY 10th, 1869.

THE SHELTERING ARMS is now five years old, and upon this day of its Fifth Annual Meeting, the Trustees devoutly thank and bless the Giver of all good for success hitherto, for present prosperity, and for the fair promise of the future. Having passed safely through the third and fourth years of corporate existence, with a work ever enlarging, the Trustees considered when entering with the summer of 1868, free of debt, upon the fifth year, that their day of experiment was over. The enterprise was no longer dressed in the attraction of novelty. The name had lost its romance through much repetition, and become familiar to all ears. Yet its first friends, for the most part, remained steadfast, and new accessions to the ranks of their co-workers had enabled the Trustees to meet the increased expenses and extend their accommodations. It was, nevertheless, with some unwillingness that the Trustees accepted the necessity forced upon them by the opening of the new drive, of purchasing ground, and erecting thereon large buildings. Having, however, no alternative, they addressed themselves with brave hearts to this great undertaking, and now report their walls up, and the roof in progress of construction, with every payment thus far met by gifts received, and the land paid for, with the exception of $9,000.00 mortgage resting upon it when purchased. The outlay upon this permanent property has been $28,706.61.

To finish the Cottages and School House, and furnish them for use, fence, and adorn their acre of ground, there is required $30,000.00, the larger part of which is yet to be collected.

To clear off every debt, and stop the waste in payment of interest, must be the sixth year's task. Can this desired end be reached? If our friends are as liberal in the new year as the last, should their numbers increase in the same ratio, the anniversary of 1870 will find the Institution free of debt, and ready for the next step in progress in the erection of "the Innocents' Hospital." We would enlist all interested in caring for homeless little ones, to exert themselves to the utmost in our behalf. Besides paying the costs of our permanent property, we must prepare for our increased expenses in maintaining the four families, or 120 children in the new quarters. These current expenses, together with support of the little paper, amounting during the year past to $12,667.78, will probably be increased the coming year to $15,000.00.

In returning thanks to contributors, the Trustees would especially acknowledge the assistance received from Churches, Sunday-schools, young ladies' schools and societies, forty-nine in number, in the States of Maine, New Hampshire, Massachusetts, Connecticut, New York, and New Jersey. As the donations from this source are, in large measure, due to the interest in our cause fostered by the little monthly paper, we may reckon the expense of publication and the pains of its preparation well bestowed.

To the members of the Ladies' Association of The Sheltering Arms, the Trustees are deeply indebted. It is owing to their care and supervision that the monthly paper has been made attractive, and has brought many friends and gifts to the Institution. The ladies have not only occupied themselves in the preparation of this paper, but have further, through the collection of subscriptions for current expenses, and of donations towards their Cottage, added largely to the receipts of the Treasury.

Various suggestions of the ladies have moreover been followed out, to the manifest benefit of the Institution, and the division of its burdens among a larger number. An article entitled, "Live Dollies," written for the December number of the paper, by one of the ladies, proposed that persons should undertake to provide for a child's wardrobe. The plan commended itself to many readers, and resulted in adding considerably to the number of our children clothed by an individual, a family, or a class. Twenty-three girls and boys are now clad in garments made for them by individuals or associations.

During the year, 123 children have been inmates of the House, the number constantly there, being 95. It has pleased our Heavenly Father to call to himself two of this number, one a little girl of 5 years, Lena McQueen by name, the other, Mary Caroline Sager, aged 15 years. Mary, who had been residing a few months with a family in New Jersey, returned to the House last Autumn stricken with a fatal illness. Our present Infirmary not being well adapted for the reception of such a case, she was, when very ill, kindly received at St. Luke's Hospital. The gentle nursing and constant attention of that institution soothed her suffering. We thank them for it; she enjoyed the religious ministrations of St. Luke's, and now sleeps, we trust, in Him, to whom two years before, in confirmation, she had give her heart and life. We laid her body to its rest with the twelve already sleeping in that dormitory from which only the coming of Christ will awaken them.

The Medical Department of the Institution has been under the charge of Dr. F. A. Utter, to whom the Trustees tender their thanks for his kind services gratuitously rendered.

The Trustees would, also, at this time renew their acknowledgment of the services rendered by the Sisters of St. Mary. It is chiefly owing to their co-operation that the wishes of the officers with regard to the children, have been thus far successfully carried out. What these wishes are, and what is the result of the present management are thus stated in the address of the President, read at the laying of the corner-stone of the new building in March last.

"In the management of the institution the Trustees have aimed to build up the children physically, to elevate them morally, and to fit them, so far as it lay in their power, for life or for death. The Trustees have not been turned from their purpose by the vain desire of pleasing every adviser, but have steadfastly and solely sought to save those intrusted to their keeping.

"The experience and observation of many years had convinced the originators of the institution that religious education, to be of the greatest value to children, must be connected with some positive teaching. Accordingly, from the beginning the pastor of the institution has been a minister of the Episcopal Church, and the religious instruction of its beneficiaries is under the sole direction of the Rector of St. Michael's Church. Children admitted, if not already Christians by baptism, with the concurrence of parents or friends receive that sacrament; all children, without exception, in addition to instruction in Holy Scripture, are taught in the Catechism, and trained in the worship as set forth in the Book of Common Prayer. In this course, we are happy to say that we have been sustained by those not of our own household of faith, who are willing to sink their individual preferences in the belief that the children are better taught and tended here than when cast about in an unsympathizing world. We have ever found, outside of our own Church, large-hearted Christians, ready to act as members of our Board of Trustees, and a constantly increasing number of subscribers, until, as we believe, every creed and form of worship in the

City of New York, heathen excepted, counts among its followers patrons of the Sheltering Arms.

With regard to the care of the institution in its other departments, the Trustees, mindful still of the children's welfare, have faithfully desired, and in some degree, they trust, succeeded in procuring for each position in the house, in the school, and in the work-room, the persons best qualified for their posts. The Sheltering Arms will suffer by no comparison between it and any similar institution. We invite all people to visit the house and see the children at their studies, work or play, proudly confident that they will find them, in personal appearance and conduct, not inferior to the same number of inmates gathered in any home; in holiness of thought and aspiration, surpassed only by those favored ones who, through all the years of childhood, have enjoyed the oversight and benefitted by the prayers, the teaching, the example of pious parents."

Finally the Trustees desire of their friends to be held in daily memory. Words of cheer or of counsel, deeds of love lighten the burden of anxiety by the assurance that our labors, imperfect as we ourselves know them to be, draw around us the sympathy and support of the faithful and the good. Above all would we desire to be remembered when in prayer you enter the presence of Him whose favor is strength and joy and life.

T. M. PETERS, D.D.
President.

REPORT OF THE EXECUTIVE COMMITTEE.

To the Board of Trustees of The Sheltering Arms:

GENTLEMEN:—In accordance with the requirements of the By-Laws of our Institution, the Executive Committee have directed me to present you with the following Annual Report —a Report, which, under the blessing of Almighty God, should lead us all to renewed efforts to extend the bounds of the charity we have been called upon to represent.

The past year has been, in many ways, one of peculiar interest and encouraging success—new friends have been continually added to those we already had, and from many unlooked-for sources have our daily wants been supplied. Since our last Report we have been enabled to commence the new and permanent House on the land purchased some time since in Manhattanville, and before the Summer is past we hope to be fully and comfortably established therein. At the last annual meeting we were directed to carry out the long-wished-for plan of this our permanent home, and now we are enabled to report that the building is all but completed.

During the past year we have had, on an average, over ninety children continually under our care, and the record presents a most satisfactory and encouraging report in each and every department of the work; the expenses of the charity for the year have been restricted in every possible way, the health of the children has been zealously watched, and we have to record but few exceptions to the usual answer to the medical call that "all are well." Our supplies have also been on an unusually liberal scale, and afford the most positive and satisfactory proof that "The Sheltering Arms" not only fills a gap heretofore neglected in the charities of our city, but that the manner in which it has been conducted meets both the approval and requirements of those who would know that the means they can give should be bestowed where they can produce the best results. The ladies in charge of the House have fulfilled their self-imposed duties to the perfect satisfaction of every member of our committee. By no means ignorant of the remarks made in many quarters regarding the peculiar status of the sisterhood to which they belong, they have nevertheless devoted their time and energies to the work in hand, and by their constant self-denial and uniform gentleness of manner, have won from all with whom their duties have brought them in contact, a universal recognition of the high and noble charity which alone could inspire them to devote their whole life to such an arduous and unremunerative calling; for this caring for the poor, although one of the noblest and most Christlike occupations, is by no means an "inviting call," unless the heart be already prepared to follow the Master whithersoever he goeth; there are but few amongst us who can thus contentedly resign the attractions and enjoyments of the world, and when such are found we should be always ready to recognise their claims upon us for encouragement and support; of their motive and sincerity we can only judge by their life, and their life is but love in act.

The paper started some time since in behalf of the Institution, also deserves your most generous recognition and support. Under the management of the ladies' association it has constantly improved, and bears, month by month, to many a home, to many an enquiring mind, the details of our work. We are fully convinced that the news we have been enabled to disseminate through this channel has, in no small way, contributed, during the past year, to our present success.

The work done by our Ladies' Association also calls for your warmest acknowledgments. To their unwearied and unceasing interest "The Sheltering Arms" owes much of its position to-day. Since their first organization to the present time, they have continually added to the number of our contributors and supporters some of our warmest friends we now lay claim to. Under the counsel and guidance of the President of this Board, they have projected and carried through such labors of love and charity, as Fairs, Concerts, &c., as only women can successfully organize and support, and in this way have led from many otherwise unknown sources those important supplies which have enabled us to meet our daily wants.

It must, of course, be apparent to every one of us, that the success of an Institution such as we represent, and the amount of good it accomplishes, year by year, can only be truly judged of by the increase of those interested in its wellfare, and judging The Sheltering Arms by this—at once the truest and most conclusive test—we may indeed close the record of the past year with sincere thanksgiving for the good we may have been enabled, under a kind and merciful Providence, to perform, and for the strong incentive thereby furnished us, to further and ever increasing activity in the work we have undertaken.

Thus we close the history of the fifth year of our existence as a Charitable Home for those who, as yet but infants, claim from the older members of a common brotherhood, that support and assistance which our Saviour has directed those who love and would follow him to bestow upon the poor, that they may hereafter be recipients of the full blessing He has promised to pronounce to those who really love Him: "Inasmuch as ye did it unto one of these the least of my brethen, ye did it unto me."

HENRY J. CAMMANN,
Secretary.

May 10*th,* 1869.

OBJECTS OF THE INSTITUTION.

The Sheltering Arms was opened October 6, 1864, for the reception of homeless children, for whom no other institution provides.

The classes of children received are as follows:

1st. The blind and deaf mutes, until the age at which they become entitled to admission at the Asylums especially devoted to such unfortunates.

2d. Crippled children, past hope of cure, and therefore no longer retained in ordinary hospitals.

3d. Children of poor parents, obliged on account of sickness to enter a hospital, and who commit their children for a season, to our charge, with the expectation upon recovery of reclaiming their own.

4. Children rendered temporarily homeless by fire or other accident.

5. Children whose home has been broken up by the intemperance or desertion of father or mother. In such cases, the remaining parent pays according to ability a small sum monthly.

6. Children abandoned by both parents, brought to us by friends or relatives unable to find immediately a proper home and yet unwilling to lose control of the children or to place them beyond their reach.

Children placed at The Sheltering Arms are not surrendered to the Institution, but are held subject to the order of parents and relations.

All the children of sufficient age attend the school of the Institution, where they receive a common education. The larger girls are also trained to household work, under the Sisters of St. Mary, to whose charge has been committed the internal management of the House. The children attend St. Michael's Protestant Episcopal Church, and are under the pastoral care of its Rector, the Rev. T. M. Peters.

ACT OF INCORPORATION AND CERTIFICATES.

{ U. S. Rev. Stamp 5 cents. }

In conformity with the provisions of an Act entitled "An Act for the Incorporation of Benevolent, Charitable, Scientific and Missionary Societies," passed on the twelfth day of April, 1848, and the amendments thereto, the subscribers, citizens of the United States and of the State of New York, of full age, being desirous to associate themselves and to become a body politic and corporate for the purpose of establishing in the City of New York, and managing an Asylum for the reception and education of children in need of a home, do hereby make and sign this Certificate.

First. The name or title by which said Society shall be known in law shall be "The Sheltering Arms."

Second. The particular business and object of such Society shall be the establishing, founding, carrying on, and managing an Asylum for the reception and education of children in need of a home. The said business is to be carried on in the City of New York.

Third. The number of Managers of said Asylum shall be twenty-one.

Fourth. The names of the Managers of said Society for the first year shall be:

Frederick S. Winston,
Henry J. Cammann,
Hermann C. von Post,
William Alex. Smith,
William J. Beebe,
Gideon Pott,
William K. Kitchen,
Peter C. Tiemann,
William B. Clerke,
William Tracy,
Simeon Draper,

James Punnett,
B. Watson Bull,
William A. Haines,
Horatio Potter,
D. Tilden Brown,
Robert S. Howland,
Benjamin H. Field,
John H. Riker,
Charles H. Pond,
William B. Asten.

IN WITNESS WHEREOF, we have hereunto subscribed our names and affixed our seals in the City of New York, the third day of October, in the year of our Lord one thousand eight hundred and sixty-four.

WM. K. KITCHEN, [L. S.]
WM. ALEX. SMITH, [L. S.]
J. PUNNETT, [L. S.]
F. S. WINSTON, [L. S.]
D. T. BROWN. [L. S.]

STATE OF NEW YORK, }
CITY AND COUNTY OF NEW YORK, } ss.

{ U. S.
Rev. Stamp
5 cents. }

On this third day of October, one thousand eight hundred and sixty-four before me personally appeared William K. Kitchen, Frederick S. Winston, William Alexander Smith, James Punnett, and D. Tilden Brown, to me known to be the individuals described in and who executed the foregoing instrument, and severally acknowledged that they executed the same for the uses and purposes therein mentioned.

MYER J. ISAACS,
Notary Public,
New York City.

I approve of the foregoing Certificate of Incorporation, and consent to the filing thereof in the office of the Secretary of State and also in the office of the Clerk of the City and County of New York, the latter being the place of business of said incorporation.

New York, October 8th, 1864.

WM. H. LEONARD,
Justice, &c.

(Endorsed), filed October 8, 1864.

STATE OF NEW YORK,
OFFICE OF THE SECRETARY OF STATE.

I have compared the preceding with the original Certificate of Incorporation of "The Sheltering Arms," with acknowledgment thereto annexed, filed in this office on the tenth day of October, 1864, and hereby certify the same to be a correct transcript therefrom and of the whole of said original.

[L. S.] Witness my hand, and seal of office of the Secretary of State, at the City of Albany, this tenth day of October, one thousand eight hundred and sixty-four.

ERASTUS CLARK,
Deputy Secretary of State.

STATE OF NEW YORK,
CITY AND COUNTY OF NEW YORK, } ss.

I, HENRY W. GENET, Clerk of the said City and County, do certify that I have compared the preceding with the original Certificate of Incorporation of "The Sheltering Arms" on file in my office, and that the same is a correct transcript therefrom and of the whole of such original.

[L. S.] IN WITNESS WHEREOF, I have hereunto subscribed my name and affixed my official seal, this 12th day of October, 1864.

H. W. GENET,
Clerk.

THE SHELTERING ARMS in Account with J. S. BREATH, Treasurer.

1868.				Dr.
May 1	To Expenditure for Permanent Home			$28,796 01
to	"	"	Bread	1,831 02
1869,	"	"	Meat and Fish	1,323 14
May 1.	"	"	Milk	1,035 23
	"	"	Groceries and Vegetables	2,082 50
	Carried forward,			$35,068 50

	Brought forward,	$35,008 40	
To Expenditure for Fuel		701 50	
"	"	Gas and Water	401 60
"	"	Wages and Labor	1,104 54
"	"	Repairs and Alterations	743 22
"	"	Tax	244 48
"	"	Rent of School House	150 00
"	"	Insurance	113 44
"	"	Household Materials	334 05
"	"	Printing & Advertising	484 48
"	"	Stamps & Stationery	120 72
"	"	Salaries and Collection	1,447 17
"	"	Sundries	481 69
"	"	Balance	188 84
			$41,653 23

Cr.			
May 1	By Balance of last Report	$33 03	
to	" Donations	25,884 26	
1869	" Annual Subscriptions & Paper	865 50	
May 1.	" Comptroller of the State	861 01	
	Award of damages by Boulevard	11,900 00	
	Received for Board	2,108 83	
			$41,653 23

NEW YORK, May 29, 1869.

At a meeting of the Finance Committee of The Sheltering Arms, held this day at the Bank of America, the account of the Treasurer for the year ending April 30th, 1869, was examined, compared with the vouchers and found correct, the same showing total receipts, including balance from previous year, amounting to $41,653 23, total expenditures amounting to $41,464 39, and a balance thus remaining on hand May 1, 1869, of $188 84.

H. C. VAN POST, *Chairman*.
WM. B. CLERKE,
J. PUNNETT.

ANNUAL SUBSCRIBERS.

—:o:—

Mrs. D. B. Allen...................................	10 00
Mrs. Ash	10 00
Annual Subscription...............................	5 00
Mrs. E. E. Anderson...............................	5 00
Mrs. H. D. Aldrich, per Miss Kemble....	10 00
Mrs. Hugh Auchincloss	5 00
Mrs. Elizabeth Brittan............................	5 00
Mrs. James Brooks.................................	5 00
Miss Amy W. Boardman, through Miss Kemble.......	5 00
Mrs. James Brooks, 2d Donation, through Mrs. Lee....	5 00
Mrs. D. B. Bodell, through Miss Tiemann............	5 00
Miss Nellie Blodgett	25 00
Mrs. F. J. Bumstead, through Miss Holmes	5 00
Mrs. Edwin T. Butler, through Mrs. Gilman	5 00
C. W. Cooper, through Miss Cooper....	10 00
George Cooper, through Miss Cooper.	5 00
William Cooper, through Miss Cooper	10 00
Mrs. Colden, through Miss Kemble.......	5 00
Miss Mary Cooke, '68, '69, through Miss Kemble......	10 00
Mrs. J. J. Coddington, through Miss Kemble..........	5 00
Mrs. Henry Cram, through Miss Kemble,.............	5 00
Mrs. Josepha J. Case (Mrs. Lee).....................	5 00
Miss Cunard, through Mrs. H. C. Von Post...........	5 00
Miss Kate Cammann	3 00
H. H. Cammann, through Miss Cammann	5 00
Mrs. R. L. Cutting, through Miss Kemble............	5 00
Mrs. J. J. Coddington, through Miss Kemble	10 00
Mrs. F. W. Coggill.................................	5 00
Mrs. Wm. P. Dixon.................................	10 00
Miss Delaplaine	5 00
Mrs. D. B. Dash, through Miss Kemble..............	5 00
Mrs. James Geddes Day, through Miss Kemble	5 00
Mrs. G. B. Docharty, through Mrs. Gilman............	5 00
Mrs. Wm. P. Dixon, 2d Donation...................	10 00
Mrs. D. M. Edgar.	5 00

Mrs. H. Everdell..	5 00
Mrs. James A. Edgar, through Miss Kemble..........	5 00
Miss Emmet, through Mrs. Von Post.................	3 00
Mrs. Fitzgerald	10 00
Miss M. Glover, through Miss Holmes...............	5 00
Mrs. Gerry, through Miss Kemble....................	5 00
Miss J. B. Gerry, through Miss Kemble..............	5 00
Miss M. M. Gaudy, through Miss Kemble	5 00
Miss Lillie C. Hall, through Mrs. Hall...............	5 00
Mrs. Daniel Hoag...................................	10 00
Miss M. E. Horner..................................	10 00
Mrs. P. Hanford, through Mrs. Gilman..............	5 00
Mrs. Ogden Hoffman	5 00
Mrs. P. R. Hoffman, through Miss Kemble...........	10 00
Mrs. A. S. Hewitt, through Miss Tiemann...........	10 00
Mrs. J. C. Hull, through Miss Chauncey	3 00
Mrs. Watson Hildreth, through Miss Chauncey	5 00
Mrs. C. W. Hull, through Miss Chauncey...........	5 00
Mrs. Charles Heywood (Mrs. Gilman)	5 00
Mrs. C. H. Isham, through Miss Pierson............	5 00
Miss Mary S. Jones, through Miss Kemble..........	5 00
Charles A. Jackson	5 00
Mrs. Deborah Rebecca Isaacs........................	5 00
Mrs. J. Keator, through Miss Tiemann..............	5 00
Miss E. Kemble	5 00
Miss E. Low, through Miss Peters..................	5 00
Miss Julia A. Low, through Miss Kemble...........	5 00
Mrs. Wm. P. Lee, through Miss Kemble	5 00
Mrs. Walter H. Lewis, through Miss Kemble........	5 00
Mrs. C. Livingston, through Miss Kemble...........	5 00
E. L. Molineux, through Miss Tiemann	5 00
B. C. Morris, Jr....................................	5 00
Mrs. J. T. Metcalfe, through Mrs. Von Post.........	10 00
Mrs. J. B. Murray, through Miss Kemble...........	5 00
Mrs. Isaiah Mankin, through Miss Kemble..........	5 00
Mrs. A. B. Morrell	5 00
Mrs. Bache McEvers, through Mrs. Von Post	5 00
Samuel Newby.......................................	5 00

Mrs. Geo. B. Ogden, through Miss Kemble...	5 00
Mrs. Hobart Onderdonk (Mrs. Gilman)................	5 00
Miss S. E. Pierson, through Miss Kemble.............	5 00
Mrs. Geo. P. Quackenbuss, through Miss Newby......	5 00
Mrs. Mary Ann Reeder, Varick, N. Y.	5 00
" Sylvanus Reed, through Miss Lee..	5 00
Miss Geraldine Reed, " "	5 00
Mrs. G. A. Robins, through Miss Kemble....	10 00
" M. A. Reeder, 2d Donation.................	5 00
" L. A. Rodenstein, through Miss Tiemann........	5 00
The Misses Renshaw, through Miss Chauncey.........	10 00
Mrs. Thomas Rutter, " "	5 00
Gustav Schwab.....	10 00
Mrs. Shedden, through Miss Holmes..........	5 00
" G. R. Schieffelin..........................	5 00
" Wm. A. Smith, through Miss Kemble...........	5 00
" Augustus Schermerhorn, through Miss Kemble...	5 00
" A. T. Sackett.	10 00
" R. S. Tucker, through Miss Kemble	5 00
" Theodore Timpson, through Mrs. Lee	5 00
" E. L. Trowbridge, " Miss Kemble........	5 00
" Dan'l F. Tiemann, " " Tiemann	5 00
Miss Martha C. Tiemann, " " "	5 00
Mrs. H. C. Von Post...........................	10 00
" A. J. Vanderpool, through Miss Kemble.	5 00
Miss C. H. Van Wyck......	5 00
Hermann C. Von Post.	100 00
Miss E. Von Post, through Mrs. Von Post....	5 00
H. F. Webster, through Miss Kemble.	5 00
Miss A. Wilkes, " " "	5 00
" G. Wilkes, " " " ....:......	5 00
" H. R. Wilkes," " "	5 00
Wm. Whitlock, Jr., through Mrs. Von Post	10 00
Mrs. Wm. H. Wisner, through Miss Kemble	10 00
" Robert Winthrop, " " "	5 00
" H. D. Wyman, " " "	10 00
" S. Wetmore, " " "	5 00
" D. B. Williamson.	5 00

Mrs. S. H. Whitlock, through Mrs. Von Post..........   5 00
"   S. J. Zabriskie.............................. 10 00

LIST OF DONATIONS.

All Saints' Church, Briar Cliff, Whit-Sunday Offertory, through Rev. R. B. Post...............	$1 20
A Friend..	20 00
Miss Minnie Adams.................................	3 40
A Friend, $2; a Friend, for Shoes, $2 50...........	4 50
All Saints' Church, Briar Cliff....................	50
Through Mrs. Aborn—B. F...........................	36 20
Mrs. A..	25 00
A Small Token from F. S. H........................	3 00
A Friend, $5; a Lady Friend, $2...................	7 00
John Alstyne......................................	50 00
Mrs. Aaron Arnold.................................	10 00
Albert's Offering.................................	33
A Friend, through Miss Chauncey...................	30 00
C. F. Alvord......................................	5 00
George C. Allen...................................	5 00
William H. Aspinwall..............................	100 00
D. H. Arnold......................................	10 00
Miss A. E. Alsop..................................	5 00
H. E. Ahrens......................................	1 00
American Merchants' Union Express Co..............	25 00
Mrs. A. A. Alvord.................................	5 00
Mrs. Peter Ammerman...............................	5 00
J. W. Alsop.......................................	25 00
Lloyd Aspinwall...................................	25 00
Benjamin Aymar....................................	20 00
Mrs. Elizabeth Aymar..............................	5 00
Mrs. R. T. Auchmuty...............................	10 00

Mrs. James Bridge..	5 00
Katie Barstow, Annie W. Brown, Nellie Delano, Mary B. S., Julia A. Shaw, Olivia Brown, Louise Bonnell, Lilly Macy, Dickie Anthony, and Sammy Shaw...	3 90
Rev. Joseph Brewster..	5 00
Little Anna Bumstead..	2 00
Master Elliott Bumstead......................................	2 00
Thomas Barron, through H. J. Cammann..............	50 00
A. B. Berard..	2 40
N. P. Bailey—B. F., through Miss Cammann..........	20 00
James L. Bogert..	25 00
Henry K. Bogert..	25 00
D. C. Birdsall..	5 00
Boynton, Richardson & Co..................................	5 00
Mrs. Japhet Bishop..	25 00
C. P. Burdett..	25 00
Miss J. Brinckerhoff...	10 00
Mrs. John Bloodgood...	10 00
Henry J. Barbey..	20 00
Mrs. V. Brown..	5 00
S. L. M. Barlow..	5 00
James A. Benedict...	5 00
N. A. Baldwin..	25 00
Mrs. William F. Beekman...................................	5 00
Mrs. J. H. Barre..	10 00
G. Banyer..	10 00
S. W. Barnard..	5 00
Stephen Brush..	10 00
Mrs. Adelia Broose..	5 00
J. V. B. Bleecker...	5 00
William Barton...	5 00
Mrs. Martha C. Babcock....................................	5 00
Sylvanus Bedell, through Miss Tiemann.................	5 00
Bridget..	1 00
Mrs. G. A. Brown, S. Orange, N. J......................	5 00
William J. Beebe...	100 00
William Betts..	10 00
Daniel C. Blodgett...	10 00

George Barclay	25 00
J. H. Beckman	5 00
Charles Barton	1 00
Mrs. H. C. Beach	9 00
Miss R. Blauvelt	1 00
Calvin Burr	20 00
James Bryce	10 00
Cornelius Bogert	25 00
James Baker	5 00
O. M. Bogert	5 00
Miss J. M. Boardman	20 00
Mrs Clift	10 00
Little Children, through Mrs. Little	1 25
Comptroller of the City, for damage occasioned by opening Boulevard	11,000 00
Christ's Church, Piermont, through Rev. S. G. Hitchcock	5 00
Poor Children of the Church of the Nativity, N. Y., their earnings	10 00
Mrs. J. B. Church, Jr.	5 00
W. B. Clerke, for Publication of Paper	20 00
Christ's Church, Rye, N. Y., through American Church Missionary Society	41 55
Church of the Redeemer, N. Y., through Rev. J. W. Shackleford	10 50
Collection in Trinity Chapel—B. F.	211 36
Ella Virginia and Little Geo. Coggill	5 00
Peter Cooper, Golden Wedding Fund	50 00
C., through H. J. Cammann—B. F.	15 75
John Caswell	50 00
M. H. Caswell	5 00
W. B. Clerke	25 00
Mrs. Peter Cooper—B. F.	5,000 00
Children's Missionary Box, Portchester, N. Y.	6 72
R. L. Cutting	25 00
Thomas W. Clerke, through W. B. Clerke	10 00
Mrs. H. Colt	5 00
Jay, Cooke & Co., through Miss Kitchen	50 00

F. W. Coggill	25 00
A. B. Clark	5 00
John J. Cisco	25 00
Mrs. H. H. Crocker	5 00
Mrs. Martha Coles	25 00
Mrs. Mary Clarkson	5 00
Mrs. J. B. Church	5 00
Mrs. N. Chandler	5 00
F. P. Chase	2 00
George Chesterman	10 00
M. & H. Clarkson	50 00
Comptroller of State	801 01
Christ's Church, Watertown, Conn., through Rev. Wm. H. Lewis	40 00
W. L. Chamberlain	5 00
C. B. Collins	25 00
Mrs. S. G. Courtney	5 00
D. A. Cushman	50 00
Miss M. G. Corlies	10 00
J. Collis	5 00
A few Children of Grace Church, N. Y., through Rev. H. C. Potter, D. D	25 00
W. A. Camp	5 00
J. M. Calvocoressi	25 00
Church of the Transfiguration, through Mrs. W. C. Gilman	25 00
Mrs. Elie Charlier	10 00
H. K. Corning	50 00
James F. Cox	10 00
Mrs. Wm. Cotheal	5 00
Proceeds of Concert at Dr. Ward's, through Mrs. Wm. P. Lee—B. F	900 00
John B. Cornell—B. F	$50 00
Henry Clews—B. F	10 00
Cash, $1, $5, $2, $1, $5, $2, $10, $5, $5	36 00
Cash, $2, 10, $5, $2, $25, $1, $4, $2, $5, $10, $1	67 00
Cash, $5—B. F	5 00
Cash, $10, $3, $10, $1, $1, $20, $1, $2, $25	73 00

Cash, $10, $1, $2, $1, $2............................	10 00
Miss F. A. Cooper, through Mrs. Hall...............	5 00
Rev. George B. Draper, D. D.......................	5 00
Mrs. S. Draper, through H. J. Cammann............	25 00
The Misses Draper, through H. J. Cammann........	25 00
J. H. Draper, " "	25 00
Through Miss Drake...............................	100 00
James F. De Peyster...............................	25 00
H. E. Davies......................................	5 00
Mrs. Wm. H. Draper...............................	5 00
" Douglass....................................	5 00
" David Dows.................................	25 00
E. J. Dunning.....................................	5 00
Mrs. A. Denison...................................	5 00
Fred'k De Payster—$100, $100, $300, B. F..........	500 00
Charles Denison...................................	5 00
W. B. Dinsmore...................................	25 00
Miss Dix, Easter Offering..........................	10 00
Mrs. Philip Dater..................................	10 00
Miss Dater..	10 00
" Helen Dater...................................	10 00
Mrs. S. Daubeny, Sing Sing........................	5 00
J. B. Dickinson....................................	5 00
"D."—B. F..	50 00
"D. A. W."..	10 00
A. Duryea...	5 00
"D."...	20 00
Mrs. Susan D......................................	5 00
" Thos. Eggleston—B. F., through W. M. Kingsland..	20 00
E. L. H., through Miss Holmes.....................	5 00
Mrs. Henry Eagle, through Mrs. Gilman............	5 00
Henry Eyre.......................................	10 00
Tracy R. Edson....................................	10 00
Easter Offering of Calvary Church, N. Y. Sunday School, through Rev. E. Washburn, D. D.........	273 29
Easter Offering of Sunday School of St. Clement's Church, N. Y., through Rev. Theodore A. Eaton...	00 07

S. C. Evans..	5 00
Easter Offering of the Annandale Parish School, through Rev. R. B. Fairbairn....................	33 00
Easter Offering of St. John's Church, Stamford, Conn..	20 00
" " children " " "	8 34
" " boys, Class 4, in Sunday School of St. Paul's Church, New Haven, Conn.............	15 00
Easter Offering of Sunday School of St. James' Church, Great Barrington, Mass., through Rev. H. Olmsted,..	25 70
Easter Offering of Christ's Church, Poughkeepsie, (of which $22 63 is from the pupils of Cottage Hill Seminary..	27 91
Mrs. Smith Ely.......................................	10 00
James F. Fuller, through H. C. Cammann............	25 00
George W. Fuller, " " "	10 00
J. D. Fish, " " "	10 00
Mrs. J. M. Farr......................................	5 00
Florence, Jessie, and Fanny, of Glen Cove, L. I........	1 50
A Friend, through James Punnett....................	10 00
J. M. Fisk...	10 00
A Friend, $2, $2....................................	4 00
W. H. Ford..	10 00
Mrs. L. B. Field.....................................	5 00
Mrs. H. Fales..	5 00
Thomas H. Faile.....................................	100 00
Miss M. L. Frost.....................................	5 00
J. P. Girard Foster...................................	10 00
A Friend, for Easter Uniform........................	25 00
H. C. Fahnestock....................................	50 00
Benjamin H. Field...................................	100 00
Mrs. W. O. Fitzgerald................................	1 00
Proceeds of a Fair held by the Young Ladies' Bible Class and Christ's Little Folk, of the Church of the Incarnation, through Miss Van Horne—B. F......	210 00
S. H. Fish...	15 00
Mrs. W. A. Freeborn.................................	10 00
F. C. H..	5 00

William H. Fogg	100 00
Proceeds of a Fair held by the Young Ladies of Mrs. Steers' School	500 00
Mrs. Isaac Gibson	2 00
G. T.	0 50
Thomas Garner, through his Executors	1,880 00
Samuel Graydon	25 00
A. Graham	10 00
Mrs. George T. Gilman	10 00
" George Griswold	10 00
" J. Grafton	10 00
Charles C. Goodhue	10 00
Mrs. Frederick Goodridge	10 00
" Wm. C. Gilman, B. F.	50 00
" S. K. Green	3 00
"St. Michaels and All Angels," 1868, Gracie's Birth-day Offering	50 00
Azel Graham—B. F.	500 00
"G. B." through H.	20 00
T. P. Grinnell	5 00
Hobart Hall, Young Ladies of	2 39
Henry J. Hoffmann	10 00
Miss Lillie C. Hall	5 00
Mrs. Huntington	2 00
" O. E. Hosmer	3 00
Hatch, Foote & Co.	5 00
James M. Hartshorne	25 00
Miss Emily Hollingsworth, Portchester	5 00
S. V. Hoffman	25 00
L. C. Hamersly	5 00
J. Hendricks	5 00
"Helping Hand" of St. James' Church, Newtown, L. I., through Rev. Sam'l Cox, D. D.	75 00
Mrs. E. S. Higgins	10 00
" J. Howe	5 00
V. G. Hall	25 00
Mrs. V. G. Hall	25 00
" Hodge	2 00

Mrs. G. Hatch.	2 00
Rev. E. A. Hoffmann, D. D.	25 00
James A. Hearn, through Miss Tiemann.	2 00
Geo. A. Hearn, through D. S. Jackson, Jr.	25 00
Frances D. Harrison.	10 00
Mrs. Sidney S. Harris, through Mrs. Gilman.	10 00
Miss Holland's Sunday School Class in St. Matthew's Church, Jersey City.	5 00
The Misses Hadden.	25 00
Mrs. Frances Hoyt, through Miss Gilman.	2 00
M. P. Hosack.	3 00
Harnden and National Express Co.	25 00
C. C. Haight—B. F.	500 00
Miss Alice Haven—B. F.	10 00
" Nina Haven—B. F.	10 00
J. E. F's. Thank Offering *Pro Patria*.	20 00
Richard Irwin.	25 00
Mrs. Wm. B. Ireland.	5 00
George R. Jackson, through H. J. Cammann.	25 00
Mrs. W. L. Jenkins.	10 00
D. S. Jackson, Jr.	10 00
Mrs. H. A. Johnston.	10 00
F. P. James.	10 00
Rev. Wm. A. Johnson.	2 00
Miss N. M. Jones, B. F.—.	5 00
George Jones.	25 00
Edward Jones.	25 00
Mrs. S. R. Johnson.	5 00
William M. Kingsland.	20 00
William M. Kingsland—B. F.	400 00
Arthur Kimber through H. J. Cammann—B. F.	250 00
Mrs. A. M. Kalbfleisch, through Miss Cooper.	10 00
Mrs. J. P. Kernochan.	25 00
Edward King.	5 00
Mrs. F. H. Kalbfleisch, B. F.—through Miss Cooper.	5 00
Katie & Daisey, Easter Offering.	5 00
Mrs. Peter V. King.	5 00
P. R. Kearney.	15 00

Mrs. George Keys	5 00
Mrs. E. Ketoltas	10 00
Frank E. Kernochan	10 00
Kitty	00
Charles Kneeland	25 00
Isaac L. Kip	10 00
Miss Louisa Lawrence—B. F. through Mrs. Gilman	2 00
Mrs. Liddell	1 00
E. Livingston	10 00
Maria E. Livingston	25 00
Wm. C. Lee	5 00
Mrs. M. Lockwood	10 00
Mrs. E. R. Lamson	10 00
Miss Julia A. Low	25 00
E. H. Ludlow	10 00
Miss Kate Lawrence	5 00
Mrs. Cornelia Livingston	5 00
A. A. Low & Brother	100 00
A. N. Lawrence	10 00
Edwin C. Litchfield	100 00
Mrs. R. J. Livingston	25 00
Daniel LeRoy	5 00
Mrs. Walter H. Lewis	10 00
Miss Lawrence, through Mrs. Gilman	3 00
Mrs. P. M. Lydig	2 00
Miss R. Lydig	1 00
Wm. P. Lee—B. F.	100 00
M. R. C.	2 00
William Weyman Mali	100 00
Charles Mali	10 00
Thomas Morrell	25 00
Thomas McMullen—B. F.	10 00
Henry Meigs, Jr.	20 00
Mrs. Meigs	5 00
Zophar Mills	5 00
E. Matthews	25 00
N. A. Murdock	10 00
Henry Morrison	3 00

Josiah Macys Sons..............................	100 00
Mrs. Peter Morris..............................	10 00
Thos. Middleton, through H. C. Von Post.......	25 00
Mrs. H. G. Marquand...........................	5 00
A. B. McDonald................................	25 00
Miss L. E. Morgan.............................	5 00
L. G. Morris..................................	25 00
Isaac P. Martin...............................	25 00
George Moke...................................	10 00
Mrs. L. P. Morton.............................	5 00
Henry Morgan..................................	20 00
R. L. Mulford.................................	5 00
John R. Maurice,..............................	25 00
Edward Minturn, through Miss Kemble...........	30 00
Francis Many..................................	50 20
M. L. B. Martin...............................	50 00
R. H. Macy....................................	20 00
R. H. McCurdy.................................	10 00
Levi P. Morton—B. F...........................	100 00
Samuel F. B. Morse—B. F.......................	50 00
Member of St. Paul's Church, New York, through Rev. Dix......................................	200 00
Morties Offering, through Rev. Mr. Sill.......	6 37
Mrs. North, Stratford, Connecticut............	5 00
George F. Nesbitt.............................	3 00
Mrs. S. P. Nash...............................	10 00
Through Miss Newby, Easter Uniform............	5 00
Mrs. E. H. Nichols............................	10 00
Offerings in St. Michael's Church, New York...	55 00
Offerings in St. Michael's Church, New York, for fuel..	100 00
W. Oothout....................................	20 00
J. V. Onativia................................	20 00
Thank Offering from Mrs. Charles Milner, through "Sister"......................................	25 00
Miss Mary C. Phelps...........................	2 00
Edward D. Peters, Boston......................	25 00
Mrs. George H. Peters, do.....................	10 00
P. H. H.......................................	10 00

Mrs. Jno. J. Phelps, through Mrs. H. C. Von Post	10 00
Master Horace Porter—B. F.	15 00
W. W. Parkin	10 00
C. L. Perkins	10 00
John Pyne	5 00
A. Pell, Jr.	6 00
Mrs. A. M. Pell	5 00
Samuel Philips	5 00
Mrs. Gideon Pott	5 00
Mrs. S. J. Penniman	5 00
Percy R. Pyne	25 00
G. W. Pell	5 00
Edmund Penfold	50 00
J. J. Petit	25 00
Dora Parks	1 00
William Paul	50 00
L. H. Pignolet	20 00
Howard Potter	50 00
Penny Collection—B. F.	6 00
Charles Peace, Jr.	5 00
Penny Savings, through Lent, of Nettie Willie & Louis of Trinity Church S. School, Brooklyn, Connecticut, through F. B. Garnett	0 00
J. G. Pearson—B. F.	10 00
John R. Platt	25 00
William Powell	5 00
Mrs. D. Parish	5 00
George P. Quackenboss	5 00
J. H. Riker	50 00
Miss Rathbone	1 00
Richard & his Mother for blind Minnie	1 25
T. W. Riley	10 00
T. Reynolds	5 00
J. Renwick	10 00
Miss Reed	10 00
Mrs. M. A. C. Rogers	10 00
W. P. Reed	25 00
W. Redmond, Jr.	5 00

Wolcott Richards	5 00
Miss Mary L. Reed	1 00
C. B. Ransom	25 00
Theodore Roosevelt—B. F.	25 00
Miss D. E. Ritter—B. F. through Miss Kemble	5 00
Second Class in St. Anns Church, Matteawan, for blind Minnie, through Rev. H. E. Duncan	80
St. James' Church Poquetannock, through Rev. Jas. Adams	2 00
S. School of St. Ambrose Church, N. Y., through R. W. Bootman	11 00
14th Class in S. School of St. Ann's Church, Matteawan, for Blind Minnie Fund	1 00
E. W. Sackett	5 00
Mrs. Jno. F. Seamen—B. F. through Mrs. Cammann	25 00
Collection in St. George's Chapel of Free Grace	20 00
Children of the S. School of the Church of the Good Shepherd, Hartford, Connecticut, through the Rev. Henry W. Nelson, Jr	17 00
S. School of St. Paul's Church, Franklin, N. Y., earnings of some of the Pupils, through the Rev. Octavus Applegate	5 00
M. Seligman, through H. J. Cammann	5 00
S. School of St. Michael's Church, N. Y.	20 77
S. School of St. James' Church, N. Y., through Mr. Kellogg	19 28
S. School of St. Mary's Church, N. Y, through Rev. Charles C. Adams	20 00
St. Peter's Church, N. Y. through the Rev. Dr. Beach,	45 15
Mrs. Jno. H. Sprague—B. F. through W. M. Kingsland	20 00
Sunday School of St. Albans' Church, N. Y., through Rev. C. W. Morrell	50 00
St. James' Church, Hyde Park, N. Y. Collection, through Rev. Dr. Purdy	17 00
St. Michael's Church, S. School	1 00
Thomas Suffern	25 00
S. School of St. Chrysostomis Chapel, through Rev. Thomas H. Sill	10 24

A Class in St. Ann's Church, Mattcawan, for Blind Minnie Fund.................................	2 62
David Stewart.................................	100 00
Thomas T. Sturges............................	25 00
W. C. Schermerhorn...........................	15 00
"S. E. W." through Mrs. H. C. Von Post.......	10 00
Mrs. B. B. Sherman...........................	10 00
S. K. Satterlee...............................	5 00
Mrs. Charles A. Sherman......................	5 00
Mrs. Rutherford Stuyvesant....................	5 00
J. Seligman...................................	5 00
R. L. Schieffelin.............................	5 00
Miss Helen Sands.............................	1 00
Mrs. A. B. Sands.............................	5 00
Mrs. George R. Schieffelin....................	10 00
Mr. and Mrs. A. V. Stuyvesant................	20 00
Mortie Schuyler, Blind Minnie Fund...........	1 00
Eugene Schieffelin............................	10 00
Mrs. J. A. Strang.............................	5 00
Mrs. N. Sullivan..............................	5 00
Mrs. Augustus Schermerhorn...................	50 00
Mrs. Geo. T. Strong—B. F. through Miss Kemble....	5 00
S. T. Skidmore...............................	5 00
James C. Spencer.............................	25 00
Mrs. Smith...................................	2 00
Mrs. C. V. A. Schuyler, for Easter Uniform....	2 00
Mrs. E. H. Stoughton.........................	5 00
Horatio G. Stevens............................	25 00
Floyd Smith..................................	5 00
W. J. Sherwood...............................	10 00
J. Stokes.....................................	50 00
S. School of St. Paul's Church, Franklin, through A. S. Miller, Warden.......................	5 50
Hamilton R. Searles..........................	10 00
Alfred Schermerhorn..........................	25 00
Frederick W. Stevens.........................	25 00
Mrs. Margaret Smith..........................	5 00
E. B. Sutton.................................	5 00

Samuel S. Sands...	20 00
S. School of All Angels' Church, N. Y., through J. N. Heffernan..	10 00
A. V. H. Stuyvesant, B. F..................................	20 00
Tithe System..	100 00
Mrs. W. H. Tillinghast, through Mrs. Gilman..........	10 00
Townsend & Davis..	10 00
Peter C. Tiemann...	52 00
James Tinker..	10 00
Mrs. C. Totten...	5 00
Miss Emma Townsend.....................................	3 00
T. G. Thomas..	5 00
Mr. and Mrs. C. T. Tillinghast............................	10 00
Miss H. A. Townsend......................................	10 00
William D. Thompson.....................................	25 00
Mrs. William D. Thompson...............................	40 00
Mrs. A. G. Thorpe..	5 00
George H. Talman..	10 00
S. C. Thompson...	10 00
William Tilden..	10 00
Two Little Girls...	2 00
U. S. Express Co..	25 00
C. Van Santvoord...	10 00
Mrs. Van Ness...	1 00
Gen'l E. L. Viele—B. F., through Miss Kemble........	25 00
C. W. Van Ness...	2 00
Mrs. H. C. Von Post, for Easter Uniform..............	5 00
Mrs. A. Vanderpool..	10 00
C. H. Van Brunt...	10 00
Mrs. A. J. Vanderpool—B. F., through Miss Kemble...	15 00
William H. Voorhis...	2 00
Richard Vose..	5 00
Mrs. J. M. White..	25 00
"W. A.," through Dr. Peters...............................	12 50
Mrs. Dan'l Williams, Augusta, Maine...................	10 00
Mrs. Charles W. Whiley, the beginning of a fund having especial reference to children under ten years of age, made temporarily homeless by fire...	50 00

J. D. Wolfe, for Minnie to buy oranges....	5 00
Mrs. H. D. Wyman.................	1,000 00
Horace Williams, Clinton, Iowa.	100 00
Rev. Wm. T. Wilson................	61 26
Weston & Gray....................	100 00
E. Wade, Jr.,.....................	25 00
Mrs. Wright, Binghamton, N. Y.......	5 00
J. H. Wainwright.................	5 00
H. A. Wilmerding................	10 00
Mrs. J. L. Wallack................	5 00
Mrs. J. S. Williams................	5 00
Mrs. Edward White................	5 00
Mrs. Dr. Ward, through Miss Cammann........	3 00
Wells, Fargo & Co.'s Express	20 00
Mrs. G. H. Wisner.	3 00
Mrs. William Whitney.............	5 00
William R. Welling...............	5 00
Mrs. C. L. R. White...............	5 00
Samuel Wetmore...................	20 00
Mrs. A. M. Ward..................	20 00
S. C. Williams....................	5 00
Mrs. C. L. R. White, for Easter Uniform, through Miss Kemble............	5 00
"W. M.".........................	10 00
T, Whittemore....................	10 00
Mrs. J. H. Watson.................	5 00
W. P. Wallace....................	2 00
M. E. Walke.....................	2 00
"W. D. M."....................	10 00
Augustus H. Ward—B. F...........	25 00
John D. Wolfe—B. F..............	5,000 00
Miss Wood	0 50
E. M. Young	10 00
Young Ladies' Penance Society........	10 00

DONATIONS FOR CHRISTMAS.

B. C. Morris, Jr.................	$5 00	
A Little Girl with a Merry Christmas......	5 00	
Carried forward................		$10 00

Brought forward,	–	$10 00
H. J. Hoffman	10 00	
William Voorhees	3 00	
A Friend	2 50	
Mrs. S. J. Zabriskie	20 00	
" D."	5 00	
St. Andrew's Church, Stamford, Conn.	10 00	
Mr. and Miss Ferguson	35 00	
C. O. L.	5 00	
Mrs. J. T. Metcalfe	5 00	
Mrs. H. C. Von Post	5 00	
Miss Emily Von Post	5 00	
Mrs. Thomas Morrell	10 00	
Wm. M. Kingsland	5 00	
The Misses Stevens	10 00	
Jane Devereaux	0 25	
Mrs. D. T. Brown	5 00	
Mrs. Geo. R. Schieffelin	5 00	
Mrs. B. H. Field	10 00	
David H. Knapp	5 00	
Mr. and Mrs. W. A. Smith	10 00	
A Friend in Maine	10 00	
Lewis G. Morris	10 00	
Fordham Morris	5 00	
Mrs. Waring	5 00	
D. Jackson, Jr.	5 00	
Mrs. Wotherspoon	10 00	
Andrew Keating	5 00	
Townsend & Davis	5 00	
		$230 75

FOR THANKSGIVING.

Mr. and Mrs. H. C. Von Post	$10 00	
Mrs. J. T. Metcalfe	5 00	
William P. Lee	5 00	
Mr. and Mrs. Wm. A. Smith	10 00	
Mrs. Forrester	2 00	
Mrs. Anderson	2 00	
		$34 00
Received for the Paper		$71 50

DONATIONS OF CLOTHING, ETC.

MAY, 1868.
- From the Bible Class of St. John's Church, Stamford, Conn., 13 new Aprons.
- Lent Work of the Children of Emmanuel Church, Stamford, Conn., 13 new Garments.
- Mrs. D. F. Tiemann, 1 dozen Towels.
- Mrs. Orr, 1 Apron.
- St. Ann's Sunday School Sewing Society, through Miss Comstock, 14 Aprons, new, and 6 Dresses.
- Mrs. Phillips, Flowers for the Annual Festival.
- Mrs. Wm. H. Lindsley, 49 yards of Calico.
- Mrs. G. R. Schieffelin, 2 new Dresses.
- Miss C. L. Gardiner and Miss R. T. Vose, Boston, 28 new Garments and 4 pairs knitted woolen Stockings.
- Miss E. W. Gardiner, Gardiner, Maine, Slates, Pencils, and Thimbles for the Nursery School.
- The Ladies' Benevolent Society of St. Ann's Church, N. Y., 22 yards Calico.
- Mrs. J. A. White and Miss M. E. Price, 20 new Aprons.
- Mrs. D. Huntington, Books for the Children.

JUNE, 1868.
- Acker & Merrall, Groceries, value $30.
- House of Mercy, Material for Dresses.
- Miss Kittie Bostwick, bundle of Clothing.
- Mrs. J. C. Vark, 10 Aprons.
- The Women's Bible Class, St. John's Parish, Stamford, Conn., 19 new Garments.
- St. John's Mission School, Stamford, Conn., from a few little girls, 9 new garments.
- Unknown, Story Books and 2 pairs of Parlor Skates.
- Unknown, Old Shoes.
- Mr. H. J. Cammann and friends, 150 Baskets of Strawberries.

JULY, 1868.
- Made by the Children of the Parish School of St. Ann's Church, Mattenwan, N. Y., 2 large Patchwork Quilts.
- Knitted by an old Lady of 98 Years, 10 pairs of Stockings.

JULY, 1868.
St. Ann's Church, Matteawan, 16 Dresses and 24 Undergarments.
Sewing School of St. James' Church, Roxbury, Mass., through the Rev. G. S. Converse, 20 Pillow Cases and 20 Undergarments.
Unknown, a large quantity of Clothing for the Boys, partly worn.
Julia Peters, 1 Apron.

AUGUST, 1868.
Mrs. Dr. Bumstead, 1 Suit Clothes, 3 Boy's Belts, 1 pair Shoes.
Julia Peters, 1 Apron.
Mrs. Ten Eyck, Vegetables.
Ladies of St. Michael's Church, Cake for the Children.

SEPTEMBER, 1868.
Mrs. E. H. Davies, Portland, Maine, Clothing.
Miss C. L. Gardiner, Boston, Mass, 6 new Aprons.
Mrs. T. M. Peters, Great Barrington, Mass., Clothing.
Mr. Blakely, Basket of Apples.
Mrs. Zabriskie, Cake.

OCTOBER, 1868.
Miss Thorpe, Clothing.
Mrs. Miller, 5 pairs of Stockings, 1 pair of Mittens, 1 pair of Leggings, 1 Hood and 6 Scarfs, 1 Sontag and woolen Yarn.
Mrs. S. Comstock, 57 pairs of new Shoes.
Mr. Davis and Mr. Dorlan, 100 copies of the *Standard Bearer*.
Miss Kate Mason, Clothing.
Mrs. N. A. Baldwin, Milford, Conn, 1 large box of Clothing.
Miss M. H. Keeler, Clothing.
Mrs. Cary, Clothing.
Mrs. W. E. Ross, 75 yards of Blue Check.
Rev. Dr. Peters, 1 Coat.
Mr. C. H. Baldwin, 1 piece of Woolen Goods, value $28 95.
Unknown, 1 piece of Muslin, 6 new Garments, and a large quantity of Worsted Yarn and Mats.
Mrs. Blackhurst, Clothing.
Miss Comstock, Clothing.
Mrs. Tweddle, half-worn Shoes.

OCTOBER, 1868.
 Mr. Gray, Apparatus for a Paralytic.
NOVEMBER, 1868.
 Mrs. Conklin, Clothing.
 Mrs. Theodore Timpson, Englewood, N. J., 7 pairs knitted woolen Stockings.
 Mrs. Blackhurst, Clothing for the Boys, and Books and Papers.
 Mrs. W. C. Gilman, Clothing and Shoes.
 Mrs. Bogert, Clothing.
 Mrs. Alex. Smith, a piece of Calico.
 Mrs. G. K. Sheridan, Clothing and Shoes for the Boys.
 Mrs. Grout, 4 pairs of Stockings and Calico.
 Mrs. Miller, 1 Hood, 17 pairs of Stockings, and 9 Skeins of Yarn.
 Mrs. W. M. Kingsland, Clothing for the Boys.
 Mrs. Whiting, Great Barrington, Mass., 2 parcels Clothing.
 Mrs. T. M. Peters, 2 boxes Clothing.
 Ladies' Society of St. James' Church, Great Barrington, Mass., Fancy Articles.
 Mrs. Dr. Metcalfe, 3 pairs of knitted woolen Stockings.
 Mrs. P. W. Bedford, 10 packages of Candy.
 J. D. Wolfe, 3 packages of Candy.
 J. D. Wolfe, for Thanksgiving, 35 Mince Pies.
 Freddy and Julius Dossoir, 2 Suits for Boys.
 A Friend, Candies.
 A Friend, 1 Turkey.
 Mrs. Willington, 1 Turkey.
 Mr. W. M. Kingsland, 1 Turkey.
 Mrs. Jessie G. Keator, 1 barrel of Vegetables.
 Mrs. Dr. Chamberlain, Clothing and Shoes.
 Mrs. Grout, 1 Basket Apples.
 Mrs. T. M. Peters, 1 barrel of Apples.
 Mrs. Jno. B. Murray, 9 pairs of knitted woolen Stockings.
 Industrial School of St. Ambrose Church, Patchwork for a Quilt.
DECEMBER, 1868.
 Mrs. Bachmann, 7 new Garments.
 G. F. C. Thompson, 4 new Garments.

DECEMBER, 1868.

Mary G. Pinkney, 1 piece Canton Flannel, 2 pieces unbleached Muslin.

Mrs. Zabriskie, Clothing, Basket of Apples, Toys, and Books, for Christmas.

The old Ladies of St. Luke's Home Benevolent Society, 20 new Aprons.

N. M. M., 4 pairs of knitted woolen Stockings.

Miss Frances Williams, 31 Ribbon Bows for the Boys.

Miss Ferguson, 9 Calico Dresses, 4 Aprons, 16 Flannel Undergarments, 6 Canton Flannel Undergarments, 6 Muslin Undergarments, 5 pairs Woolen Stockings, and 6 pairs Cotton Stockings.

Mrs. P. W. Bedford, Candies.

Mrs. J. H. Walker, Christmas toys.

The Misses Stephens, 12 Dolls, Dressed.

Mrs. Henry Everdell, Boys' and Girls' Clothing, Outer and Undergarments, Shoes and Stockings.

Mrs. C. F. Heywood, Dolls and other Toys for Christmas.

Kitty Everdell and her two little brothers, for the Christmas Tree, 100 Cornucopias and Candy to fill them.

Mrs. Wm. P. Lee, A Box of Dried Fruit, Citron, Currants and Raisins.

Mr. J. D. Wolfe, Candies and Oranges for all the Children.

Nelly and Emma McGunn, 2 large Cornucopias, filled with Candies.

Mrs. Wm. H. Lindsley, 11 pairs of knitted woolen Stockings, 1 piece of Calico, 12 Boxes of Candy.

Mrs. D. F. Tiemann, 120 New Year Cakes.

Mr. Wm. Taylor, through Mrs. D. F. Tiemann, Large Box of Toys and Ornaments for Christmas Tree.

Mrs. Jessie G. Kentor, 24 Articles of Clothing.

Miss Jessie H. Kentor, a doll's carriage and 6 boxes of candy, for the Christmas tree.

Mrs. Dr. Metcalfe and Mrs. H. C. Von Post, 100 cornucopias, filled with candy, and 9 books.

A lady of St. Paul's Church, Eastchester, N. Y., 3 pairs of knitted woolen stockings, 4 pairs of knitted cotton stockings, 5 muslin and 4 flannel undergarments.

DECEMBER, 1868.
  Miss S. R. 12 dolls, dressed, and a box of toys, Christmas tree.
  Mrs. Zeiger, a box of cake and sugar toys.
  Mr. J. D. Wolfe, 50 mince pies.
  From a member of St. Ann's Church, for deaf mutes, 2 turkeys.
  Acker, Merrall & Condit, figs, prunes, lemons, and oranges.
  Thomas C. Hopps, 765 Sixth street, 6 pairs of shoes.
  Sunday School of the Church of the Redeemer, Yorkville,
      through Mr. Kemble, Toys for the Christmas tree.
  Miss Ingersoll, 25 lace stockings, filled with candies.
  Miss Furness, Toys.
  Mrs. Wm. Beebe, Books.
  "Cousin Willie," Rocking chair, for Minnie.
  Mrs. Wm. Guion, 3 packages of cakes.
  Miss Cooper, dolls and candies.
  Miss Brewster, 6 Undergarments, 2 Dresses, Dolls.
  Mrs. McGinniss, Toys and Books.
  Katy and Daisy Blake, 16 Flannel Undergarments, 29 Canton
      Flannel Undergarments.
  Mrs. G. R. Scheiffelin, 2 Toy Tea Setts, 1 Box of Soldiers, 1 Box
      of Building Blocks.
  Gertrude F. Riker, an easy Chair for Willie Stanley.
JANUARY, 1869.
  Mr. R. Prior, 100 New Year Cakes and 1 loaf of Fruit Cake.
  Mr. H. Wagner, 1 Turkey and 29 pounds of Beef.
  "Verein" 4 Muslin Undergarments and 15 Canton Flannel.
  Mrs. W. C. Gilman, Bundle of Clothing for the Boys.
  Master Willie Carter, a Rocking Horse.
  Unknown, half worn Shoes.
  Mrs. Groat, 2 Dresses.
  Mrs. A. Suydam, New Brunswick, N. J., 5 pairs Socks.
  Mrs. Reeves, 3 Sacks and 1 Dress.
  House of Mercy, 3 Dresses and 1 Quilt.
  Unknown, 1 Barrel of Vegetables.
  Mrs. A. S. Hewitt, Parlor Croquet Table and Game.
  From the Cottage Hill Seminary, Poughkeepsie, through Rev.
      G. T. Rider, a box of valuable fancy articles.
  Mrs. Withington, Candies and Oranges.

JANUARY, 1869.
  Mrs. Pliny F. Smith, Clothing.
  Mrs. James Townsend, Clothing & Shoes.
  Mr. Hopp, Shoes.
  Miss Dunham, 10 pairs Socks.
  Mrs. Coddington, 7 Caps, 2 Hats, 16 pairs Stockings, 5 pairs Shoes, 5 bundles Yarn.
  Verein, 24 Canton Flannel Petticoats,
FEBRUARY, 1869.
  Mr. William Goulding, 3 pieces of Ribbon, for the girls' hats for Easter.
  Miss Emmett, 9 pairs of Stockings.
  From the Ladies' Sewing Society of South Orange, 27 New Garments.
  From the Verein Sewing Society, through Mrs. James Heeney, 25 New Garments.
  Anonymous, 11 new Garments.
  Acker & Merrall, Groceries, value $30.
  Mr. D. B. Bedell, Crockery, through Miss Tiemann.
  From the Midnight Mission, a bundle of Infant Clothing.
  From Mr. William Handley, West Hoboken, a number of Pictures.
  All Saints' Parish, Neversink, N. J., through Miss Guion, School Books—1 dozen Spellers, 1 dozen Readers, 1 package Copy Books.
MARCH, 1869.
  Children of St. John's Church, Stamford, Conn., Easter flowers,
  Verein, 21 new Garments.
  Mrs. N. P. Bailey, 1 Sack, Workbox, Brush and Comb, and several Games.
  A Friend, 9 Collars for the boys.
  Mrs. F. Edson, 12 pairs of Socks.
  Mrs. L. Morris, 13 pairs of Stockings.
  Mrs. Wm. H. Lindsley, 60 yards of Dress Material and 6 pairs of Stockings.
  Midnight Mission, Clothing.
  Mrs. Hayden, Clothing.
  Miss Tiemann, Towels and Crockery.

March, 1869.
  Mrs. Archibald, Buns for Good Friday, Worsted and Toys.
  Mrs. Jas. N. Paulding, Clothing.
  Young Ladies' Penance Society, 55 new Garments.
April, 1869.
  Mrs. Stanton, Clothing.
  Mrs. Caswell, 35 new Garments.
  Mrs. Johnson, (blind), 6 new Garments
  German Industrial Mission, Oranges, Cakes, and Candies.
  Little Richard Boyd, a Scrap-Book.
  Girls' Sewing Class of St. Andrew's Parish, Stamford, Conn. Easter gift, 16 Aprons (new) and 20 Handkerchiefs.
  Mary Bradstreet Chadwell, Toys and Books.
  Susy Gifford, through Mr. H. Cammann, a Dress and Apron for Blind Minnie.
  Mrs. James L. Stratton, 26 new Garments.
  Mrs. L. Frank, through Mrs. Stratton, 7 Aprons and 2 Dresses.
  Mrs. T. A. Emmett, 3 pieces of Calico.
  Mrs. Haydin, 3 Shirts.
  Miss Henrietta Haight, 15 new Garments.
  Miss Caswell, 1 dozen Towels and 7 Undergarments.
  Mrs. W. Cortlandt Nicoll, members of Ladies' Association of the Church of the Resurrection, N. Y., 19 new Garments.
  A Friend, 19 new Aprons.
  Willie Pomeroy, 50 Oranges.
  Mrs. Louis F. Therasson, 1 Crib and 1 small Bedstead, with bedding, 1 Pincushion, 1 Hat, and 2 Undergarments,
  Mrs. Therasson, Walking Basket for lame child.
  Miss Tiemann, 7 pairs Socks.
  Mrs. Auchincloss, Oranges and Hommy.
  Mrs. Atwell, Burlington, Vermont, 2 pairs Stockings, 3 Undergarments.

THE SHELTERING ARMS,
Founded in 1864.
10th Avenue and 129th Street.

"THE SHELTERING ARMS."

SIXTH ANNUAL REPORT.

NEW YORK.

1870.

NEW YORK:
W. C. ROGERS & CO., STATIONERS AND PRINTERS,
26 JOHN STREET.

1870.

Trustees of "The Sheltering Arms."

President.

Rev. THOMAS M. PETERS, D. D., Address, B'way, cor. 90th St.

Vice-Presidents.

FRED'K S. WINSTON,	Address, 144 Broadway
WM. ALEX. SMITH,	" 40 Wall Street
WM. J. BEEBE,	" 149 Front St.

Secretary.

HENRY J. CAMMANN. Address, 8 Wall Street.

Treasurer.

J. S. BREATH, 300 Mulberry St.

Visitor.

Rt. Rev. H. POTTER, D. D., D. C. L., L. L. D.. - 38 E. 22d St.

Trustees.

HERMANN C. VON POST,	68 Broad Street.
BENJ. H. FIELD,	127 Water street.
D. TILDEN BROWN, M. D.,	Manhattanville.
PETER C. TIEMANN,	Manhattanville.
WM. B. CLERKE.	25 Broad Street.
WM. H. FOGG,	82 Burling Slip.
THOS. WATT,	430 Fifth Avenue.
J. B. CHURCH, Jr.,	11 Pine Street.
WM. P. LEE,	326 Fifth Avenue.
WM. M. KINGSLAND,	110 Fifth Avenue.
Rev. H. E. MONTGOMERY, D. D.,	200 Madison Avenue.
FRANKLIN EDSON,	19 Whitehall Street.
CHARLES F. STRONG,	68 Wall Street.
WOODBURY G. LANGDON,	51 West 36th St.
ABRAM S. HEWITT,	9 Lexington Avenue.

Physician.

L. A. RODENSTEIN, M. D., - - Manhattanville.

Consulting Physician.

ABRAHAM JACOBI, M. D., - 110 West 34th Street.

Ladies Association of "The Sheltering Arms."

Miss M. CHAUNCEY,	30 East 35th Street.
" S. E. KITCHEN,	Park Bank.
Mrs. WM. P. LEE,	326 Fifth Avenue.
Miss S. B. NEWBY,	314 West 28th Street.
" L. PETERS,	Broadway, cor. 112th St.
" J. A. TIEMANN,	Manhattanville.
" M. A. COOPER,	Bushwick, Long Island.
Mrs. R. W. ABORN,	43 West 39th Street.
Miss S. E. PIERSON,	24 Broadway.
" LIZZIE HOLMES,	123 Fifth Avenue.
Mrs. ROBERT WEIR,	23 West 10th Street.
Miss F. COTHEAL,	26 University Place.
Mrs. JOHN DE RUYTER,	67 Madison Avenue.
Miss KATE BELL,	20 West 20th Street.
Mrs. WOODBURY,	121 West 41st Street.

OBJECTS OF THE INSTITUTION.

"The Sheltering Arms" was opened October 6, 1864, for the reception of homeless children, for whom no other institution provides.

The classes of children received are as follows:

1st. The blind and deaf mutes, until the age at which they become entitled to admission at the Asylums especially devoted to such unfortunates.

2d. Crippled children, past hope of cure, and therefore no longer retained in ordinary hospitals.

3d. Children of poor parents, obliged on account of sickness to enter a hospital, and who commit their children for a season to our charge, with the expectation upon recovery of reclaiming their own.

4th. Children rendered temporarily homeless by fire or other accident.

5th. Children whose home has been broken up by the intemperance or desertion of father or mother. In such cases, the remaining parent pays according to ability a small sum monthly.

6th. Children abandoned by both parents, brought to us by friends or relatives unable to find immediately a proper home and yet unwilling to lose control of the children or to place them beyond their reach.

Children placed at "The Sheltering Arms" are not surrendered to the Institution, but are held subject to the order of parents and relations.

All the children of sufficient age attend the school of the Institution, where they receive a common education. The larger girls are also trained to household work. The children attend St. Mary's Protestant Episcopal Church, and are under the pastoral care of the Rev. T. M. Peters.

ACT OF INCORPORATION AND CERTIFICATES.

{ U. S.
Rev. Stamp
5 cents. }

In conformity with the provisions of an Act entitled "An Act for the Incorporation of Benevolent, Charitable, Scientific and Missionary Societies," passed on the twelfth day of April, 1848, and the amendments thereto, the subscribers, citizens of the United States and of the State of New York, of full age, being desirous to associate themselves and to become a body politic and corporate for the purpose of establishing in the City of New York, and managing an Asylum for the reception and education of children in need of a home, do hereby make and sign this Certificate.

First. The name or title by which said Society shall be known in law shall be "The Sheltering Arms."

Second. The particular business and object of such Society shall be the establishing, founding, carrying on, and managing an Asylum for the reception and education of children in need of a home. The said business is to be carried on in the City of New York.

Third. The number of Managers of said Asylum shall be twenty-one.

Fourth. The names of the Managers of said Society for the first year shall be:

Frederick S. Winston,
Henry J. Cammann,
Hermann C. von Post,
William Alex. Smith,
William J. Beebe,
Gideon Pott,
William K. Kitchen,
Peter C. Tiemann,
William B. Clerke,
William Tracy,
Simeon Draper,
James Punnett,
B. Watson Bull,
William A. Haines,
Horatio Potter,
D. Tilden Brown,
Robert S. Howland,
Benjamin H. Field,
John H. Riker,
Charles H. Pond,
William B. Asten.

IN WITNESS WHEREOF, we have hereunto subscribed our names and affixed our seals in the City of New York, the third day of October, in the year of our Lord one thousand eight hundred and sixty-four.

       WM. K. KITCHEN, [L. S.]
       WM. ALEX. SMITH, [L. S.]
       J. PUNNETT, [L. S.]
       F. S. WINSTON, [L. S.]
       D. T. BROWN. [L. S.]

STATE OF NEW YORK, } ss.   { U. S. Rev. Stamp 5 cents. }
CITY AND COUNTY OF NEW YORK.

On this third day of October, one thousand eight hundred and sixty-four before me personally appeared William K. Kitchen, Frederick S. Winston, William Alexander Smith, James Punnett, and D. Tilden Brown, to me known to be the individuals described in and who executed the foregoing instrument, and severally acknowledged that they executed the same for the uses and purposes therein mentioned.

      MYER J. ISAACS,
        Notary Public,
        New York City.

I approve of the foregoing Certificate of incorporation, and consent to the filing thereof in the office of the Secretary of State and also in the office of the Clerk of the City and County of New York, the latter being the place of business of said incorporation.

New York, October 8th, 1864.

      WM. H. LEONARD,
        Justice, &c.

(Endorsed), filed October 8, 1864.

STATE OF NEW YORK,
OFFICE OF THE SECRETARY OF STATE.

I have compared the preceding with the original Certificate of Incorporation of "The Sheltering Arms," with acknowledgment thereto annexed, filed in this office on the tenth day of October, 1864, and hereby certify the same to be a correct transcript therefrom and of the whole of said orignal.

[L. S.]   Witness my hand, and seal of office of the Secretary of State, at the city of Albany, this tenth day of October, one thousand eight hundred and sixty-four.

ERASTUS CLARK,
Deputy Secretary of State.

STATE OF NEW YORK,
CITY AND COUNTY OF NEW YORK. } ss.

I, HENRY W. GENET, Clerk of said City and County, do certify that I have compared the preceding with the original Certificate of Incorporation of "The Sheltering Arms" on file in my office, and that the same is a correct transcript therefrom and of the whole of such original.

[L. S.]   IN WITNESS WHEREOF, I have hereunto subscribed my name and affixed my official seal, this 12th day of October, 1864.

H. W. GENET,
Clerk.

REPORT

OF THE

Board of Trustees,

MAY, 1870.

The last Annual Report left us with our buildings in progress, payments being made as due up to the date of closing the Treasurer's account, leaving, however, nine thousand dollars on mortgage and thirty thousand dollars required to complete the buildings. To clear off every debt and stop the waste in payment of interest was announced as the sixth year's work.

This task, impossible as it seemed, has been accomplished. Blessed be the Mover of hearts and Giver of all good. We are thankful to be able to announce that our mortgage is paid off and also all the debt incurred in finishing the buildings and fencing the grounds. Our whole property is now unincumbered. To those who have kindly given us their aid to this end we shall show our thanks by faithfully striving to make our Institution an honor to the Church of God and a blessing to our country.

The receipts for current expenses have also enabled us to meet our ever increasing outlay, encouraging us in the belief that, extend our borders as we may, the fountain of supply in faithful hearts and liberal hands will be unfailing.

We are now, therefore, free to prepare for the work announced last year as our next step onward, namely, the erection of the "Innocents' Hospital" for permanent cripples. It has for years been our desire to possess a building especially devoted to the care of such children, both in order that our own helpless little ones might be accommodated, and also that we might receive those discharged as incurable by Dr. Knight's and other hospitals. May we not hope in our next annual Report to record that this cherished wish has been gratified and the poor little ones provided for?

Our patrons are already aware that during the past year we have lost from the Institution, after five and one-half years of quiet and prosperity, its kind and constant friends, the "Sisters of St. Mary." Their devotion and self-denial, their readiness to carry out in relation to the children the wishes of the Trustees had endeared them to all connected with "THE SHELTERING ARMS." Thanks cannot repay them for all that they have been to us. Without their aid we should hardly have ventured to open our doors at the first; and throughout these years of rapid growth they have modified and in a large degree directed the development of the Institution. We shall ever remember with gratitude and pleasure this long term of faithful and unsalaried service.

The health of our large family, numbering always 90 children, and from that to 120, has been uncommonly good. For the first year in our history no child has died and few have been seriously ill. James Tilford, a cripple, remarkable for his sweet and gentle manners, has been for months sinking, and we cannot expect him long to remain with us.* With that exception the infirmary is without patients.

The whole number of children on our books since the last annual Report has been 152, of whom 117 are still in the cottages. Although only three months in our new home, we have yet throughout nearly the whole year counted from 115 to 120 children, owing to the kindness of the Trustees of the "Leake & Watts Orphan House," and their Superintendent, Mr. W. H. Guest. Repeating the generous favor of five years

---
* Since dead.

ago they received 25 children and cared for them nearly eight months while our new building was in progress. We were thus enabled to take in the most pressing cases from among the applicants.

Largely increased as is our accommodation by the erection of this first row of cottages, we are as ever forced to refuse almost all the daily demands for the admission of homeless children. Owing to the number of boys in our care exceeding the number of girls, two of our new cottages are appropriated to families of 30 boys each. The John D. Wolfe Cottage shelters the small boys; the Jas. E. Montgomery Cottage the larger ones. The Cottage of the Ladies' Association is devoted to the nursery children of both sexes, intended also to count 30, but at present actually reaching 33. The Mrs. Peter Cooper Cottage receives the 30 larger girls.

It is our hope by this new system of distribution to break up in some degree the Institution feeling and make a nearer approach to the family relation. In order to accomplish this object, we propose placing at the head of each cottage a lady to stand in the relation of mother to the children, and in that capacity to have the superintendence and control of the occupants of her cottage out of school-hours. Under this direction the inmates of the cottages for the larger children, divided into companies of ten each, will be expected to do the work in the dormitory and keep in order the play-room and bath-room of the family. Two of the cottages are already thus provided for. From among those offering their services we shall select the best persons to be found to take charge of the remainder. We trust also that the love of Christ will move yet other ladies to offer their services, until all our posts of responsibility and work are in this manner permanently filled. An allowance, sufficient to cover their personal expenses, will be made to these ladies, whom we hope to organize into an Association, having their home and connection with "THE SHELTERING ARMS." There will then in time become necessary for the reception of the superannuated or disabled a separate cottage, which may also serve as a place of occasional or periodical rest for all from the fatigue of constant labor.

Some of these new features are suggested by the arrangement of our buildings dividing the children into families. Other changes, tending to do away with the Institution atmosphere, and bring to bear upon each child as much as possible of the family influence, will be introduced from time to time, as they may be found practicable. In all respects the aim of "THE SHELTERING ARMS" will be to train the children according to the teachings and spirit of our Church, and to educate them to fill the place of Christian men and women in American life. In the confidence of former years that we shall be sustained in our present scale of usefulness, and yearly enlarge our number, we prepare our plans, and prayerfully await God's time and blessing.

We cannot close this Report without acknowledgement of the continued services of the "Ladies' Association of The Sheltering Arms." In collecting funds for the Institution, articles for the paper, and clothing for the children, and, above all, by their active exertions in connection with the Grand Bazaar they have greatly aided the President and Executive Committee and furthered the cause which they have espoused. They have our grateful thanks.

THOMAS M. PETERS,
President.

REPORT OF THE EXECUTIVE COMMITTEE.

—:o:—

To the Board of Trustees of The Sheltering Arms:

GENTLEMEN:—At no period in the history of our Institution has your Executive Committee been called upon to lay before you a more important Report than the present one, in which, as in accordance with the requirements of the By-laws, they will give you an account of all that has transpired since last you met. It is the history of that portion of the life of "THE SHELTERING ARMS" that closes the sixth year of its existence—a portion of its life that has been strangely diversified by light and shadow—a portion of its life that has witnessed a rapid and successful development of the purposes we had in view in its organization, and, above all and before all, a portion of its life that must ever stand prominently forth in its history, as THAT on which the God of the orphan and the destitute has so visibly set his seal that the work we have in hand is His work, and that as He has so signally crowned our efforts with success, so we should arouse ourselves to renewed exertions and to a just appreciation of the magnitude of the interests committed to our care.

Remember, we gather together to-night to close and witness the sixth page in our Book of Record and commit it to the safe keeping of the past. It cannot be altered, it cannot be obliterated; WHAT WE HAVE WRITTEN, WE HAVE WRITTEN; and this thought should be present with us to-night, that we may approach our deliberations and councils as to the future management of this Charity in such a spirit, that when our duties and labors shall be forever finished, we may receive that higher, nobler approbation of a faithful stewardship, which only an approving conscience can give. Let us place a firm reliance in all we do upon that Infinite Power which overrules the results of all human exertions, and without whose all-powerful supervision no institution can possibly succeed.

In the internal management of the House during the past six months we have nothing especially important or striking to note. The system inaugurated at the commencement has been so fully developed and adhered to that this part of our daily history is a tale easily told. It is simply the record of daily duties cheerfully performed; daily responsibilities met and discharged; daily blessings thankfully enjoyed. The children, in such an institution as this, soon become familiarized with and attached to this daily routine, and, like a well-disciplined army, they willingly obey their leaders, knowing that they themselves are the recipients of the blessings bestowed, and conscious of the kind care heaven has provided for them in this, their home. They have, of course, their own peculiar sorrows and joys—sorrows, when perchance death calls one of their number away, or, when the remembrance of a Parent's never-to-be-forgotten smile and voice is missed, as memory asserts over their infant minds its powerful sway— joys, when some kind heart and hand go forth from the busy turmoil of the world to cheer THEIR hearts with some unexpected pleasure, which, to their imagination, breaking in as it does upon their dark life with the brightness of the noonday sun, contains in its enjoyment all the wonder and mystery of oriental enchantment. We say, upon their DARK lives, for remember we are speaking of the children of the unfortunate poor, and it were well for all of us, did we but know by our own experience, how much true pleasure can be gathered round their path, at a very small outlay of expense and time on our part. It is only by personal contact with those children committed to our care that we can teach them of Him who is THEIR God as well as OUR God; THEIR Father as well as OUR Father; that we can exert an influence over them, "making the world they live in, and weaving about them the webs of good or evil, which shall leave their impress on their souls."

The two most important events, in all their bearings, during the past winter, have been the completion of and removal into our new Building, and the Grand Bazaar, held for the purpose of removing all indebtedness from our land and house. The House itself has fully answered, in all its arrangements and conveniences, our expectations, and it has been universally conceded by those who have visited us since its completion that in its every detail it is most admirably adapted to the requirements of such an Institution. This result is due in a very great measure to the able and judicious manner in which the building was attended to by the architect, Mr. Charles C. Haight, and to that gentleman your Committee would here express their sincere thanks for the courtesy and attention with which he was always ready to receive and thoroughly examine into any alterations or supposed improvements they might suggest.

The full Report of the Bazaar will be laid before you by the Committee this evening and we need therefore only say that in its conception, arrangement and result, it was worthy the cause it sought to aid—worthy the many kind and charitable hands and hearts by which it was managed—worthy the city whose inhabitants are always so prompt to give when true charity stands and cries in her streets for the alleviation of the sufferings of the poor. It is most probable that the amount realized from the Bazaar will remove all indebtedness, and we shall then own, unencumbered, our own house and land, with full accommodation for one hundred and twenty children, and, above all, we are surrounded by a host of friends who will see that our current expenses will be fully provided for. Upon such a Record, gentlemen, we call upon you this evening to look with us and join in fervent thanksgiving to the Giver of all good, to the Great King, Eternal, Invisible, who has willed that not one of His weakest lambs should perish from neglect, but that all should find mercy and rest in the sheltering arms of His own holy love. This, gentlemen, closes our account for the past six months of the Institution. We need not now comment further on the Past, but let us rather close our Page of Record here, knowing that as our work has prospered so it WILL prosper, if we but trust in God, and keep ever in view the ONE GRAND OBJECT for which we have been banded together, striving to carry out in the true spirit of Christ the golden rule, "to care for the poor and needy, and to do unto all men as we would they should do unto us."

Six years have passed and the Record is closed and sealed; the page of the coming year lies before us clean and without mark. Be it ours to see that its Record shall be to the honor and glory of God, and to the temporal alleviation and the eternal benefit of those, THE CHILDREN OF THE POOR, who shall be committed to our care.

HENRY J. CAMMANN,

Secretary.

THE SHELTERING ARMS in Account with J. S. BREATH, Treasurer,

1870.			Dr.
May 1.	To Expenditure for New Home............		$35,704 08
"	" Bread......................		1,346 53
"	" Meat and Fish.............		804 45
"	" Milk......................		1,009 20
"	" Groceries and Vegetables...		1,917 45
"	" Fuel......................		655 50
"	" Gas, Water and Express....		574 25
"	" Wages and Labor...........		1,275 05
"	" Repairs...................		154 54
"	" Insurance.................		242 30
"	" Household Material........		264 80
"	" Printing and Advertising...		935 46
"	" for Stamps and Stationery..		257 10
"	" Salaries and Collection.....		1,899 63
"	" Furnishing New Building..		1,477 25
"	" Interest on Loans..........		1,724 52
"	" Sundries..................		574 41
"	" Balance on hand...........		1,097 68
			$52,005 85

1870.		Cr.	
May. 1.	By Balance of last Report......	$168 84	
	" Donations..................	12,871 41	
	" Annual Subscriptions & Paper	900 00	
	" Special for Christmas and Thanksgiving............	202 85	
	" Minnie's Picture...........	9 12	
	" Comptroller of the State.....	1,540 43	
	" " " City......	1,000 00	
	Received for Board..........	2,184 20	
	Loans......................	33,100 00	
			$52,005 85

NEW YORK, October 13th, 1870.

At a meeting of the Finance Committee of "The Sheltering Arms," held this day, the account of the Treasurer for the Year ending April 30th, 1870, which shows a balance remaining on hand of $1,097.68, was examined and compared with the vouchers, and found correct.

H. C. VON POST,
WM. H. FOGG,
WM. B. CLERKE.

ANNUAL SUBSCRIBERS.

A

Mrs. H. D. Aldrich....................................	$10 00
Mrs. Auchincloss.....................................	10 00
Mrs. Aaron Arnold....................................	10 00

B

Mrs. C. C. Baldwin...................................	5 00
Miss A. W. Boardman, $5, $5.................	10 00
Mrs. D. C. Birdsall...................................	5 00
Mrs. Edwin T. Butler................................	5 00
Mrs. John Boyd, Jr..................................	5 00
D. B. Bedell...	5 00
Mrs. W. P. Dixon.....................................	10 00
Miss Nellie Blodget.................................	25 00
Miss Hattie T. Bryce...............................	5 00
Mrs. James Brooks..................................	5 00
Mrs. M. Baldwin......................................	3 00

C

Miss E. C. Cooper...................................	5 00
Mrs. John Caswell, $5, $5........................	10 00
Miss Kate Cotheal, $3, $5........................	8 00
Miss A. H. Cooke....................................	5 00
Miss M. G. Corlies...................................	5 00
H. H. Cammann......................................	5 00
William Cooper.......................................	10 00
C. W. Cooper...	10 00
J. C. Cooper..	5 00
Mrs. H. Colt...	5 00
Mrs. H. A. Cram.....................................	5 00
Miss E. Cooper.......................................	5 00
Mrs. J. Coddington..................................	5 00
Mrs. Colden...	5 00
Mrs. J. J. Coddington..............................	5 00

Miss M. Cooke	5 00
Miss Mary Cunard	5 00

D

Mrs. DeWitt, Augusta, Maine	5 00
W. H. Draper, M. D.	10 00
Miss Delaplaine	5 00
Mrs. D. B. Dash	5 00

E

Mrs. D. M. Edgar	5 00
Mrs. J. L. Englehart	5 00
Mrs. James A. Edgar	5 00
Miss Emmet	3 00

F

Mrs. Fitzgerald	10 00

G

Mrs. Wm. H. Guion, $10, $10	20 00
Miss M. M. Gandy, $2, $5	7 00
Miss M. Glover	5 00
Mrs. H. T. Gerry	5 00
Miss Jeannie Gerry	5 00

H

Mrs. Goold Hoyt	5 00
Mrs. John C. Hamilton	5 00
Miss M. E. Hamilton	3 00
Miss M. F. Horner	10 00
Mrs. Chas. F. Heywood	5 00
Miss Emily Hollingsworth	5 00
Mrs. Francis C. Hall	5 00
Miss Lillie C. Hall	5 00
Miss Nellie Hale	1 00
Mrs. A. S. Hewitt	10 00
Mrs. C. W. Hull	5 00

Mrs. J. C. Hull	3 00
Mrs. P. Hanford	0 00

I

Mrs. Chas. H. Isham	5 00

J

Mrs. C. A. Jackson	5 00
Miss M. S. Jones	5 00

K

Mrs. A. M. Kalbfleisch	5 00
Miss Ellen Kemble	5 00
Mrs. J. P. Ogden Kemble	5 00
Mrs. Jessie G. Keator	5 00
Mrs. George Keyes	5 00

L

Mrs. T. Lambard, (Augusta, Maine)	5 00
Mrs. A. Lambard, do. do.	5 00
Miss Katie Lambard, do. do.	5 00
Miss E. Low	5 00
Mrs. Wm. P. Lee	5 00
Mrs. C. Livingston	5 00
Mrs. N. Lawrence	5 00
Miss Julia A. Low	5 00

M

Mrs. Isaac P. Martin	5 00
Mrs. Henry Meigs	5 00
Mrs. H. McKim	5 00
Mrs. J. B. Murray	5 00
Mrs. Isaiah Mankin	5 00
Mrs. A. B. Morrell	5 00
Mrs. J. T. Metcalfe	10 00
Mrs. B. McEvers	5 00
John Moulson, Jr., $10, $10	20 00

N

Mrs. J. P. Nazro, $3, $3	6 00
Miss S. B. Newby	5 00
Mrs. North	5 00

O

Mrs. Alfred Ogden	5 00
Mrs. Hobart Onderdonk	5 00
Mrs. G. B. Ogden	5 00

P

Horace Porter	5 00
E. D. Peters	20 00
Miss S. E. Pierson	5 00

Q

Mrs. Geo. P. Quackenboss	5 00

R

Mrs. Sylvanus Reed	5 00
Miss Geraldine Reed	5 00
Misses Renshaw	10 00

S

Mrs. Catharine L. Spencer	10 00
Mrs E. Shedden	5 00
Miss H. Stanley, (Augusta, Maine)	5 00
Mrs. A. T. Sackett	10 00
Mrs. Augustus Schermerhorn	5 00

T

Mrs. T. Timpson	5 00
Miss Tracy	5 00
Mrs. Wm. Travers	5 00
Miss K. Tracy	5 00
Mrs. R. S. Tucker	5 00

Mrs. D. F. Tiemann	5 00
Miss Martha Tiemann	5 00
Mrs. E. L. Trowbridge	5 00

V

Miss A. Van Buren	2 00
Mrs. H. C. Von Post	10 00
Miss Von Post	5 00
Mrs. A. Vanderpool	10 00

W

C. S. Weyman	5 00
Miss G. Wilkes, $5, $5	10 00
Miss H. K. Wilkes, $5, $5	10 00
Mrs. D. E. Wheeler, $10, $10	20 00
H. F. Webster	5 00
Mrs. D. Williams, (Augusta, Maine)	5 00
Mrs. H. D. Wyman	10 00
Mrs. John S. Williams	5 00
Mrs. R. Winthrop	5 00
Mrs. W. H. Wisner	10 00
Miss C. L. R. White	5 00
Mrs. D. B. Williamson	5 00
Miss A. Wilkes	5 00
Mrs. S. H. Whitlock	5 00
William Whitlock, Jr.	10 00
Mrs. J. H. Watson	5 00
Mrs. Chas. W. Whiley, an. "69" special	10 00

SHELTERING ARMS LEGION OF ONE DOLLAR.

COMPANY 1.

EMILY DICK, Minnie Wiley, G. S. Stringfield, Suzie Gorham, S. & M. Coates, Minnie Ferguson, Annie Brierly, Clara Yenni, Sarah E. Mackenzie, Sarah Smith, Harrie V. D. W. Sheridan.

COMPANY 2.

JULIA T. PETERS, Ruth Tiemann, Paul Tiemann, Elsie Tiemann, Benj. F. Tiemann, Andrew Peters, John P. Peters, W. L. Sandford, Irving J. Kitchell, W. R. Peters.

COMPANY 3.

EMILIE HEISER. Julia Peters, Evoline Hicks, John Heiser, Charlie Heiser, Fred. Brown, C. E. Smith. Math. Elgars, Emma Grube, Charles H. Grube, Emma Hochrein.

COMPANY 4.

KITTIE JACKSON, D. S. Jackson, D. S. Jackson, Jr., Willie Jackson, Lillie Jackson, A. V. Williams, Frederika Conrad, Maynard Ollifle, Arthur Davis, Ralph Townsend, Willie Bleakly.

SCATTERING.

Rev. R. T. S. Lowell, D. D., Miss Sarah Wheeler, Mrs. Isaac Hartshorne, Mrs. R. Goldsmith, Miss Helen Field, Miss Matilda Sorrill, Miss Emma Newby, Miss Bessie Greenfield, Miss Mattie Kane, Mrs. J. N. Wells, Miss A. Radcliffe, Richard V. Boyd, Jno. L. Cadwalader, Wm. J. Paulding, Louisa Driver, Mrs. Boyce, Mrs. Willington, Mrs. W. DeF. Day, Miss F. Cotheal, Miss Lizzie Holmes, Mrs. Pratt, Mary J. Tuckerman, Florence Melville, Miss A. D. Robins, Mrs. O. E. Hosmer, Mrs. E. B. Hartshorne, Little Michael, J. Gibson Jaffray, Miss H. Bushnell, Mrs. G. M. Ogden, Mrs. D. B. Ogden, Mrs. Cadr. E. Ogden, G. M. Ogden, Jr., Mrs. Walter R. Leggat, Mrs. W. H. Ludlow, Mrs. Gen. Sanford, Miss Alice Sanford, Annie F. Tweed, Helen Sand, Jno. Fletcher, Mrs. Geo. W. Read, Mrs. L. M. Seymour, Mrs. S. S. Fitch, Carrie Swan, M. K. Leute, Alice Paulding, Louis Johnson, W. C. Rhinelander, Jr., Harry B. Parsons, Carrie H. Burgess, Mrs. Nathan Cleaves, R. R. Chadwick, Mrs. Chas. P. Cooper, Mrs. W. E. Vermilyea, Miss Lavinia Brooks, Mrs. W. O. Fitzgerald, Miss C. A. Butler, Mrs. J. C. Sproull, Mrs. E. A. Whately, S. M. Taylor, Mrs. A. F. Carter, Miss Eunice C. Long.

DONATIONS.

A.

Mrs. "A. M. B."	$5 00
Mrs. "A. M."	2 00
T. P. Allyn	10 00
R. H. Arkenburgh	5 00
Alms box, $7.55, $13.93, $9.16	30 64
"A. V. R."	10 00
Mrs. J. V. H. Arnold	5 00
"Anonymous," B. F.	10 00
Thro. Mrs. R. W. Aborn	17 00
J. S. Abecasis	10 00
Richard Amerman	5 00
Mrs. Arthur Amory	10 00
Mrs. R. T. Auchmuty, thro. H. J. Cammann	100 00
C. F. Alvord	5 00
Mrs. Wm. B. Astor, Jr., B. F. Miss Kemble	15 00
Mrs. Aaron Arnold, B. F.	10 00
Wm. H. Aspinwall	100 00
Mrs. Alonzo Alvoord	5 00
"A"	5 00
John B. Aycrigg	5 00
J. W. Alsop	25 00
Benjamin Aymar	10 00
Mrs. Richard Alsop	10 00
Mrs. W. C. Arthur	5 00
American Merchants' Union Express Co.	25 00
Mrs. William Alsop	5 00

B.

Thomas Barron, $50, $25	75 00
Matthew Bird, $5, $5	10 00
W. Blackstone	5 00
William Bloodgood	10 00
Daniel G. Bacon	5 00
J. O. Bartholomew	5 00

Annie Brierly ; Minnie fund, $2, $2, $2	6 00
A. V. Blake	10 00
Mrs. F. J. Bumstead, for beds	10 00
Edward E. Brown	5 00
Miss Sarah Burr	20 00
" Birth day," for bedstead and mattress, thro. Rev. H. E. Montgomery, D.D.	10 00
Mrs. E. A. Bull, for bedstead	5 00
Mrs. G. F. Betts	5 00
J. A. Bostwick	25 00
Mr. & Mrs. D. T. Brown, in Memorium	100 00
P. R. Bonnett	5 00
Mrs. Edward Baldwin	10 00
W. B. Bend	25 00
Edward A. Boyd	10 00
Mrs. A. Boody	5 00
D. W. Bruce	20 00
Elliott Bumstead, to buy a bed	5 00
Stewart Brown	100 00
Mr. and Mrs. John H. Boynton	20 00
C. Butler	5 00
Mrs. Henry Barclay	10 00
Mrs. N. P. Bailey, B. F. thro. H. J. Cammann	25 00
G. Banyer, thro. Miss Kemble, $10, $10	20 00
Robert Bettner, B. F.	2 00
Mrs. Boyce	3 00
Miss A. Bleakley	2 00
E. O. Brinckerhoff	5 00
Henry Bergh	5 00
F. C. Barlow	5 00
Misses Bridge, St. Catharine's Hall	10 00
Charles E. Beebe	25 00
H. K. Bogert	25 00
James L. Bogert	25 00
William Betts	20 00
Wm. Smith Brown, thro. F. S. Winston	20 00
B. F. Button, B. F., thro. Miss Hall	25 00
" B. K"	2 00

Mrs. Japhet Bishop............................	25 00
Mrs. John Bloodgood...........................	25 00
William C. Bryant.............................	10 00
Mrs. R. M. Brinkerhoff........................	5 00
V. H. Brown...................................	5 00
Stewart Brown, B. F...........................	500 00
Mrs. L. F. Battelle...........................	5 00
Miss Benkard, thro. Benkard & Hutton...........	50 00
Mrs. Wm. F. Beekman...........................	5 00
S. W. Barnard.................................	5 00
W. N. Beach...................................	5 00
Mrs. S. Brush.................................	5 00
Mrs. William Barton...........................	5 00
Mrs. Adeline Breese...........................	5 00
J. Bleecker, U. S. N..........................	5 00
Mrs. John Byers...............................	5 00
William J. Beebe..............................	100 00
Marcus Beach..................................	10 00
Mrs. D. C. Blodgett...........................	10 00
J. H. Beekman.................................	5 00
Daniel Butterfield, thro. H. J. Cammann........	50 00
Miss J. Brinckerhoff..........................	10 00
Mr. and Mrs. J. R. Boyd.......................	10 00
O. M. Bogart..................................	5 00
Cornelius Bogert..............................	25 00
C. F. Blodgett................................	5 00
C. Braker, Jr.................................	25 00
Baker & Kitchen, Miss Kitchen..................	25 00

C.

CASH.

$10, 5, 1, 10, (25, H. M.,) (25, J. H. V. C.,) (10, R. H.,) (W. E., 5,) (S. B., 25,) 8, 2, 5, 5, 2, 2.50, 10, 2, 5, 1, 10, 10, 100, 10, 2, 5, 10, 5. $5, 2, 5, 10, 10, 2, 5, 10, 2, 5, 1, 2, 1, 5, 1, 50, 2, 5, 15, 10, 5, 20, 1, 2, $25, 5, 1, 2, 10, 5, 10, 3, 5, 50, 5, 2, 1, 2, 10, 10, 1, 1, 5, 5, 5, 5, 10, $1, 2, 1, 1, 2, 1, 2, 2, 2, 1, 10, 5, 5, 5, 3, 2, 1, 5, 3, 10, 2, 3, 5, 5, 5, 1. $5, 5, 1, 1, 5, 5, 5, 3.

Mrs. Wm. Campbell.............................	2 00

Miss Mary Canard	50 00
T. C. Chardavoyne	20 00
do. Impromptu, through Mrs. J. A. Mitchell	5 00
Mrs. J. M. Constable	10 00
Coleman & Co	5 00
J. C. Carter	10 00
Concert at Dr. Ward's, additional $15, $12, $6	43 00
I. W. Cooper	10 00
David M. Clarkson, (Heidelbergh) through Adam Norrie	50 00
Condensed Milk Co	25 00
Mrs. Colden	5 00
"C. P. L." for B. F., through Dr. Peters	100 00
Church of the Intercession through the Am. Church Missionary Society	6 35
Mrs. Cornelia L. Crary	5 00
John Caswell, $50, $100—B. F	150 00
Wm. F. Cary	50 00
William E. Curtiss	10 00
Geo. C. Colburn	5 00
Mrs. Oswald Cammann, bedstead and mattrass	10 00
Cyrus Curtiss	25 00
Mrs. "C. H."	5 00
James S. Cushman	5 00
Chamberlain of the City N. Y	1,000 00
J. A. Cone	25 00
Frederich Chauncey	10 00
Sanford Cobb	5 00
Charity Box of two little girls, L. and H	5 00
Israel Corse	25 00
Henry Chauncey	25 00
Robert R. Crosby	10 00
Le Grand B. Cannon	10 00
Mrs. Peter Cooper, 10 bedsteads and mattrasses	100 00
Church of the Mediator, (So. Yonkers, N.Y.) through Rev. M. T. Wilson	50 84
Miss Crocker	5 00
R. L. Cutting	5 00

Mrs. R. L. Cutting..	5 00
Ten Children of Sing Sing, through Mrs. Wiltse.....	2 00
Thomas Clapham..	25 00
George P. Clapp...	25 00
John J. Cisco..	25 00
Mrs. H. H. Crocker...	5 00
"C. L. W."...	10 00
Mrs. Martha E. Coles......................................	10 00
Mrs. Mary Clarkson..	5 00
"Cash" B. Fund...	3 00
Mrs. N. Chandler..	5 00
Christ's Church, Rye, N.Y., through Rev. Reese F. Alsop	23 50
Geo. A. Clark and brother................................	5 00
James Clinch..	5 00
W. L. Chamberlain...	10 00
Mrs. E. R. Cole..	5 00
Henry Chauncey..	15 00
Comptroller State of N. Y................................	1,549 43
Mrs. William Campbell....................................	2 00
George Chesterman..	25 00
Coleman House...	5 00
Mrs. N. W. Chater, through Mrs. Gilman.............	5 00
Christ's Church, Riverdale, N. Y., S. D. Babcock's Easter Offering, by the hand of Rev. Geo. D. Wildes, Rector...	100 00
Peter Cooper Golden Wedding Fund..................	50 00
H. R. Clark, through the Rev. Dr. Twing.............	5 00

D

Mrs. T. W. Dwight...	3 00
Wm. P. Douglas..	25 00
"D." for building fund.....................................	50 00
Miss Drake...	4 50
John H. Draper...	25 00
Uriah H. Dudley..	10 00
William Dennistoun..	20 00
P. Dickie...	5 00
Mrs. H. Drisler..	3 00

Mrs. H. W. Dolson	10 00
Mrs. Anson Dodge	5 00
H. C. De Rham	25 00
" D."	20 00
Dix and Morris	20 00
"Donation"	20 00
C. J. DeWitt	5 00
E. DeWitt	5 00
Mrs. Anna M. Dudley	10 00
" D. H."	25 00
Charles DeRham	20 00
J. F. DePeyster	25 00
E. A. Duyckink	5 00
E. J. Dunning	5 00
Mrs. David Dows	25 00
Mrs. Wm. A. Dooley	5 00
Wm. B. Dinsmore	25 00
James Dater	5 00
E. Delafield, M. D	10 00
Mrs. W. Butler Duncan—B. F.	20 00

E

Henry Ellsworth	20 00
John M. Emerson	5 00
Wm. M. Evarts	25 00
" E. W. D."	20 00
Amos R. Eno	25 00
Mrs. Augustus Embury	10 00
Mrs. D. M. Edgar	10 00
Mrs. Alfred H. Easton	10 00
J. Edgar	5 00
Mrs. Sarah J. Egleston	10 00
" E. M."	2 00
A. B. Embury	5 00
James Emott	25 00
Tracy R. Edson	10 00
Wm. C. Emmel	5 00
" E. A. M."	5 00

S. C. Evans	5 00
D. B. Eaton	10 00
H. Elsworth	10 00
Easter Offering of Christ's Church, Sheffield, Mass., Rev. J. A. Penniman	4 00
Easter Offering of Christ's Church, Watertown, Conn., Rev. W. H. Lewis, D. D., of which $20 from Dr. Peters' class in S. School, N. S. Perry, teacher	58 21
Easter Offering of Annandale Parish School, Rev. R. B. Fairbairn, D. D., Warden of Stephens' College	50 00
Easter Offering S. S. All Angels Church, N. Y.	10 00
Easter Offering St. John's Parish, Stamford, Conn., Rev. W. Tatlock	7 70
Easter Offering Trinity Chapel, N. Y.	5 00
Easter Offering S. School St. James' Church, New London, Conn., (of which $2.61 was left by Percie B. Spaulding, a former pupil of the school, who died at Panama of fever	12 00

F.

Charles Fox	5 00
E. E. Freligh	5 00
Jed. Frye	5 00
Florie, Jessie, Louie and Charlie, Glen Cove, L. I., through Miss Little	1 25
R. C. Ferguson	25 00
S. J. Fatman	5 00
A. Morton Ferris	10 00
"A Friend," thro. Mrs. Day	10 00
"A Friend" at St. Luke's Church, Matteawan, thro. Rev. H. E. Duncan	2 00
"A Friend"	10 00
P. H. Frost	10 00
"A Friend," by Miss Murray, B. F.	5 00
"A Friend," Augusta, Maine	5 00
C. B. Foote	10 00
J. D. Fish	25 00
Mrs. J. M. Farr	5 00

Mrs. William P. Furniss...	50 00
"A Friend," thro. Mrs. Day, B. F...	4 00
J. M. Fisk...	10 00
H. W. Ford...	10 00
Mrs. Morris Franklin...	5 00
E. L. Ferry...	10 00
J. P. Girard Foster...	10 00
"A Friend," thro. Mrs. Nazro, B. F...	10 00
Sands H. Fish...	10 00
"A Friend"...	2 00
James C. Fargo...	25 00
"A Friend," for Minnie fund...	1 00
"A Friend"...	1 50
Mr. and Miss Ferguson, furnishing fund...	100 00
"A Friend"...	50 00
Friendship's Offering...	50
Miss Fanny Fleeman, B. F...	1 00

G.

Mrs. O. D. F. Grant...	5 00
Mrs. William T. Garner...	15 00
Mrs. Ann J. Garner...	5 00
G. G. Gray...	20 00
Peter Gilsey...	10 00
A. Gilsey...	5 00
B. L. & Ira Greenback & Co...	10 00
Arthur Gillender...	10 00
B. W. Griswold...	10 00
Mrs. Harriet H. Garner...	5 00
J. H. Gautier...	50 00
C. F. Gostenhofer, thro. H. J. Cammann...	50 00
Winthrop S. Gilman, B. F...	5 00
Mrs. Geo. F. Gilman...	5 00
A. A. Gallatin...	5 00
"G. V."...	1 00
Mrs. C. R. Green...	5 00
Mrs. Thos. P. Grinnell...	5 00
C. C. Goodhue...	10 00

Mrs. Spencer K. Green........................... 5 00
Mrs. A. Grosvenor............................... 5 00

H.

Mrs. Angelica L. Hamilton, $10, $25 .... 35 00
H. J. Hoffman, $10, $10.......................... 20 00
Mrs. Henry E. Hawley............................ 5 00
Mrs. T. H. Hubbard, Rome, N. Y., thro. Fred. Hubbard. 100 00
Robert J. Hubbard............................... 25 00
G. G. Howland.................................. 25 00
D. Hoadley..................................... 25 00
Wilson G. Hunt................................. 5 00
A. G. Harmon................................... 10 00
Mrs. J. P. Hilliard.............................. 2 00
Mrs. Peter S. Hoe............................... 10 00
Jacob Hays..................................... 10 00
Mrs. E. Holbrook................................ 5 00
Mrs. R. Hoe, Jr................................. 5 00
Benjamin Huxton................................ 5 00
R Haydock..................................... 5 00
Mrs. Allan Hay.................................. 10 00
Mrs. P. Hubbard, for beds........................ 50 00
D. T. Hoag..................................... 10 00
George A. Hearn................................ 25 00
William Heath.................................. 10 00
P. H. Holt. 25 00
Rev. S. G. Hitchcock............................. 2 00
H. L. L.. 5 00
Robert Hewitt, B. F., thro. Miss Hall.............. 5 00
Miss Howes, B. F., thro. Mrs. Gilman.............. 10 00
S. V. Hoffman.................................. 25 00
John A. Hardenburg............................. 10 00
Mrs. Alice T. Hallet............................. 15 00
Mrs. W. Ogden Hegeman......................... 5 00
Mrs. E. S. Higgins............................... 10 00
Mrs. J. Howe................................... 5 00
Valentine G. Hall............................... 25 00
Mrs. Valentine G. Hall........................... 25 00

Rufus Hatch	100 00
J. C. Harrison	10 00
Misses Hadden	10 00
Mrs. J. C. Hamilton	50 00
Charles Henschel—B. F.	10 00
Com'rs and Mrs. Hitchcock, Cold Spring, Putnam Co., for bedstead and mattrass, through Miss Kemble.	10 00
Wm. Habishaw—B. F., Miss Kemble	5 00
" H. S. W."	20 00
" H. M. B."	2 00
Harding, Colby & Co.	10 00
F. C. Havemeyer	10 00
" H. L. M"	5 00

I & J

Miss Margaret Inglis	5 00
Mrs. Jonesbury	75
B. Johnson & Sons	5 00
Mrs. Margaret Iselin	5 00
Frederick E. Ives	20 00
Mrs. Rebecca Jones	5 00
Mrs. F. U. Johnson	5 00
Stephen Johnson	10 00
Adrian Iselin	50 00
Frederick M. Jones	20 00
Mrs. J. F. Johnson	5 00
Mrs. T. R. Jackson	5 00
George R. Jackson	25 00
T. J. Jeremiah	5 00
Mrs. Illius—B. F., through Mrs. Gilman	5 00
W. R. T. Jones	10 00
" J. A. U."	5 00
" J. C " of Liverpool—B F., through S. T. S.	10 00
" J. C." through Mrs. H. S. F.	3 00
" J. M."	10 00
J. H. V. C.	20 00
" J. J. A."	5 00
Miss Inglis	5 00

Richard Irvin	25 00
"J. W. B."	10 00
"J." through Wm. Alex. Smith	20 00

K

George G. Kellogg	5 00
Thomas B. Kerr	10 00
Isaac C. Kendall	5 00
Mrs R. E. Kelly	10 00
Wm. M. Kingsland	20 00
Andrew Keating	21 00
J. Knower	10 00
Charles Kneeland	50 00
Edward King	10 00
Mrs. Joseph Knapp	5 00
Mrs. Peter V. King	5 00
Mrs. E. Keteltas	10 00
Mrs. Jessie G. Keator, for Mattrass	6 00
Miss Jessie G. Keator, for Bedstead	4 00
Edward Kearny—B. F.	10 00
Mrs. P. R. Kearny	5 00
Charles P. Kirtland—B. F., through Mrs. Lee	100 00
Kitty	37

L

Charles A. Lambard, $10, $25	35 00
Miss Kate Lawrence—B. F.	10 00
J. Lane, $10, $10	20 00
Loui Lee, Minnie Fund	1 37
Cyrus J. Lawrence	10 00
Mrs. T. J. Leslie	10 00
Annie, Thomas W. and Jas. B. Ludlow	1 50
John T. Long	10 00
Job Long	10 00
Miss Lawrence—B. F.	5 00
Mrs. W. E. Laight	5 00
Cyrus H. Loutrel	5 00

Mrs. R. E. Livingston............................	10 00
A. Limbert, $5, Louis Limbert, $1.................	6 00
William Lottimer................................	25 00
Mrs. M. M. Livingston...........................	10 00
Miss M. E. Lockwood............................	10 00
Miss Julia A. Low...............................	25 00
Joseph Larvegue.................................	25 00
Lewis Livingston................................	10 00
Mrs. G. W. Livingston...........................	5 00
R. J. Livingston................................	25 00
Mrs. Pierre Lorillard............................	25 00
Mrs. "L. K."—B. Fund..........................	20 00
E. Livingston...................................	15 00
Charles F. Lockwood............................	10 00
Mrs. W. H. Lewis...............................	10 00
A Laboring Man................................	1 00
E. H. Ludlow	10 00
"L. P.,".......................................	2 00
Little Boys' Savings Bank........................	1 00

M

Mrs. Allan McLane..............................	50 00
Mrs. R. W. Martin, Jr...........................	25 00
Tasker H. Marvin................................	50 00
George Merritt..................................	50 00
John H. McKim	25 00
Charles E. Milnor...............................	20 00
Mrs. J. Mildeberger.............................	5 00
S. C. Milbank...................................	5 00
Mrs. John McKesson.............................	5 00
Charles A. Miller................................	5 00
"M. M. H.".....................................	5 00
John H. Morris..................................	5 00
William Mackay.................................	10 00
Nelson Merrell—through Miss Kitchen.............	5 00
C. G. Mitchell...................................	5 00
Rutson Mawry...................................	5 00
J. G. McDonald.................................	10 00

J. Martin, Jr...	10 00
A. P. Man..	10 00
Allan McLane—through Rev. Dr. Houghton.........	100 00
H. Meigs...	10 00
"Mother," Augusta, Maine.............................	10 00
Charles Mali..	10 00
Zophar Mills..	5 00
Richard Mortimer.......................................	25 00
George W. McCollum..................................	10 00
J. Moulson, Jr..	10 00
Fordham Morris, B. F..................................	5 00
Mrs. T. T. Moran.......................................	5 00
Morewood & Co..	10 00
H. A. Wilmerding......................................	10 00
Josiah Macy's Sons....................................	25 00
Mrs. J. Morrison.......................................	5 00
A. B. McDonald..	25 00
Mrs. Peter Morris......................................	5 00
Lewis G. Morris—through H. J. Cammann..........	50 00
Isaac P. Martin...	25 00
Miss L. E. Morgan.....................................	5 00
R. L. Mulford...	10 00
John Miller...	5 00
Thomas D. Middleton..................................	5 00
Mrs. W. S. Mayo.......................................	10 00
H. E. Moring..	5 00
Henry Morgan..	25 00
Miss M. S. Mortimer...................................	3 00
James Moir...	5 00
John R. Maurice..	25 00
Edward Morgan...	20 00
R. H. McCurdy...	5 00
M. L. B. Martin..	5 00
Mrs. Jno. W. Minturn, B. F...........................	10 00
Richard Mortimer, B. F................................	100 00
Mrs. S. Mendelson.....................................	5 00
Mrs. Mahan, (West Point, B. F.).....................	5 00
Miss Moore. B. F.......................................	1 00

'M. P.''... 2 00
Mrs. "M. A. C. R."...................................... 10 00
Minnie's Pictures, $9, $12............................ 21 00

N

Henry D. Noyes, M. D. 5 00
Wm. H. Neilson.. 10 00
H. W. Nieman.. 5 00
Mrs. F. H. Nichols.................................... 5 00
Wm. Niblo, through B. H. Field.................. 100 00

O

James D. Oliver....................................... 10 00
Offering in St. Ann's Church, N. Y., Bertie's Birthday Gift.. 3 00
O. and A. (two fatherless children) $5, $10..... 15 00
Mrs. E. H. Owen....................................... 5 00
Thomas Owen.. 10 00
Old New Yorker (pr. S. T. S.) Miss Holmes..... 5 00
C. V. R. Ostrander.................................... 10 00

P

James A. Patterson................................... 5 00
Orlando B. Potter..................................... 25 00
Samuel N. Pike, $5, $5.............................. 10 00
James W. Patterson.................................. 10 00
Samuel R. Platt, $25, $25........................... 50 00
John Pondir... 50 00
Augustus Proal.. 9 00
John E. Parsons...................................... 10 00
J. Pickard... 10 00
Colonel F. E. Prime, B. F. (Kemble).............. 5 00
Miss A. Paulding   do. 3 00
James K. Pell.. 10 00
J. Kent Pell, Jr.. 5 00
Royal Phelps... 100 00
W. W. Parkin... 10 00

Mrs. C. L. Perkins	5 00
Mrs. Alfred Pell	5 00
J. D. Pell	5 00
Mrs. S. H. Palmer	5 00
Mrs. Geo. C. Peters	10 00
Mrs. S. T. Peters	10 00
Geo. W. Powers	20 00
Mrs. A. M. Pell	5 00
Eleazer Peet	5 00
Mrs. S. J. Penniman	25 00
Mrs. I. W. Pierson	10 00
J. J. Petit	5 00
C. R. Pennlman, B. F., through Mrs. McKim	20 00
Mrs. John J. Phelps, through Mrs. Von Post	10 00
Levi Pawling	5 00
Mrs. M. Pettigrew	10 00
Mrs. J. Peck	5 00
Mrs. Daniel Parish	5 00
O. B. Potter	25 00
Chas. Peace, Jr	5 00
Penfold, Schuyler & Co	25 00
Mrs. Sarah E. Parkin	3 00
Proceeds of a musical and literary entertainment by the pupils of Seabury Hall, N. Y., through Miss M. L. Frost, principal	52 23
Pupils of Misses Woodham's School, N. Y. City, for bedstead and mattress	10 00

Q

T. W. Quincey, through Mrs. Lee	3 00
Mrs. M. M. Quackenboss	10 00

R

Mrs. W. G. Ray	5 00
Jacob Reess	10 00
W. C. Rogers & Co	3 07
J. F. Ruggles	2 00

J. H. Riker	10 00
Edward C. Richards	10 00
Chandler Robbins	20 00
Mrs. Wm. Remsen	5 00
Thomas T. Read	10 00
Douglas Robinson	10 00
" R. S. C."	25 00
C. T. Raynolds, $5, $5	10 00
Mrs. Mary Ann Reeder	5 00
Miss A. M. Reed	5 00
Wm. Ransom	2 00
J. Renwick	10 00
A. H. Reynolds	5 00
J. C. Runkle	5 00
L. M. Rutherford	10 00
Matthew P. Read	25 00
Geo. P. Rowell	10 00
W. C. Rhinelander	100 00
Wm. Redmond, Jr	25 00
Mrs. G. A. Robbins	10 00
" R. H. B."	10 00
Chas. B. Ransom	25 00
Miss Roundey, Boundbrook, N. J.	5 00
Mrs. L. A. Rodenstein, through Miss Tiemann	5 00
Mrs. Henry V. Ryder	2 00
" R. F. & C." through Mr. Punnett	20 00

S

Mrs. Catharine L. Spencer, B. F.	100 00
Charles F. Southmayd	10 00
Mrs Charles S. Spencer	5 00
L. L. Sturges, $5, $5	10 00
George P. Smith	10 00
Sunday School of St. James', Hamilton Square, thro' M. A. Kellogg	26 00
Sunday School, St. Michael's Church, N. Y.; Class B, $1.98; Class E, $1.45	3 43

Sunday School St. Michael's Church, Brooklyn, N. Y., to be used by some poor boys for shoes............	15 00
Sunday School, Christ's Church, N. Y................	9 85
Sunday School, St. Michael's Church, N. Y..........	43 88
Sunday School, Church of the Holy Apostles, N. Y.; Miss Adele Seymour's Class...................	4 50
Gustav Schwab, $10, $10......................	20 00
Sunday School of Church of the Resurrection, N. Y.; Miss M. L. Frost's Class.....................	5 00
Sunday School of St. Barnabas, Infant Class, for Blind Minnie Fund................................	26 00
St. Michael's Church, N. Y., of which, $10 for bed and bedstead....................................	17 49
Sunday School of Trinity Church Mission, Columbus, Ohio, for support of James Porter, through A. N. Whiting, $10, $10, $10.......................	30 00
Oscar E. Schmidt...........................	10 00
Charles F. Sanford..........................	25 00
"S. D."...................................	5 00
Mrs. John Stephens.........................	5 00
Mrs. J. Schmelzel...........................	10 00
Henry F. Spaulding.........................	25 00
"S. B. L." and "M. H. C.," beds and mattrasses......	10 00
St. Michael's and All Angels' 1869; Gracie's Birth-day Offering...................................	50 00
Mrs. J. Slade...............................	10 00
John Sneeden..............................	50 00
Mrs. J. C. Sanford...........................	5 00
Douglas and Katie Sloan......................	5 00
James Rufus Smith..........................	25 00
Mrs. Helen Stuyvesant.......................	20 00
Wm. Alexander Smith........................	50 00
Mrs. Charles H. Smith........................	10 00
"W. B. H."..................................	5 00
Mrs. Caleb Tangier Smith.....................	25 00
B. Schlesinger..............................	100 00
James L. Schieffelin.........................	10 00
Mr. Sabbaton...............................	5 00

Alexander T. Stewart	100 00
Mrs. A. V. H. Stuyvesant, two beds and mattrasses	20 00
Mrs. J. Sonneborn	5 00
E. H. Schermerhorn	15 00
Sunday School of Christ's Church, N. Y., through Rev. Dr. Ewer	8 00
Mrs. Wm. H. Stewart	5 00
Robert Stuyvesant, B. F., through Mrs. McKim	20 00
Savings Bank of Mrs. Lewis' Children	2 18
S. School of St. James' Church, Hyde Park, for a bed	10 00
Mrs. C. V. R. Schuyler, B. F., Mrs. Gilman	5 00
Miss Stadrall	5 00
William H. Scott	10 00
S. School of St. Chrysostom Chapel, N. Y., through Rev. T. H. Sill	35 66
S School of St. Mary's Church, N. Y., through Rev. Chas. C. Adams	13 00
Mrs. Smith	2 00
Miss Suffern	10 00
David Stewart	100 00
S. School of the Church of Holy Apostles, N. Y., thro' Miss Newby	31 00
Stamford Manufacturing Co.	10 00
W. C. Schermerhorn	20 00
Ira Starr	2 00
Mrs. B. B. Sherman	10 00
Jno. A. Stevens	25 00
W. N. Seymour	5 00
George W. Smith	5 00
C. W. Sandford	5 00
Sunday School of St. George's Church, Newburgh, N. Y., through Rev. Octavius Applegate	81 75
S. L. M. B.	20 00
Miss Gertrude Sackett, B. F.	3 00
Mrs. C. A. Sherman	5 00
Robert Soutter	20 00
Mrs. Rutherford Stuyvesant	5 00
J. and W. Seligman	25 00

Mrs. A. B. Sands	5 00
A. V. H. Stuyvesant	10 00
Mrs. A. V. H. Stuyvesant	10 00
Mrs. J. W. Southack	5 00
Eugene Schieffelin	10 00
Mrs. Lewis A. Sayre	10 00
Mrs. G. M. Simonson	5 00
Mrs. Stephens	5 00
W. R. Sands	5 00
James C. Spencer	25 00
W. L. Sanford	10 00
Mrs. L. Stewart	5 00
Henry D. Sedgwick	5 00
Emily, Florence, and Theresa Shiff	3 00
Mrs. Isaac H. Smith	5 00
Mrs. Stacey, B. F., Miss Cammann	3 00
Miss Stacey, " "	2 00
Mrs. Edwin Stoughton	5 00
Mrs. H. G. Stevens	25 00
Miss "S. E. W."	10 00
J. B. Slawson	10 00
Floyd Smith	5 00
Joseph Sampson	100 00
Mrs. N. Sands	5 00
Savings of Maria Poole, 2½ years old	2 00
Special Contribution from Gracie	25 00

T

Wm. W. Todd	10 00
Hon. D. F. Tiemann, Minnie Fund	5 00
Miss A. Tiemann "	1 00
Miss Martha C Tiemann "	1 00
M. H. Throop	3 00
Miss Talman, through Rev. Dr. Dix	50 00
Mrs H. G Thompson	5 00
Mrs. D. H. Twiner	10 00
Mrs. Thos. B. Tweddle, B. F., Mrs. Gilman	5 00
Griffith Thomas	10 00

Mrs. Wm. M. Tweed	100 00
Miss Sarah W. Thorne, through Rev. Dr. Dix	37 00
L. Tuckerman	10 00
J. H. Titus	10 00
Mrs. Wm. Tilden	10 00
Townsend & Davis	50 00
"T. W. R."	10 00
Frederick L. Talcott	25 00
Mrs. Isaac Townsend	10 00
James Tinker	10 00
P. C. Tiemann	53 00
Miss Troupe	5 00
Miss H. A. Townsend	10 00
John J. Townsend	10 00
Peter Townsend	20 00
Mrs. T. G. Thomas	5 00
Mrs. A. G. Thorp	5 00
Wm. K. Thorn	25 00
Wm. D. Thompson, through Mrs. Dr. Smith	45 00
S. D. Tompkins	20 00
Miss E. G. Tackaberry	2 00
Geo. H. Talman	10 00
Mrs. Townsend's book	4 50

U

M. Ulshoeffer	005
Mrs. R. Upjohn, B. F.	5 00
United States Express Co.	25 00
"U. H. D."	5 00

V

John Van Santvoord	2 00
Thomas A. Vyse, Jr.	50 00
Wm. H. Voorhis	5 00
Mrs. F. L. Vultee	10 00
G. C. Verplanck	5 00
Mr. Voorhis	2 00

Mrs. J. C. Vark, B. F., Miss Comstock	5	00
C. Van Santvoord	20	00
Chas. H. Van Brunt	50	00
Mr. and Mrs. Richard Voss	10	00
Miss C. Van Wyck	5	00

W

Edward M. Willett	10	00
J. H. Wainwright B. F., Miss Kemble	10	00
John Warren	10	00
Mrs. D. Williams	10	00
Dr. Ward	10	00
Women's Bible Class of St. John's Church, Stamford, Conn., through Mrs. G. L. Brown	3	00
F. Wigand & Co.	10	00
Joseph S. R. Wood	25	00
Mrs Mary Watt	100	00
John A. Ward	5	00
E. G. W. Woerz	5	00
Mrs. James R. Wood	10	00
E. P. Wheeler	10	00
Thurlow Weed	10	00
Wm. A. Whitbeck	25	00
Widow's mite	1	00
Mrs Francis M. Wiley	10	00
Mrs. Joseph Walker	5	00
Mrs. J. C. Work	10	00
Mrs. M. H. Whitney B. F., Miss Comstock	5	00
Miss C. L. R. White, Bedstead and Mattrass	10	00
Mrs. Elijah Ward	50	00
Edgerton L. Winthrop	10	00
D. A. Wood	25	00
F. S. Winston	25	00
S. C. Williams	10	00
E. R. Ware	5	00
Mrs. Coleman Williams, B. F.	5	00
Horace Williams (Clinton, Iowa)	100	00
Miss Lillie F. Wesley	25	00

Mrs. Willington, for bed	10 00
Elias Wade, Jr.	25 00
Wm. C. White	5 00
Mrs. J. M. White	25 00
Mrs. J. L. Wallack	5 00
Mrs. A. B. Wheeler	5 00
J. Walter Wood	50 00
J. O. Ward	5 00
Mrs. A. H. Ward	10 00
Mrs. C. G. Ward	10 00
Mrs. S. S. Ward	5 00
Henry C. Ward	5 00
Mrs. Waterbury, Mrs. Gilman	3 00
T. Whittemore	25 00
Willing Helpers, Mott Haven	1 00
S. C. White	5 00
Samuel Willets	25 00
Henry Weil	5 00
Mrs. Mary F. Walke	3 00
F. Wigand & Co	10 00
Mrs. Wood	1 00

Y

Mrs. H. Young	2 00

Z

Mrs. S. J. Zabriskie	50 00
Mrs. C. Zabriskie, Jr.	10 00

——:o:——

DONATIONS FOR THANKSGIVING.

Mrs. O. Cammann	$6 50	
H. J. Cammann	2 00	
Wm. Alex. Smith	5 00	
Mrs. Alex. Smith	5 00	
Mrs. Gustav Schwab	8 00	
Mrs. H. C. Von Post	5 00	
		$31 50

FOR CHRISTMAS.

Mrs. D. T. Brown............	$5 00
R. W. Bootman..............................	5 00
Mrs. O. Cammann...	5 00
" D."......	5 00
Mrs. John A. Dix, for Turkeys	10 00
Mrs. Azel Graham	10 00
H. J. Hoffman...	10 00
Hon. D. S. Jackson	5 00
Mrs. J. T. Metcalfe.........	5 00
Emma Luly and Tony Leavitt...............	5 00
Miss Mary G. Pinckney Christmas Tree......	10 00
Horace Porter.....	5 00
Wm. Alex. Smith	5 00
Mrs. Alex. Smith	5 00
Mrs. Mary P. Roundey, Mrs. Gilman..........	2 50
H. Wagner................................	5 00
Mrs. Dan. F. Tiemann.........	5 00
Miss A. Tiemann..........................	5 00
Miss Julia Tiemann......................	5 00
Mrs. Travers, through Miss Kemble..........	5 00
W. W. Thompson............................	5 00
Miss Stephens	10 00
Frederick Hubbard..	10 00
Mrs. Valentine Hall, Tivoli, from her children	2 35
H. C. Von Post	5 00
Mrs. H. C. Von Post.......................	5 00
Miss Van Sciver, Miss Lanby and Miss Fennimore, Burlington, N. J	1 50
Miss C. L. R. White	10 00
Samuel Auchmuty Tucker	5 00
	$171 35

:0:

NAMES OF THOSE WHO PAY THE BOARD OF CHILDREN FOR CHARITY.

Mrs W. J. Beebe , ...	*Minnie.*
St John's Church, Stamford, Ct	*Bott's Boys.*
Mrs. Deyo, Yonkers	*Kittie Boyle.*

NAMES OF PERSONS WHO PROVIDE CLOTHING FOR CHILDREN.

Mrs. W. J. Beebe	*Minnie.*
The Misses Tiemann	*Maggie Hill.*
Mrs. W. P. Lee	*Angeline.*
Mrs. W. C. Gilman	*Ella Stanley.*
Mrs. F. C. Bogart	*Frank Talmadge.*
The Misses Heywood	*Joe Lynch.*
The Misses Cooper	*Jennie Smith.*
Mrs. Charles Kneeland	*Minnie Foley.*
Miss M. A. Green	*Walter Sarrington.*
St. Luke's S. School, Charleston, N. H.	*C. F. Sarrington.*
Miss Chittenden	*Geo. and John Botts.*
Miss Edith Newbold	*Eliza Wright.*
Miss Annie Cooke	*Annie Bagan.*
Miss Hoyt	*Maggie Boyce.*
Mrs. Schwab	*Robt. Oliver.*
Miss Butler Duncan	*Hiram Bagan.*
Miss Ogden	*Annie Stuart.*
Miss Edith Hartshorne	*Michael Bagan.*
Miss Lockwood	*Maggie Tilford.*
Miss Bessie Greenfield	*Maggie O'Rourke.*

DONATIONS IN CLOTHING, ETC.

MAY, 1869.

Miss Tiemann, 7 pairs of Socks.

Mrs. Atwill, Burlington, Vt., 3 Undergarments, 3 pairs of Stockings.

Mrs. Auchincloss, Oranges and Hominy.

Miss Chittenden, 5 pounds of Candy, and Books.

Miss Cutting, through Miss Kemble, 7 Undergarments, 4 Dresses and 1 Apron.

Thank-offering from Little Jennie Miller, "Books read to me in a sick-room."

MAY, 1860.
- Mrs. Gookin, through Mrs. W. C. Gilman, half-worn Shoes and a bundle of Clothing.
- Sewing-School of St. James' Parish, Boston Highlands, Mass., 58 Under-garments, 31 Pillow-Slips, 5 Pocket-handkerchiefs.
- Young Ladies' Penance Society, 6 Dresses and 17 Aprons, Patch-work for a Quilt.
- Mrs. T. M. Peters, 2 bundles of Clothing.
- Miss Chittenden, Clothing, and 1 soft Ball.
- Miss Wiltse, 24 Dresses, 54 Under-garments, 2 Aprons, 1 Sack.
- Mrs. Wm R. Travers, through Miss Kemble, 1 Boy's Suit, 1 Hat, 3 Coats, 2 pairs of Shoes, 2 Scarfs, 8 pairs of Stockings.
- Mrs. Robert Weir, 1 box of Pieces.
- Mr. Welling, through Miss Drake, 1 piece of Blue Check.
- Langley, Satterlee, Blackwell & Co., through T. R. Keator, 1 case of Straw Hats.
- Mrs. I. T. Williams, Fordham, N. Y., Clothing.
- Freddie M. Burr, 2 pairs of Worsted Stockings.
- Katie Lambard, a quantity of beautiful Toys.
- The Lent Work of a few young Ladies of Calvary Church, N. Y., 6 Under-garments, and 4 Aprons.
- Mrs. H. D. Wyman, 7 Common Prayer Books.
- Mrs. George Sheridan, Clothing.
- A Friend, 2 Dresses.
- Lottie Draper, Gt. Barrington, Mass., box of Clothing.
- George F. C. Thompson, Clothing.

JUNE, 1869.
- J. N. Paulding, 16 University Place, Clothing.
- (Three Missions of St. John's Church, Stamford, Conn.) The Women's Bible Class, 11 new Under-garments; The Cove Mission, 2 Bibbs, 2 Aprons, 4 Under-garments, all new; Emmanuel Church Mission, 7 new Under-garments.
- Sunday School Sewing Society of St. Ann's Church, N. Y., 13 Under-garments, ten pairs of Worsted Leggings.
- Mrs. H. H. Hayden, 17th Street and Irving Place, Clothing, &c.
- Mrs. P. F. Smith, Clothing.
- Lane, Son & Co., 1 bag of fine Meal.
- Miss Travers, 2 Dresses.

JUNE, 1869.
  G. F. C. Thompson, Clothing.
  Mrs. L. P. Morton, 2 large packages of Cake.
  Mrs. G. P. Trigg, 260 West 23d Street, Clothing for the Boys.
  J. D. Wolfe, Strawberries for all.
  Miss Jean Gerry, 5 pairs knitted Stockings.
  Mrs. G. Schwab, 2 packages of Cakes, for all.
  Mrs. Johnson, Cake and Fruit.
  Mrs. J. P. Thompson, Boys' Clothing,
  Mrs. Humy, 30 new Garments.

JULY, 1869.
  Through Miss Webbe, Brooklyn, 6 Under-garments
  R. L. Mulford, 1 half barrel Pickled Tongues.
  The Old Ladies' Sewing Society, St. Luke's Home, Hudson St., 5 pairs knitted Cotton Stockings, and the making of 4 Dresses and 3 Sheets.
  Mrs. Wm. Guion, 8 Flannel Skirts.
  House of Mercy, Vegetables.
  A Friend of the House, Clothing.
  Mrs. J. T. Williams, Fordham, a Crib, Chair and Carriage.
  Mr. Blakely, Apples.
  Mrs. Mix, through D. T. Brown, M. D., a Metropolitan Organ.

AUGUST, 1869.
  A Friend, Stamford, 10 new Aprons.
  Mrs. T. M. Peters, 1 Overcoat.
  House of Mercy, Vegetables.
  Mrs. Frederick Saunders, Brooklyn, N. Y., Peaches, for all.
  Mrs. J. J. Merrifield, through Miss Kate Comstock, a quantity of Clothing and Shoes.
  Mrs. T. M. Peters, 2 baskets Tomatoes and 1 of Squashes.
  From Minnie and Mattie Dorlon, Brooklyn, a Feast for the Nursery Children.

SEPTEMBER, 1869.
  A Friend, bundle of Clothing.
  Mr. McGann, a quantity of Corn.
  Mr. A. S. Clark, a basket of Peaches.
  Mrs. C., 13 Aprons and 1 Dress.

SEPTEMBER, 1869.
  Old Ladies' Sewing Society, St. Luke's Home, Hudson St., 18 Aprons.
  Dr. Peters, 2 baskets of Squashes.
  Mrs. Phillip Van Volkenburg, 1 piece of Blue Check.
  Mrs. B. W. Foster, Bananas and Pears.
  Miss Brierly, a basket of Tomatoes.
  A Friend from Trinity Church, New York, a number of " Young Christian Soldiers " and " Children's Guests."
  Mrs. Brewster, a basket of Peaches.
  Mrs. Carey, bundle of Clothing.
OCTOBER, 1869.
  Through Mrs. H. Von Post, 14 pairs of Knitted Woolen Stockings.
  Poor Children of the Church of the Nativity, N. Y., 6 pairs of new Shoes.
  Mrs Case, a Miniature Hand Organ.
  Miss Stewart, a Cloth Cape.
  Mrs. Oswald Cammann, 1 dozen Sheets and 1 dozen Pillow-cases, new.
  S. B. L. and M. H. C., 23 new Garments, 1 pair new Shoes, and several half-worn Garments.
  Miss L. Chittenden, 12 pairs of new Shoes.
  Mrs. Blake, 2 pairs of Knitted Cotton Stockings.
  Miss Kate Wilcox, Plainfield, N. J., 2 half-worn Dresses.
  Mrs. Homoyard, a large bundle of half-worn Clothing, and a quantity of Story-Books, Picture-Books, Papers and Toys.
  The Willing Helpers, St. Mary's Church, Mott Haven, through Mrs. Starbuck, 11 new Garments, Nuts and Candies.
NOVEMBER, 1869.
  Emily and Ella Dick, a box of Grapes for the Nursery Children.
  Miss E. J. Butterworth, 5 Dresses, 3 Aprons, and 1 Canton Flannel Skirt.
  G. F. C. Thompson, Bundle of Clothing.
  Miss Moore, 2 Dolls and Picture-Books.
  Mrs. W. M. Kingsland, 1 Turkey for Thanksgiving.
  Mr. John D. Wolfe, 100 Mince Pies for Thanksgiving.
  Mrs. Willington, a box of Oranges for Thanksgiving.

NOVEMBER, 1869.
  Miss Brewster, Candies for the Nursery, Thanksgiving.
  Mrs. C. Pierson, 1 Dozen Spools of Sewing Cotton.
  Mrs. Thomas Tweddle, bundle of Clothing.
  Mrs. Chas. H. Wilmerding, bundle of Old Linen, 11 Large School Charts, and a quantity of Games, Toys and Ornaments.
  N. A. Baldwin, 1 Case Straw Hats, 4 Cases Velvet Hats.
  Mrs. R. M. Shaw, 1 new Overcoat, large quantity of valuable Clothing, partly worn.

DECEMBER, 1869.
  Mrs. W. B. Smythe, half worn Shoes.
  Mrs. C. V. A. Schuyler, 178 Front St., bundle of Clothing, half worn.
  The Children of Mrs. Thomas Watt, 430 Fifth Ave., 1 piece of Muslin and 27 yards of Calico.
  Mrs. S. F. Sackett, 14 W. 34th St., large bundle of valuable Clothing, partly worn.
  Miss Bessie Greenfield, No. 2 Nassau Street, 1 pair of Boots.
  Mrs. Travers, 6 new Under-Garments.
  Mrs. T. M. Peters, Clothing.
  Andrew Peters, a quantity of "Pleasant Reading for stormy days."
  C. L. Case, Clothing.
  Hiram Paulding, Huntington, Long Island, 1 barrel of Apples.
  Mrs Wm. Tweed, 41 W. 36th St., large quantity of valuable Clothing.
  Acker, Merrall & Condit, 132 Chambers street, 1 bag of Salt, 1 bag of Indian Meal, 1 bag of Rice, 1 bag of Prunes, 1 bag of Sugar, 1 package of Chocolate, 1 box of Macaroni, 1 box of Oranges, 3 large and 3 small Brooms.
  Unknown, 3 pairs of Crutches.
  Mr. Handley, Several Pictures.
  Friendship's Offering, 1 pair of Knitted Stockings.
  Mrs. G. Sheridan, large bundle of Boy's Clothing.
  Mrs. and Miss Kemble, large box of Toys and Books.
  Mrs. H. Anderson, a bundle of valuable Clothing.
  Mrs. Dickerson, a bundle of valuable Clothing.

DECEMBER, 1869.

Mrs. V. Hall, Tivoli, N. Y., a box of Clothing and Toys.
Mrs. Keator, a box of Toys, a barrel of vegetables.
Mrs. Schlesinger, 1 piece of Calico, 1 pair new Blankets, 15 new Books and a bundle of Woolen Goods.
Mrs. W. H. Lindslay, 12 Woolen Hoods, 6 Woolen Cloaks, 6 Boys' Comforters.
Mrs. Bogert, a bundle of Clothing.
M. S., 10 handsome Illuminations framed.
Kittie and Daisy Blake, a box of Toys, a large dressed Doll, and about 118 yards of Dry Goods.
Mr. Prior, 8 dozen New Years Cakes.
Mr. J. D. Wolfe, 100 Mince Pies.
American Church Press Co., 50 Carols.
Miss Stephens, 2 dozen dressed Dolls.
Mrs. H. Anderson, 1 dozen dressed Dolls.
Mrs. Lee, material for Children's Plum Pudding.
Mrs. Brierly and Daughters, Dolls and Fancy Articles for Christmas Tree, Hood, Mittens, and Scarf for Minnie, and Scarf for K. Hart.
Mr. M. S. Coburn, 4 boxes Fancy Soap.
Mr. W. B. Taylor, box of Toys, through Miss Tiemann.
Misses Furniss, large basket of Toys.
Miss Luie Lee, 100 Oranges.
Freddie Burr, 6 Dolls, dressed and named.
Y. Y. Y., large quantity of Toys.
W. H. Fowler, 2 dozen Oranges.
Miss Brierly, 3 dressed Dolls and a number of Woolen Articles.
Mrs. Spencer K. Green, 107 E. 37th street, Clothing.
Miss A. L. Green, 107 E. 37th street, 8 pounds Candy.
Dr. Metcalfe, 14 pairs new Shoes.

JANUARY, 1870.

Mrs. Tiemann, New Year Cakes for all.
Mrs. R. Tweed, 6 Boxes of Candy.
Mr. T. Back, 6 Pounds of Candy.
Mrs. Peter Cooper, 18 pairs of New Cotton Stockings.

JANUARY, 1870.

Three American Ladies, Liverpool, England, through Mrs. Amanda Guion, 1 Piece of Serge, 4 Pieces of Serge-Poplin, 4 Pieces of Linsey Woolsey, 3 pieces of Calico, 5 Yards of Flannel, 20 pairs of Stockings, 18 Sontags, 35 Books and 1 Packet of Reward Cards.

A Parishioner of S. Paul's, East Chester, through Rev. W. S. Coffey, 5 pairs of Woolen Stockings, 5 pairs of Cotton Stockings, 5 yds. of Calico and 6 Under-Garments.

Rev. N. F. Ludlam, a Picture-Book for the Nursery.

Seven Happy Little Girls, Bergen Point, 3 prs. of Stockings, 10 Dresses, 6 aprons, 8 Under-Garments, 1 pair of Mittens, 1 Woolen Sack, 4 Dolls dressed, Books, Cards and Picture-Papers.

Miss Burnay and Miss Hunt, 4 Aprons, a piece of Flannel.

Mrs. Robert Weir, a Child's Blanket.

Mr. and Mrs. James N. Paulding, a bundle of Clothing and a quantity of Worsted

Miss Grace Wilkes, 6 pairs of Knitted Woolen Stockings.

Miss Nettie Sterling, the 23d Psalm with Music.

Miss Kilbourne, St. Luke's Home, Hudson St., N. Y., the Little Wonder Sewing Machine.

Wm. R. Welling, through Miss Drake, 1 piece of Blue Check.

Mrs. Robert Hoe, a quantity of Toys, a Music-Box and a loaf of Fruit-Cake.

Theodore Irwin, Oswego, N. Y., made and given by, 1 pair of Mittens and 1 pair of Cuffs.

Miss Lillie C. Hall, 2 Transparencies.

Mrs. Spencer, a bundle of Clothing.

From Mrs. Dubois, Mrs. Schism, Mrs. Campbell, Mrs Teter, Mrs. Holsestopple, Mrs. Shulman, Miss Stella Pulver, The Misses Kelly, Mr. Ostrander, from Anandale, through R. M. Hayden, 1 barrel of Apples, Nuts, Cakes and Crackers.

FEBRUARY, 1870.

Mrs. Dr. Williams, 1 dozen of Boys' Collars.

Mrs. T. M. Peters, a basket of Clothing.

Miss MacWilliamson, 3 Dolls for the Infirmary.

The O. N. Society, 5 Handkerchiefs and 3 Bibles.

FEBRUARY, 1870.

  John D. Locke & Co., 135 pieces of Tin and Japanned Ware.
  Mrs. Van, Toys and Books.
  Mrs. J. J. Phelps, through Mrs. H. C. Von Post, 12 pairs of Woolen Stockings and 1 pair of Mittens.
  Baby Chase, 1 pair of Stockings and a Scarf.
  Mrs. S. P. Nash, a trunk of Valuable Clothing.
  Mrs. A. E. Weir, Plate-Warmer.
  The House of Mercy, Mail-Bag.
  Mrs. P. C. Schuyler, 10 new Garments, 2 packages Illumined Texts.
  Mrs. John B. Murray, 6 pairs of Woolen Stockings.

MARCH, 1870.

  Mrs. De Ruyter, 12 Aprons.
  The Willing Helpers St. Mary's Church, Mott Haven, 27 white Aprons, 2 Bibs, and 2 Under-Garments.
  Unknown, 5 yards of Cloth for the Boys.
  Through Mrs. D. T. Brown, 4 pairs knitted Woolen Stockings, 3 white Aprons, and 7 Needle-Books.
  From Little Elsie Tiemann, on her Birthday, Ice-cream and Cakes for every one.
  Mr. Wm. M. Kingsland, 12 pairs of new Shoes.
  Mrs. Theodore Hopkins, Burlington, Vt., 12 Aprons.
  Mrs. T. M. Peters, 3 bundles of Clothing.
  Miss Peters, Half-worn Shoes and Stockings.
  Miss Kate Comstock, Half-worn Shoes.
  Pupils of Miss Barlow's School, 29 Sheets and 50 Pillow Cases.
  An Unknown Friend, 1 pair of Stockings.
  A Friend, "A Trifle."
  Acker, Merrall & Condit, 30 pounds of Rice.
  Miss Juliet Little, 5 new Garments.
  Mrs. Cuyler Van Vechten, School-Books and Picture-Books.
  Bowman & Blewitt, several boxes of Carbolic Acid Soap.
  A Constant Friend, Stamford, Ct., 14 pairs of new Shoes.
  Emma and Allie Beebe, Candy for the Nursery.
  Mrs. H. H. Hayden, Clothing.

MARCH, 1870.
  Through the Rev. H. E. Duncan, Matteawan, N. Y., 20 Dresses, 48 Under-garments, 16 pairs of Stockings and several Fancy Articles.
  Mr. S. Coburn, 1 pair of new Shoes.

APRIL, 1870.
  Arthur De Forest Wheeler, 1 Game of Parlor Croquet.
  The O. N. Society, 5 Aprons, 2 Bibs, 5 Under-garments, 5 Handkerchiefs.
  Mrs. Gerry, 8 new Garments.
  Mrs. Laidlaw, N. J., 10 yards of Calico.
  Mrs. Julius Siemann, bundle of Clothing.
  Mrs. Archibald, 2 Woolen Wrappers.
  Mrs. S. E. Getty, Yonkers, bundle of Clothing for the Boys.
  Miss Heiser, Clothing for the Boys.
  The Ladies' Sewing Society of St. Ann's Church for Deaf Mutes, 18 Garments.
  Mary L. Reed, Cohoes, 2 Pillow Cases and a Patch-work Quilt.
  A Friend in Cohoes, 3 pairs of knitted Woolen Stockings.
  Mrs. Harriet Strong, 3 pairs of Socks.
  Miss Annie Paulding, Huntington, L. I., 5 pairs of Socks and 2 Flannel Shirts.
  Mrs. Samuel Gore, Braintree, Mass., through the Sisters, a Marble Shelf for the medicine closet and an easy Chair for the sick children.
  A Friend, through the Sisters, a Writing-Desk and 5 Tables for the Infirmary.
  Mrs. J Tinker, Clothing.
  Archie Bull, 3 Story Books.
  Mrs. R. V. McKim, a large box of Toys.
  The Willing Helpers, St. Mary's Church, Mott Haven, 3 Aprons.
  Mrs. S. Gore, Braintree, Mass., 5 small Trays.
  Mrs. Tiemann, Colored Easter Eggs for all the Children.
  Freddie M. Burr, a beautiful Picture-Book, an Easter Gift to the Boys of the Sheltering Arms.
  The Sisters, through the Rev. C. C. Adams, Oranges and Cakes for all the children.
  Mrs. J. D. Wolfe, 56 Dolls.

APRIL, 1870

Mrs. Tiemann, 2 new Calico Dresses, 6 new Under-garments.
Mrs Boothe, through the table of the Earnest Workers, a Picture.
Bazaar, 12 volumes of Parley's Cottage-Library.
Mrs. Benj. Field, a Croquet Game.
W. J. Pollock, 4 dozen Neck Ties
Mrs. Stringfield, Two Ornamental Crosses.
Bazaar, 26 Hats for Girls.
Bazaar, 6 volumes for Library.

PRAYERS

TO BE USED BY THE FRIENDS OF

"The Sheltering Arms."

ALMIGHTY and most merciful Father, whose well beloved Son, our Saviour, did welcome the young children to His arms and bless them, look with pity, we beseech Thee, upon these little ones committed to our care, that, being shielded from temptation and delivered from evil, they may glorify Thy holy name, and finally, by Thy mercy, obtain everlasting life, through Jesus Christ, our Lord. AMEN.

OH, Lord God and Heavenly Father! infinite in love and full of mercy, send down thine Holy Spirit, as upon all friendless children and orphans, so especially upon these little ones, whom Thou hast given into our keeping, grant that the old Adam in these children may be so buried, that the new man may be raised up in them.

Grant that all sinful affections may die in them, and that all things belonging to the Spirit may live and grow in them.

Grant that they may have power and strength to have victory, and to triumph against the devil, the world, and the flesh.

Grant that, being dedicated to Thee, they may also be endued with heavenly virtues, and everlastingly rewarded, through Thy mercy, O blessed Lord God, who dost live and govern all things, world without end. AMEN.

"The Sheltering Arms."

SEVENTH ANNUAL REPORT.

NEW YORK,
1871.

Incorporated October, 1864.

New York:
E. WELLS SACKETT, STATIONER AND BOOK AND JOB PRINTER,
CORNER WILLIAM & PINE STREETS.

Officers of "The Sheltering Arms."

PRESIDENT.
REV. THOMAS M. PETERS, D. D.............Address, Broadway, cor. 99th St.

VICE-PRESIDENTS.
FRED'K S. WINSTON...144 Broadway.
WM. ALEX. SMITH..40 Wall Street.
WM. J. BEEBE...104 Wall Street.

SECRETARY.
PETER C. TIEMANN..Manhattanville.

TREASURER.
J. S BREATH...306 Mulberry Street.

VISITOR.
RT. REV. H. POTTER, D. D., D. C. L., LL. D...............38 East 22d Street.

TRUSTEES.
HENRY J. CAMMANN ....8 Wall Street.
HERMANN C. VON POST......................................68 Broad Street.
BENJ. H. FIELD...127 Water Street.
D. TILDEN BROWN, M. D....................................Manhattanville.
WM. B. CLERKE,...24 Broad Street.
WM. H. FOGG,..32 Burling Slip.
THOS. WATT,..439 Fifth Avenue.
J. B. CHURCH, Jr..11 Pine Street.
WM. P. LEE...326 Fifth Avenue.
WM. M. KINGSLAND,..116 Fifth Avenue.
REV. H. E. MONTGOMERY, D.D..........................209 Madison Avenue.
FRANKLIN EDSON...19 Whitehall Street.
CHARLES F. STRONG..68 Wall Street.
WOODBURY G. LANGDON...................................719 Fifth Avenue.
ABRAM S. HEWITT,..9 Lexington Avenue.
E. WELLS SACKETT,..56 and 58 William Street

PHYSICIAN.
L. A. RODENSTEIN, M. D......................................Manhattanville.

CONSULTING PHYSICIAN.
ABRAHAM JACOBI, M. D......................................110 West 34th Street.

Ladies' Association of "The Sheltering Arms."

VICE-PRESIDENT.
MRS. WM. P. LEE..326 Fifth Avenue.

SECRETARY.
MISS M. CHAUNCEY..................   ....53 West 36th Street.

TREASURER.
MRS. B. F. CORLIES.............................   ....29 Union Square.

MEMBERS.
MRS. R. W. ABORN................................43 West 39th Street.
MISS S. E. KITCHEN ....Park Bank.
" S. B. NEWBY..................   ....314 West 28th Street.
" L. PETERS..................   ....Broadway, cor. 112th Street.
" J. A. TIEMANN..................   ....Manhattanville.
" M. A. COOPER.............................Bushwick, Long Island.
" LIZZIE HOLMES.................................123 Fifth Avenue.
" F. COTHEAL..........................   ....28 University Place.
MRS. JOHN DE RUYTER.............   ....75 Madison Avenue.
MISS KATE BELL.................................20 West 20th Street.
" HOFFMAN...Cornwall, N. Y.
MRS. A. S. HEWITT ....9 Lexington Avenue.
MISS MONTGOMERY..............................209 Madison Avenue.
MRS. GEO. B. DRAPER..................Fifth Avenue, corner 130th Street.
MISS GERALDINE REED........... ....Corner 38th Street and Park Avenue.
" CHITTENDEN..................................Inwood, N. Y. City.
" JANE WILLIAMS......................:Yonkers, Westchester Co.
MRS. E. WELLS SACKETT...........................136 West 125th Street.
MISS AUGUSTA SLADE...............................5 East 38th Street.
" WILSON..................................127 West 46th Street.
MRS. R. F. WARE..............................138 West 36th Street.
MISS S. S. RICHMOND..Manhattanville.
" CATLIN....................................286 Madison Avenue.
" CHARLOTTE B. ARNOLD......................   ....Station R, Harlem.
" ANNIE P. CHURCHILL.......... ....5 Gramercy Park.
" WOLFE.....................................13 Madison Avenue.
MRS. JOHN MUNRO....................... ....14 West 36th Street.
" ISAAC P. MARTIN............................Fort Washington, N. Y.
MISS SCOTT..40 East 41st Street.
" HELEN BEACH..220 2d Avenue.

OBJECTS OF THE INSTITUTION.

"THE SHELTERING ARMS" was opened October 6, 1864, for the reception of homeless children, for whom no other institution provides.

The classes of children received are as follows:

1st. The blind and deaf mutes, until the age at which they become entitled to admission at the Asylums especially devoted to such unfortunates.

2d. Crippled children, past hope of cure, and therefore no longer retained in ordinary hospitals.

3d. Children of poor parents, obliged on account of sickness to enter a hospital, and who commit their children for a season to our charge, with the expectation upon recovery of reclaiming their own.

4th. Children rendered temporarily homeless by fire or other accident.

5th. Children whose home has been broken up by the intemperance or desertion of father or mother. In such cases, the remaining parent pays according to ability a small sum monthly.

6th. Children abandoned by both parents, brought to us by friends or relatives unable to find immediately a proper home, and yet unwilling to lose control of the children or to place them beyond their reach.

Children placed at "THE SHELTERING ARMS" are not surrendered to the Institution, but are held subject to the order of parents and relations.

All the children of sufficient age attend the school of the Institution, where they receive a common education. The larger girls are also trained to household work. The children attend St. Mary's Protestant Episcopal Church, and are under the pastoral care of the Rev. T. M. Peters.

REPORT

OF THE

Board of Trustees,

MAY, 1871.

THE Seventh year of this Society's labors is ended, and we proceed in brief annals to add its history to the pages of former years. We cannot do so with entire satisfaction, whether regarding the work or ourselves. The last year has been one of unparalleled pressure for admission to our care.

Our constantly-proclaimed purpose of enlarging, if possible, our accommodations until the door should never be shut against any one from those classes for whom our ministrations are intended, has perhaps invited to our threshhold this throng of worse-than-homeless little ones. To make room for the saddest and most needy cases we have again and again gone over our list of inmates, removing from the Cottages one and another for whom provision comfortable or profitable to themselves might be made. We have added a bed, and a bed, and a bed, until we have exceeded by 10 the number we proposed to shelter, and now, having been obliged during the year to postpone or refuse 272 out of 368 applicants, count always 130 children.*

---

* It is some consolation, amid the imperfections of our own work, to witness the establishment of other Institutions in our Church for the same classes of destitute children admitted here. If we count but 130, as many more are under Christian training in the House of the Good Shepherd, Rockland County, and the Children's Fold and the Shepherd's Fold in the City of New York. May the Lord bless their labors, and increase their means of usefulness.

During the year ending May 1st, 96 were admitted, and 83 removed. Two have died: James Tilford, a sweet, patient cripple; and Katy Long, a little girl whose soul remained in her feeble body but two months after her reception.

The large number of the admitted and discharged is due to an attempt to make the Institution especially useful as a temporary home for children in emergencies soon passing away. Several were with us during the illness of father and mother, others were brought to remain until some day of household calamity should be overpast.

The many changes referred to are unpleasant to us, because breaking, in some cases, the attachments of years; detrimental to the order and good appearance of our households from the constant removal of disciplined inmates to make room for untrained and often exceedingly rough material; and further, the most pressing cases are almost invariably and necessarily of those whose friends can pay no board, so that in receiving them we are diminishing still further our already scanty receipts from that source, and are forced to depend upon the charitable for a still larger proportion of the seventeen or eighteen thousand dollars annual expenses.

An anecdote, related of himself by the head of an Institution for children, has helped us to fix our principle of action, and under adverse circumstances steadily to practise it.

The person referred to, upon taking charge of an asylum, found the children quite a secondary consideration with all the officials, whose chief thought seemed to be their own ease. His endeavors at reform were met with remonstrance from the employes most in need of the process. Their own comfort as to quarters, food and hours was interfered with, for the sake of all those "*troublesome young-ones.*"

After enduring a few weeks of those complaints, the Superintendent one day called together the adults, who in various capacities had charge of the children, and with solemn face stated the inconveniences they were all enduring, closing with the suggestion that a petition be prepared and unanimously signed, setting forth their grievances and praying the Trustees to remove both boys and girls altogether from the house.

When the good appearance and order of our Institution, manifestly to our eyes, suffer from the frequency of these changes, we admit to ourselves that everything would be more quiet, satisfactory, attractive, and to all, inmates and visitors, more pleasant, if we took only little children and retained them until grown. As we did not, however, establish "THE SHELTERING ARMS" for our own comfort, and do not propose to conduct it, having chief regard to making it a show Institution, these thoughts are put to sudden flight as enemies.

Again, some of our good friends are much concerned (and we ourselves at times a little), because 90 of our children pay nothing and the remaining 40 less than one-half the cost of their joint maintenance, leaving over $14,000 to be collected in donations and otherwise—a constant dragging burden.

We could readily convert "THE SHELTERING ARMS" into a cheap child's lodging-house and boarding-school, and a very useful Institution such would be; again, we could in brief space fill the cottages if we required one-half board as an indispensable condition of reception. The former class of children can, however, be cared for elsewhere; there is some hope that the latter may be, but when by the side of such there stands at our door one for whom it is a home here for a while, or misery and squalidness, perhaps death, if turned into the street, we send the whole pay or half pay to others, and take in the utterly friendless and destitute. If we are The Sheltering Arms of Christ, we can do no otherwise. Thn such was our first purpose, to do for Christ's sake, and like to Christ, we endeavor always to bear in mind. By that principle we accept or reject. In no other course can we have both God and man and our own conscience on our side.

If the expenses of "THE SHELTERING ARMS" are thus increased, we can point with satisfaction to the fact that, notwithstanding the additional service required by our plan of cottages and distinct families, and the necessity of keeping a hired man, we still have but little exceeded the annual average cost of each child as heretofore estimated—viz., $135.

In the support of the Institution and its enlargement, we ask all interested to act for us. Many, pleased with the work, yet leave the financiering to others' activity. Being entirely without endowment, $1,000 excepted, we depend upon the constant flow of offerings, little and great, made for His sake to whose work we are called. Let every well-wisher do a double benefit by being a collector as well as personal contributor. Interest the children of Sunday and other schools; form societies to work for our aid. A reference to our acknowledgments of money and material will show a wide-spread interest in the success of this Charity. We trust to embrace within an ever-extending circle, a yearly-increasing company of friends, enlarging in like ratio our accommodations, purchasing ample grounds and erecting new cottages beyond the limit of streets and pavements, bidding every homeless child to find here the best substitute we can offer for a father's protection and a mother's nurture.

For the good health of the children during the past year, we have been constant in gratitude to Him who has watched over us. Besides the two mentioned above, but one child, little Ida Holmes, has been seriously ill. She still occupies a bed in the Infirmary, having for companions three cripples, one little blind child, and the nurse's baby, a year ago seemingly sinking into the grave but now full of health. Our physician, Dr. L. A. Rodenstein, takes a warm interest in the welfare of the Institution ; and to his suggestions are due, we believe, in some degree, the continued good health of our households during a sickly season. His unceasing solicitude for the lives of the children in case of the appearance of an epidemic, has induced the Trustees to purchase for an isolated infirmary a small brick house adjoining our grounds, and in his opinion well adapted to the purpose. The cost of purchasing and putting it in proper order will be from $5,500 to $6,000. For this expenditure we ask for special contributions ; the amount thus far received or pledged being about nine hundred dollars.

The little monthly paper has been continued during the past year, the Ladies' Association greatly lightening the burden by collecting material. The Association has been enlarged to somewhat over 30 members, and has been organized in a more formal manner by the adoption of a Constitution and By-Laws. They have contributed to the relief of the Treasury by collecting funds and otherwise aiding the Institution.

For the Superintendence of the House we are indebted, as during all the years of our existence, to the devotion of woman, working in love for Christ's sake. The services of Miss Richmond, thus offered, have been gratefully accepted by the Trustees. It is their hope and her's that, moved by the Holy Spirit, others will associate themselves with her in these labors. The plan proposed is that adopted at St. Barnabas' House with reference to the sisters of the Good Shepherd and also elsewhere ; namely, the appropriation to each lady, thus giving her time, of a sum sufficient to cover necessary personal expenses while laboring with us. In case of permanent dedication to the work, it is our purpose, in the future, to have a cottage and life-long home and support for those whose years may be prolonged beyond their strength to labor.

The School, under the charge of the Misses Cleaveland, has been refurnished and in many respects improved. We have every reason to be satisfied with the thoroughness of their system and the progress of the Children.

The past year has added to the record of the Board of Trustees one sad day, namely, that in which it was called upon to part with James Punnett, one of the original incorporators of "THE SHELTERING ARMS," and a liberal patron of this Charity. To him is largely due the acquisition, at a low price, of the ground on which stand the new cottages. May God raise up, in this careless world, others like him in faith, charity and truth.

Before closing this Report, we would refer every reader to the Treasurer's return, by which it will appear that, as is our custom, we come to our anniversary without funds in hand even for a month's expenses. Commence at once to collect for our summer wants. During your recreations and vacations have many thoughts for us, and gather, as you may find opportunity, the grains and little gifts for our daily bread.

Finally, accept our thanks as Trustees for your willing co-operation, and remember us when you come into the presence of Him, to whom, for all good received or accomplished, we render the chief honor and praise.

T. M. PETERS.
President.

THE SHELTERING ARMS in Account with J. S. BREATH, Treasurer.

1870.			DR.	
May 1—To Expenditure on New Home			$7,905	25
"	"	Bread	1,589	29
"	"	Meat and Fish	1,298	42
"	"	Milk	1,313	07
"	"	Groceries and Vegetables	2,102	17
"	"	Fuel	702	91
"	"	Gas, Water, Express & Car fare	572	74
"	"	Wages and Labor	3,360	89
"	"	Insurance	217	75
"	"	Household Material	1,441	41
"	"	Printing and Advertising	1,123	32
"	"	Stamps and Stationery	335	73
"	"	Salaries and Collection	2,109	63
"	"	Loans Paid	42,000	00
"	"	Interest on do	1,072	23
1871.				
Apr. 31— "	"	Church Sittings	125	00
"	"	Corporation Assessment	685	97
"	"	Sundries	273	46
			$68,222	64

1870.		CR.	
May 1—By balance from last Report		1,097	68
" Cash proceeds of Bazaar through Wm. Alex'r Smith, Treasurer		52,311	03
" Cash from Comptroller of the City		900	00
" " " " " State		1,244	57
" " Annual Subscriptions and Paper		543	00
" Cash Special for Thanksgiving and Christmas		206	26
" Cash Donations		10,259	25
1871.			
Apr. 31— " " Board received		1,584	67
Due Treasurer		76	18
		$68,222	64

NEW YORK, June 12, 1871.

At a meeting of the Finance Committee of "The Sheltering Arms," held this day, the account of the Treasurer for the year ending April 30th, 1871, was examined, compared with the vouchers and found correct, the same showing a balance due the Treasurer on the 1st May, 1871, of $76.18.

H. C. VON POST,
WILLIAM H. FOGG, } *Auditing Committee.*

BUILDING FUND,
RECEIPTS AND EXPENDITURES.

RECEIPTS OF THE BAZAAR.

Committee No. 1, Hall and Tickets.................	$9,332 80
Committee No. 2, Flowers,.........................	1,959 38
" " 3, Dry Goods, etc...................	114 63
" " 4, Jewelry, etc......................	3,035 70

Of this $100 was a special contribution from Miss Newberry of Chicago, and $100 a contribution of Miss Iselin.

Committee No. 5, Fancy Articles, etc................	816 23
" " 6, Fine Arts, etc....................	5,394 05
" " 7, Optical Instruments, etc...........	509 00
" " 8, Books and Household Articles......	1,726 11
" " 9, Refreshments, etc.................	2,254 44
Ladies' Association of Sheltering Arms...............	1,239 57

The Church of the Holy Communion sent a valuable contribution to this table.

St. Michael's Church, Bloomingdale.................	862 41
Trinity Parish.....................................	1,511 79
Church of the Incarnation..........................	7,234 27

This includes the receipts for the Post Office which was inaugurated under the auspices of the Committee of this Church, also $1,000 given by Mrs. Salisbury for the endowment of a bed.

Grace Church......................................	2,395 90
St. Thomas' Church................................	2,301 47

Of which amount $500 was the gift of Mrs. George Kemp, and $631 57 the proceeds of the table of the Twilight Circle, a society of St. Thomas' Parish.

Calvary Church....................................	3,147 35
St. Mark's Church.................................	3,411 74

Of this amount $2,066 35 was realized from the exhibition of the pictures of Mr. August Belmont.

St. Alban's Church.................................	497 97
Church of the Annunciation........................	459 34
Church of St. John the Baptist.....................	103 72
Church of the Holy Apostles........................	348 41

Christ Church...	$962 00
Church of the Heavenly Rest.........................	1,504 13
Zion Church...	1,501 22
Church of the Holy Sepulchre........................	294 07
St. Andrew's Church, Harlem.........................	764 87
Washington Heights Sheltering Arms Association.....	809 67
Seabury Hall..	261 12
Sowers and Reapers.....................................	265 28
New Jersey..	419 62
Table for Library..	184 01
Secretary's desk...	597 51
St. Luke's Church...	163 87
Helping Hands..	560 76
Earnest Workers...	123 00
Receipts at the Door.....................................	5,373 75
Mrs. Goold Hoyt...	16 00
Editorial Committee......................................	654 55
Waif..	10
Sundries paid Treasurer.................................	311 31
Mrs. Fleming and Mrs. Ives............................	32 00
Total Receipts...............................	$63,455 12

The Expenses of the Bazaar amounted to $9,758 37
Services of Secretary....................   500 00
Deduct amount for Special Purposes, viz:
    For Endowment.... $1,000 00
    For Library........   184 01
                               1,184 01
                                            11,442 38

There remained, therefore, of the proceeds of the Bazaar available for the Building Fund................... $52,012 74
Amount accumulated for Building Fund during the three years previous........................... 21,788 61

Whole amount received for Building Fund........... $73,801 35
Paid for land and permanent buildings to May 1, 1871................................ $78,565 54

                        J. S. BREATH, *Treasurer.*

"THE SHELTERING ARMS BAZAAR"

In account with

WM. ALEX. SMITH, Treasurer.

1870.   Dr.
          To Cash Paid

March 16.	G. F. Nesbitt & Co., Special Appeal........$	13	50
April 8.	Henry Crocker, Circulars, &c............	50	25
" 13.	" " Pass Books, &c..........	23	00
" 16.	P. C. Schuyler, Tickets, &c.............	109	85
" 25.	Julius Schlucter, Guides, &c............	383	20
" 27.	Williams Bros., Posting Bills............	45	00
" 29.	L. A. Milbank, Sundry Receipts.........	69	13
" 30.	Chas. A. Ditson, Printing Music........	68	60
" "	Albert McNulty, Insurance..............	428	00
May 2.	J. M. Lander, Music...................	880	00
" "	Thos. Martin, Banners.................	60	00
" 3.	Jno. Mahon, Bill Posting...............	36	90
" 4.	Klunder & Long, Flowers...............	40	50
" "	Francis Small, Messenger...............	40	00
" 5.	Printing & Eng. Establish't, Printing, &c.	60	00
" "	J. F. Brierly, Engraving................	20	00
" 7.	Haynes, Lord & Co., Cambrics, &c......	123	38
" "	E. Ratley, Wire Work.................	138	62
" 9.	Ward, Dickson & Co., Fancy Goods......	97	24
" 12.	E. Uhlig, Concert.....................	392	00
" "	John Mathews, Messenger..............	42	50
" 13.	W. G. Langdon, Sundry Bills...........	973	59
" "	Michael Norton, General Services........	68	00
" 18.	E. Ferrero, Rent of Hall...............	66	00
" "	Tiffany & Co., Fancy Articles............	206	25
" "	F. B. Vanderpool, Messenger............	25	00

17

To Cash Paid

May	19.	L. A. Milbank, Sundry Receipts.........	$189	00
"	"	J. H. Beckman, " "	416	08
"	"	Jas. S. Breath, Treas...................	17,000	00
"	20.	Caffrey, Benson & Wilson, Calcium Light.	54	00
"	21.	Jas. S. Breath, Treas...................	25,650	03
"	24.	Lewis Conger, Small Articles...........	58	70
"	"	William Schaus, picture...............	11	25
"	25.	W. Mackinzie, Carpenter Work.........	387	69
"	26.	W. Servers, Services..................	50	00
"	27.	37th Regiment, Gas Bills..............	180	30
"	"	Evening Express, Advertising..........	57	60
"	"	Alex. Flemming, Circulars.............	15	00
"	30.	A. W. Barnes & Son, Rent of Chairs....	30	00
"	"	Evening Mail, Advertising.............	94	08
"	31.	Lewis & Conger, Spoons...............	4	15
"	"	Jno. Clarke & Co., Earthenware........	39	75
June	1.	Tribune, Advertising....................	128	75
"	"	N. Y. Times, "	150	00
"	"	Evening Post "	75	24
"	2.	Rev. T. M. Peters, bill Henning & Schlueter	194	60
"	3.	Wm. P. Lee, Sundry Bills...............	111	00
"	4.	James Miller, Stationery, &c...........	101	25
"	"	J. S. Breath, Treas....................	5,000	00
"	7.	John Thompson.......................	38	27
"	"	M. J. Paillard, Music Boxes.............	268	00
"	"	G. J. Kraft, Mdse.....................	34	77
"	10.	Swiss Manuf'g Co., Fancy Articles......	202	09
"	13.	The World Co., Advertising............	114	30
"	15.	G. F. Nesbitt & Co., Printing, &c........	475	00
"	"	Pott & Amery, Books, &c..............	42	67
"	22.	Arthur Amory, Cash advanced.........	86	22
"	23.	P. C. Schuyler, Sundry Bills............	63	15
"	27.	L. A. Milbank, " "	28	18
"	"	Am. Bank Note Co., Engraving........	8	00
"	28.	Charlott Bearney, Wax Flowers........	22	00
"	29.	C. Vanderbilt, Jr., Car Tickets..........	33	90

To Cash Paid

July	6.	Sutton, Bowne & Co., Title Pages........	$16 00
"	"	Clark & Maynard, Paper, &c............	27 87
"	"	Walter Reid, Boquets, &c..............	47 05
"	"	N. J. Magnin, Guidin & Co., Repairing...	28 00
"	"	J. S. Breath, Treas....................	3,500 00
"	8.	The Sun, Advertising..................	187 00
"	12.	W. H. Arthur & Co., Diaries............	117 75
"	20.	J. D. Clark, Florist...................	83 25
Sept.	8.	Chas. Scribner & Co., Books...........	57 17
"	26.	Chas. L. Jones, "	12 43
Oct'r	4.	F. W. Christian, "	49 89
"	"	J. S. Breath, Treas....................	800 00
Nov.	3.	Egbert Mills, Carpenter Work..........	51 23
"	"	Jno. Wetterle, Florist.................	40 00
"	"	G. F. Nesbitt & Co., Circulars, &c......	80 50
"	"	A. F. Learned, Posting Bills............	21 40
"	"	W. E. Everdells' Sons, Engraving.......	175 00
"	5.	Lewis & Conger, Water Cooler..........	40 00
"	7.	Abraham Mead & Co., Gas Fitting.......	65 50
"	"	J. S. Breath, Treas....................	361 00
Dec.	1.	P. C. Schuyler, Testimonial, &c..........	90 00
"	6.	W. P. Lee, Sundries....................	103 93
"	"	D. Appleton & Co., Bill................	150 00
"	"	Rev. T. M. Peters, Trustee, special for bed from Ch. Incarnation................	1,000 00
"	7.	Isaac Smith's Son, Parasols, &c..........	55 32
"	"	A. W. Hale, Sundry Bills...............	30 56
"	21.	G. Collamore & Co., Bronze Figures.....	5 00
"	29.	Michael Norton, Services...............	30 00
"	30.	J. W. Smith, Flags, &c.................	77 62
1871.			
Jany.	14.	Locke & Munroe, Plumbing.............	5 25
Feby.	27.	John Bryan, Services	26 00
Mar.	28.	Tiffany & Co., Bal. Bill................	10 25
May	4.	W. P. Lee, Books......................	33 81
"	5.	J. S. Breath, Treas., balance...........	201 71

$63,455 12

1870.   Cr.
        By Cash Received,

Feby.	4.	A. S. Hewitt..........................			$25 00
"	28.	Member "Church of Incarnation"....			5 00
March	16.	Donation, H. W. T. Moll............			100 00
"	29.	Sale of Tickets (J. E. Montgomery)...			400 00
"	"	Treas. "Church of the Incarnation"..			106 31
April	18.	Donation, Miss Newberry, Chicago...			100 00
"	20.	Sale of Tickets, acc't Jno. Pyne......			75 00
"	22.	Cash W. P. Lee, Chairman..........			5,000 00
"	23.	" J. E. Montgomery.............			4,000 00
"	26.	" W. P. Lee, Chairman..........			15,000 00
May	2.	" " " "			5,000 00
"	3.	" " " "			10,000 00
"	10.	" " " "			10,000 00
"	25.	" " " "			5,000 00
June	9.	" " " "			2,000 00
"	27.	" " " "			5,000 00
Nov.	3.	" " " "			825 00
Dec.	6.	" " " "			637 81
1871.					
May	4.	" " " "			181 00
					$63,455 12

E. & O. E.
New York, 5th May, 1871.

                      WM. ALEX. SMITH, *Treasurer.*

                      New York, Sept. 7, '71.

Examined and found correct,

                By
                    W. B. CLERKE,
                        Of Auditing Committee.

FOUNDERS OF A COTTAGE BY THE GIFT OF FIVE THOUSAND DOLLARS.

Mrs. Peter Cooper (1869).
Mr. John D. Wolfe (1869).

———:o:———

ENDOWMENT OF BEDS.

By Resolution of the Board of Trustees passed on the 27th day of March, 1871, it was decided to accept endowments of beds at the rate of $1,000, the nomination of the occupant to remain in the donor for life; or of $2,000, with right of nomination in perpetuity; and that all sums so received be invested, and the interest only applied to the support of The Sheltering Arms.

NAMES OF PERSONS ENDOWING BEDS.
1871.
    Mrs. Henry Salisbury............................. $1,000 00

———:o:———

PATRONS OF THE SHELTERING ARMS, BY THE PAYMENT IN ONE YEAR OF FIVE HUNDRED DOLLARS.

1866.
    Frederick Hubbard, Robert B. Minturn, John D. Wolfe.
1867.
    Mrs. H. Rose.
1868.
    Loring Andrews, W. L. Andrews, James Punnett, Rev. T. M. Peters, D.D., H. C. Von Post.
1869.
    Frederick DePeyster, Thomas Garner, Azel Graham, C. C. Haight, Mrs. H. D. Wyman.
1870.
    Stewart Brown.
1871.
    Mrs. George Kemp.

LIFE MEMBERS, BY THE PAYMENT IN ONE YEAR OF ONE HUNDRED DOLLARS.

1865.
Wm. J. Beebe, Chas. E. Beebe, John Caswell, Thomas H. Faile, B. H. Field, W. H. Fogg, W. A. Haines, Rev. R. S. Howland, D.D., Geo. Merritt, Rev. W. A. Muhlenberg, D.D. Adam Norrie, Gideon Pott, Wm. Alex. Smith, W. K. Kitchen, S. S. Wyckoff.

1866.
Stewart Brown, Simeon Draper, Frederic G. Foster, Horace Gray, Jr., W. C. Gilman, Franklin F. Randolph, Mrs. Ogden Hoffman, Mrs. H. D. Aldrich.

1867.
W. Armstrong, Jay Cooke, Mrs. Frederick De Peyster, D. B. Fayerweather, Robt. J. Livingston, J. W. Minturn.

1868.
Mrs. S. C. Barling, Edward Jones, Rev. H. E. Montgomery, D.D., Mrs. Mary Watt, Mrs. Laura L. Wallen.

1869.
Wm. H. Aspinwall, Wm. M. Kingsland, Arthur Kimber, A. A. Low, Edwin C. Litchfield, Wm. P. Lee., Wm. Weyman Mali, Levi P. Morton, Wm. P. Furniss, David Stewart, Horace Williams.

1870.
Mrs. R. T. Auchmuty, F. A. Peters, S. D. Babcock, Mrs. T. H. Hubbard, Rufus Hatch, Charles P. Kirkland, Allan McLane, Richard Mortimer, Royal Phelps, W. C. Rhinelander, B. Schlesinger, Alex. T. Stewart, Wm. Niblo, Joseph Sampson, Mrs. Wm. L. Tweed, Mrs. Mary Watt.

1871.
J. A. Bostwick, John Bloodgood, Miss L. Peters, Cortlandt Field Bishop, A. J. Peters, Mrs. T. M. Peters, Peter C. Tiemann, Thomas Watt, Peter Cooper, Mrs. H. C. Von Post, Miss Newberry, Miss Iselin, H. W. T. Mali, Mrs. Catharine L. Spencer.

ANNUAL SUBSCRIBERS.

Mrs. Hugh Auchincloss	$10 00
Mrs. H. D. Aldrich	10 00
Mrs. Alonzo Alvord	5 00
Mrs. F. J. Bumstead	5 00
Mrs. C. C. Baldwin	5 00
D. D. Bedell	5 00
Miss Hattie T. Bryce	5 00
Mrs. H. Colt	5 00
Mrs. Colden	5 00
Miss Mary Cunard	5 00
William Cooper	10 00
C. W. Cooper	10 00
G. E. Cooper	5 00
Mrs. R. L. Cutting	5 00
Mrs. Henry Cram	5 00
Miss Kate Cothoal	5 00
Miss M. G. Corlies	5 00
W. H. Draper,	10 00
Mrs. W. P. Dixon	10 00
Mrs. J. L. Englehardt	5 00
Miss Emmet	3 00
Mrs. Alfred H. Easton	10 00
Mrs. Fitzgerald	10 00
Mrs. H. T. Gerry,	5 00
Miss Jeannie Gerry	5 00
Miss M. M. Gandy	5 00
Miss M. Glover	5 00
Mrs. C. F. Heywood	5 00
Mrs. J. C. Hamilton	5 00
Miss M. E. Hamilton	3 00
Mrs. C. W. Hull	3 00
Mrs. J. C. Hull	3 00
Miss M. E. Horner	10 00
Mrs. P. Hanford	5 00
Mrs. A. S. Hewitt	10 00
Miss M. A. Jones	5 00

Mrs. Chas. A. Jackson	$5 00
Miss M. S. Jones	5 00
Mrs. A. M. Kalbfleisch	5 00
Mrs. Jessie Keator	5 00
Mrs. George Keyes	5 00
Mrs. N. Lawrence	5 00
Mrs. W. P. Lee	5 00
Mrs. Charles E. Milnor	20 00
Mrs. H. Meigs	5 00
Mrs. B. McEvers	5 00
Mrs. J. T. Metcalfe	10 00
Mrs. A. B. Morrell	5 00
John Moulson	10 00
Mrs. E. L. Molineux	5 00
Mrs. Alfred Ogden	5 00
Mrs. Hobart Onderdonk	5 00
Mrs. A. C. Peters	5 00
Miss L. Peters	3 00
Horace Porter	5 00
Mrs. Sylvanus Reed	5 00
Miss Geraldine Reed	5 00
Miss C. T. Renshaw	10 00
Mrs. Thomas Rutter	5 00
Mrs. Mary A. Reeder	5 00
Mrs. L. A. Rodenstein	5 00
Mrs. W. Alexander Smith	10 00
Mrs. E. Shedden	5 00
Mrs. A. T. Sackett	10 00
Mrs. T. Timpson	5 00
Mrs. C. L. Trowbridge	5 00
Mrs. D. F. Tiemann	5 00
Miss Mattie Tiemann	5 00
Miss Catharine Tracy	5 00
Mrs. H. C. Von Post	10 00
Mrs. W. H. Wisner	10 00
Miss Wilkes	5 00
Miss G. Wilkes	5 00
Miss H. K. Wilkes	5 00
Hamilton F. Webster	5 00

Wm. Whitlock, Jr....	$10 00
C. S. Weyman...	5 00
Mrs. H. D. Wyman...	10 00
Mrs. J. H. Watson...	5 00
Mrs. S. H. Whitlock...	5 00

SHELTERING ARMS LEGION OF ONE DOLLAR SUBSCRIBERS.

COMPANY 1.

KITTIE JACKSON, D. S. Jackson, Willie Jackson, A. V. Williams, Maynard Olifie, Mrs. Stacey, Miss Stacey, Minnie Sommerville, John Sommerville, Frederika Conrad, Arthur Davis, Willie Bleakley, A. W. Hearn............................... $13 00

COMPANY 2.

JULIA T. PETERS, B. F. Tiemann, Ruth Tiemann, Paul Tiemann, Elsie Tiemann, Andrew Peters, W. L. Sandford, Irving Kitchell, Mary Tully, Josephine Ellicott, A. J. Peters, Minnie Wiley... $12 00

COMPANY 3.

EMILY DICK, Susie Gorham, Harrie Sheridan, Minnie Ferguson, Mrs. Weaber, Sarah Smith, Clara Yenni................. $7 00

COMPANY 4.

EMILIE HEISER, C. E. Smith, Fannie Hassell, Kate Davis, Maggie Davis, Mary Davis, Miss Buckenham, Rosalie Helser, Chas. Heiser, John Helser, Ebby Hicks..................... $11 00

COMPANY 5.

HENRIETTA M. BRIERLY, Charlotte E. Byron, Mrs. E. Lange, Addie Cooper, Jennie O'Neill, Mrs. Knapp, Anna McDermott, Mary I. Graham, Dr. Clow, Annie J. Brierly, Henry Thomas, Lottie Ferguson, Clara Lall, Bertha Schedler................. $14 00

COMPANY 6.

WILLIE H. WAITE, C. C. Waite, L. F. Feller, Geo. B. Farrar, C. Burritt Waite, Albert Clark. [10 dollars sent, but no more names] $10 00

SCATTERING.

Paul Fleury, Miss Talmadge, Freddie Ware, Miss Chittenden, Miss Hannah Lee, Mrs. J. T. Low, Mrs. W. H. Beams, Mrs. Lillie Willson, Jno. V. Wheeler, Mrs. W. E. Vermilyea, Mrs. D. E. Ritter, Miss E. M. Cotheal, Miss Lawrence, Miss E. L. Holmes, Miss F. Cotheal, J. Hendricks, J. Murray Beam, Mrs. J. A. Schmelzel, Mrs. J. Mildeberger, "For Papers," Mrs. Coleman Williams, Mrs. G. Gurnett, Mrs. E. T. Allen, "Hard Times," "W.R.B." Miss Julia Wells, S. G. Williams, Minnie Wiley, Miss C. E. Wolbert, Mrs. Geo. Richmond, Mrs. S. F. Dayton, Mrs. G. A. Seixas, Mrs. A. E. Orr, W. H. Guest, Miss Mary Tallmadge, Miss Josie Campbell, Mrs. Hanford, Miss M. L. Whitlock, Maimy Morse, Mrs. F. T. Whiting, Lilly Morse, Margaret North $43 00

DONATIONS.

A.

Alms Box...	$14 74
R. H. Arkenburgh...................................	2 00
Mrs. J. H. V. Arnold	10 00
"A. H. M."..	5 00
Mrs. R. W. Aborn...................................	5 00
Mrs. Wm. Alsop.....................................	5 00
Mrs. J. S. Abecasis..................................	5 00
Mrs. A. B. Ansbacher...............................	5 00
J. B. Alexander......................................	25 00
Mrs. Allen...	10 00
C. F. Alvord..	5 00
An American living abroad, through Mrs. Jno. A. Marsh,	50 00
Wm. H. Aspinwall...................................	100 00

American Merchants' Union Express Co.	$25 00
"A. B. C."	5 00
B. Aymar	15 00
Mrs. W. C. Arthur	5 00
Mrs. H. D. Aldrich	100 00
"Aunt Molly," for Infirmary	25 00

B

J. A. Bostwick	100 00
Bazaar held by 4 Little Girls—Isabel Morrell, Flora Work, Mattie Searles and Connie Du Flon	42 15
Annie Brierly, "Minnie fund"	2 00
Sales of Bazaar articles at Institution	25 00
Beadleston, Price & Woerz	25 00
Samuel Bonnell, Jr.	5 00
J. L. Brownell & Brothers	25 00
J. H. Baldwin	3 00
Mrs. G. W. Burnham	5 00
H. Batjer	5 00
M. G. Baldwin	10 00
Mrs. G. W. Birdsall	5 00
J. Barclay	10 00
Mrs. E. H. Byers	5 00
Mrs. S. Bartholomew	10 00
"B. S."	25 00
H. A. Burr	10 00
Mrs. B——	5 00
August Belmont	20 00
Mrs. Geo. Bell	5 00
Miss Kate Bell	5 00
Mrs. A. Boody	5 00
Mr. and Mrs. J. H. Boynton	20 00
C. Butler	5 00
Through Dr. Brown	12 00
George Barnard, D. D. S.	5 00
Mrs. P. R. Billings	10 00
William Betts	10 00
F. C. Barlow	3 00

Mrs. S. Brown....	$5 00
E. M. Block...	5 00
Miss Kate B. Bell...	25 00
Mrs. L. F. Battelle...	5 00
Mrs. J. R. Boyd...	5 00
Mrs. C. P. Burdett...	5 50
John Bloodgood...	100 00
Sylvanus Bedell...	5 00
Mrs. Bromley...	2 00
J. A. Benedict...	5 00
Wm. F. Beekman...	5 00
Edward A. Boyd...	10 00
Mrs. E. A. Boyd...	10 00
Mrs. W. N. Beach...	5 00
Mrs. W. Barton...	5 00
Mrs. Stephen Brush...	10 00
J. H. Beekman...	5 00
Mrs. W. G. Breese...	5 00
G. Banyer, for Easter Festival...	10 00
Mrs. H. C. Beach...	3 00
J. V. B. Bleecker, U. S. N...	5 00
Miss J. Brinckerhoff...	10 00
Mrs. Sarah Barclay...	20 00
Miss Mary Benkard...	50 00
James Baker...	5 00
Cornelius Bogert...	25 00
Miss Boardman...	6 00
W. Blackstone...	5 00
Thomas Barron...	50 00
Williamson Bacon...	5 00
Mrs. C. Braker, Jr...	5 00

C

Cash $1, 20, 5, 2, (5, S. A.) 3...	36 00
" $25, 2, 2, 3.50, 24.70, 1, 1, 5...	64 20
" $5, 10, 2, 5, 2, 2, 2, 5, 10, 2...	45 00
" $1, 1, 1, 2, 2, 5, 10, 5, 10, 1, 10...	48 00
" $1, 1, 1, 5, 5, 10, 15, 2, 5...	45 00

Children's Christmas Offertory of St. John's Parish, Stamford, Conn., through Rev. W. Tatlock, 1869.	$10 90
Jay Cooke & Co.	50 00
Comptroller of City of N. Y.	900 00
Cash for Gravestone.	2 00
James S. Cox.	10 00
Charles M. Congreve.	10 00
S. B. Collins.	5 00
J. S. Cushman.	5 00
"C. M.".	10 00
W. L. Cogswell.	10 00
R. S. Clark.	25 00
Mrs. F. W. Coggill.	10 00
Ella, George and Julia Coggill.	10 00
Car Fare Saved.	8 00
Mrs. Martha Coles.	10 00
Mrs. H. H. Crocker.	5 00
Thos. C. Chardavoyne, $5, $10.	15 00
George Chesterman.	25 00
Mrs. L. Clarkson.	5 00
Mrs. Smith Clift.	10 00
Mrs. N. Chandler.	5 00
James Clinch.	5 00
W. L. Chamberlain.	10 00
Mrs. B. F. Corlies.	5 00
Miss E. M. Cotheal.	4 00
E. B. Chilton.	2 00
Comptroller State N. Y.	1,244 57
Miss Minnie P. Cole.	5 00
Mrs. Charles Cole.	10 00
Mrs. D. N. Crouse.	5 00
Eight Children, for Tommy's Gravestone.	8 00
Henry Chauncey.	20 00
Wm. A. Camp.	10 00
Thomas P. Cummings.	10 00
Mrs. Wm. Campbell.	2 00
Mrs. Frederick Church.	5 00
Rev. Lyman Cobb.	5 00
Wm. B. Clerke.	50 00

29

"C. V. S. R."	$25 00
John Cinnaman, Infirmary	10 00
H. A. Coster, Infirmary	25 00
Peter Cooper, Golden Wedding Fund	50 00

D

Mrs. H. W. Dolson	5 00
P. Dickie	2 00
Theodore M. Davis	25 00
"D. W. B."	20 00
Miss C. G. Davis	3 00
E. Delafield, M. D	5 00
C. J. DeWitt	10 00
E. DeWitt	10 00
Mrs. Daniels, per D. H	20 00
C. De Rham	10 00
James F. De Peyster	25 00
E. A. Duyckinck	5 00
Mrs. David Dows	25 00
A. Denison	5 00
Charles Denison	10 00
Mrs. F. H. Delano	6 00
T. W. Dwight	3 00
George Denison	20 00
A. Dunlap, Infirmary	5 00
Mrs. G. B. Docharty	5 00
"D. H.", Cash	5 00
Mrs. W. A. Dooley	5 00

E

Wm. M. Evarts	10 00
"E. G."	2 50
Easter Offering, 1870, Calvary Ch. S. S., N. Y	162 78
Elliott, Anna and Josephine, for Maggie Haselbacher's Gravestone	60
"E. R. L."	10 00
Mrs. A. Embury	5 00
Jonathan Edgar	5 00

Mrs. E. A. Edgar	$5 00
James Emott	10 00
Mrs. Wm. C. Emmet	5 00
Endowment Fund Interest	38 50
S. C. Evans	5 00
Mrs. E. M.	2 00
H. Elsworth	10 00
Easter Offering, Christ Church, Watertown, Conn., Rev. W. H. Lewis	50 00
Easter Offering, St. James' Church, Great Barrington, Mass., through Rev. H. Olmsted, D. D.	14 75
Easter Offering, Calvary Church S. School, '71, through Mr. James Pott	108 03

F

"A Friend," for Maggie's Gravestone	10 00
"F. A. P." for do	5 80
Proceeds of a Fair held by Ida Pirsson, Eva Woodford, Lizzie Eames and Johnny Eames	25 33
Wm. M. Fliess	5 00
S. J. Fatman	5 00
N. Fisher	5 00
"F. S." Cash	5 00
Wm. W. Fessenden	5 00
D. V. H. Floyd	5 00
F. C. Field	5 00
C. B. Foote	10 00
"A Friend of Sister Ellen"	100 00
"Miss F."	25 00
"Messrs. F."	25 00
H. W. Ford	10 00
"A Friend"	5 00
E. L. Ferry	10 00
Wm. B. Fletcher	10 00
Thomas H. Falle	100 00
A. Goodrich Fay	10 00
J. P. Girard Foster	20 00
Benjamin H. Field, to constitute Cortlandt Field Bishop a life member of Sheltering Arms	100 00

"Friends," in Newark, New Jersey, for Carrie Sagars'
  Gravestone.. $8 00
"A Friend"... 10 00
"Three Little Lame Friends," for the Infirmary.......... 14 37

G

P. W. Gallaudet... 5 00
G. G. Gray... 20 00
P. Gilsey... 10 00
Miss Margaret A. Green...................................... 5 00
J. H. Gautier.. 25 00
Mrs. M. A. Grosvenor... 25 00
Mrs. Wm. T. Garner... 10 00
Sheppard Gandy... 90 00
C. T. Gostenhofer.. 25 00
Miss A. J. Garner... 25 00
J. C. Gray... 10 00
Mrs. J. C. Gray... 10 00
Mrs. Gibson... 2 00
Mrs. Geo. T. Gilman.. 5 00
Miss Grey... 2 00
Mrs. H. H. Garner.. 5 00

H

Hoffman & Williams.. 10 00
A. O. Headley... 5 00
Mrs. J. P. Hilliard... 2 00
Mrs. P. S. Hoe.. 10 00
Mrs. W. T. Hicks.. 5 00
M. M. Hendricks... 10 00
Wm. B. Hoffman.. 5 00
Mrs. R. Hoe, Jr... 5 00
Mrs. M. Hartley... 10 00
C. E. Hartung... 2 00
William Heath... 5 00
Mrs. Charles Henschel... 10 00
H. Hudson Holly... 5 00
P. H. Holt... 25 00

Mrs. Ogden Hoffman	$5 00
Miss M. C. Hoffman	3 00
Miss V. S. Hoffman	3 00
J. A. Hardenburgh	10 00
N. P. Hosack	3 00
Mrs. E. S. Higgins	10 00
J. Montgomery Hare	5 00
Valentine G. Hall	25 00
Mrs. V. G. Hall	25 00
Joseph T. Harris	5 00
Jno. R. Hurd	10 00
F. C. Havemeyer	10 00
Rev. S. G. Hitchcock	2 00
F. Hornby	10 00
Misses Hadden	10 00
Mrs. A. L. Hamilton	25 00
"H. de R," Thank Offering for Infirmary or Hospital	25 00
C. F. Heywood	5 00
Mrs. H. H. Holly	5 00

I

Mrs. Margaret Iselin	2 00
F. E. Ives	10 00
Adrian Iselin	50 00
Richard Irvin	25 00
Miss Margaret Inglis	5 00

J

Katie Herbert Jackson	1 48
Mrs. M. Mason Jones	10 00
Mrs. H. W. Johnson	10 00
B. Johnson & Sons	5 00
Mrs. T. R. Jackson	5 00
"J. C. C."	5 00
Thomas Jeremiah	5 00
Mrs. Geo. R. Jackson	5 00
Mrs. F. U. Johnson	5 00
Misses F. & R. M. Jones	20 00

Mrs. "J. Q. A."	$5 00
Mrs. H. A. Johnson	10 00
"J. M., Jr."	10 00
Mrs. J. J. C	2 00
Mrs. Colford Jones	25 00
"J. M. C."	25 00
George Jones	25 00
"J. V. N."	5 00
Miss Jones	20 00
"Jm."	5 00
Mrs. J. A. C."	5 00
"J. T. P.." for little girl's Gravestone	10

K

Wm. M. Kingsland	20 00
J. Knower	10 00
Mrs. J. P. Kernochan	20 00
Isaac L. Kip	25 00
Wm. W. Kip	10 00
Mrs. E. Keteltas	10 00
Mrs. Jno. Kerr	5 00
Charles H. Korner	10 00
Wm. M. Kingsland, Infirmary	50 00
Mrs. P. R. Kearny	5 00

L

Mrs. F. Lieber	3 00
Luie Loe's Savings' Bank for Monument to Unserer lieben Tochter	2 00
Cyrus J. Lawrence	10 00
Wm. K. Lothrop	5 00
Mrs. T. J. Leslie	5 00
F. R. Leo	5 00
W. Landon	10 00
P. Lorillard & Co	20 00
Mrs. Joseph Lawrence	5 00

Mrs. R. E. Livingston	$10	00
Mrs. H. L. Langdon	5	00
William Lottimer	20	00
Joseph Larocque	25	00
Miss Julia A. Low	20	00
Mrs. C. S. Little	5	00
Com. Jno. W. Livingston	25	00
Mrs. G. W. Livingston	5	00
A. N. Lawrence	10	00
R. J. Livingston	25	00
Mrs. Samuel Lawrence	3	00
Edward Livingston	10	00
Mrs. "L. A. J."	2	00
Donation of Ladies' Association of St. Thomas' Church, N. Y., through Miss Augusta Slade, V. P.	74	16
Josiah Lane	10	00

M

J. T. Metcalfe, B. F.	25	00
"M. G. O.", for Little Girl's Gravestone		50
Mabel, for Maggie's Gravestone	1	00
Thomas McMullen	10	00
J. H. McKim	20	00
William Mackay	10	00
William Mackey	10	00
Samuel B. F. Morse	5	00
Mrs. Peter Morris	5	00
Mrs. T. T. Moran	5	00
Mrs. H. McKim	5	00
Wm. W. Mall	25	00
Zophar Mills	5	00
Mrs. J. A. Munsell	5	00
Mrs. "M. A. C. R."	10	00
Mrs. C. Munzinger	5	00
Mrs. J. Morrison	2	00
A. B. McDonald	10	00
Mrs. L. E. Morgan	5	00

Miss M. S. Mortimer	$3 00
Mrs. L. P. Morton	10 00
Thos. D. Middleton	10 00
Mrs. Geo. A. Morrison	5 00
Mrs. S. E. Morse, Jr	5 00
James Moir	5 00
J. R. Maurice	25 00
"M. D. H."	5 00
Wm. C. Moore	5 00
"M. A. L."	100 00
Mrs. Wm. F. Morgan	5 00
Miss Anna Morgan	5 00

N

New York Condensed Milk Co	25 00
Mrs. E. H. Nichols	5 00
Nettie, Lizzie, Ellie and Josie, $5 each, for Infirmary	20 00
H. D. Noyes	5 00
H. W. Niemann	8 00

O

Mrs. E. H. Owen	5 00
Oswald Ottendorfer	20 00
Thomas Owen	10 00
C. V. D. Ostrander	10 00
William Oothout	20 00

P

J. E. Parsons	10 00
Augustus Proal	3 00
John Poudir	50 00
Mrs. W. H. Peckham	5 00
Alfred A. Post	12 00
Parishioner of St. Paul's Church, East Chester, through Rev. W. S. Coffey	2 00

Royal Phelps	$100 00
J. K. Pell	5 00
Levi Pawling	5 00
Mrs. Geo. C. Peters	5 00
Mrs. A. M. Pell	5 00
Miss Parson	5 00
Rev. T. M. Peters	249 59
Mrs. J. J. Phelps	10 00
Mrs. C. W. Pell	10 00
Mrs. J. J. Petit	5 00
William Paul	5 00
Mrs. John Pettigrew	25 00
Lilly and May Platt	5 00
Mrs. J. R. Platt	10 00
James Petit	18 17
Mrs. Geo. H. Purser	20 00
Mrs. T. M. Peters	100 00
Miss L. Peters, Infirmary	100 00
Little Marion Poole's Mite Box, and Baby Harold's first Easter Offering for the Children at the Sheltering Arms, through Mr. James Pott	10 00
John D. Phillips	10 00

Q

Mrs. M. M. Quackenbos	10 00
Mrs. Thomas Quincey	3 00
Mrs. Geo. P. Quackenbos	3 00

R

M. P. Read	25 00
E. C. Richards	10 00
C. Robbins	10 00
Mrs. Wm. Remsen	5 00
Mrs. Sylvanus Reed, proceeds of a Concert held in Mrs. Reed's drawing-room	400 00
C. T. Raynolds	5 00
Mrs. E. Robbins	5 00
James Rogers	10 00

C. B. Ransom	$25	00
Wolcott Richards	5	00
Rent for house on the grounds	64	00

S

Mrs. "S. W. E."	10	00
S. S., St. Alban's Church, N. Y.	50	00
St. Ann's Church, N. Y., Infant Class	6	00
Other Classes of do	5	92
Mission S. School, do., for the support of one baby	6	35
S. S., St. Michael's Church, N. Y., Class E	2	20
S. S., St. Paul's Church, Franklin, N. Y., through Rev. Wm. M. Ogden	6	16
St. James' Church, Great Barrington, Mass., Rev. H. Olmstead, D. D., Rector, Offering at Celebration of the Communion for the Sick	7	60
S. S. of said Church	3	40
S. S. of Calvary Chapel, 23d St., N. Y., through Rev. W. D. Walker	83	54
"Staten Island," for Gravestone	2	00
C. V. A. Schuyler & Son	25	00
Charles G. Small & Co	10	00
Mrs. J. Schmelzel	5	00
C. Swan	25	00
John Sneeden	50	00
"Stranger"	5	00
Mrs. A. Scholl	5	00
J. A. Sprague	5	00
J. Rufus Smith	10	00
"S. B. S."	5	00
J. L. Schieffelin	10	00
"S. C."	5	00
Mrs. J. Sonneborn	5	00
Charles F. Sanford	25	00
B. L. Solomon	10	00
Floyd Smith	5	00
E. H. Schermerhorn	10	00
J. Selden Spencer	5	00

R. Seaman	$10 00
Miss A. Slade	5 00
Wm. Alex. Smith	50 00
Mrs. J. W. Southack	5 00
Stamford Manufacturing Co.	10 00
Frederick Schuchardt & Sons	25 00
Mrs. Catharine L. Spencer	100 00
Otis D. Swan	90 00
Alfred Schermerhorn	25 00
J. B. Slawson	10 00
Mrs. Jarvis Slade	10 00
Mrs. Sackett	3 00
W. C. Schermerhorn	10 00
W. N. Seymour	5 00
C. W. Sandford	5 00
Mrs. R. Stuyvesant	5 00
S. S. Church of the Holy Apostles, N. Y.	44 69
"A Stranger"	5 00
Charles A. Sherman	5 00
Mrs. E. Stoughton	5 00
Sale of Old Materials	218 38
Miss "S. E. W."	10 00
Mrs. G. Schwab	10 00
A. V. H. Stuyvesant	20 00
Robert Soutter	25 00
Miss M. D. Smith	5 00
Mrs. Lewis A. Sayre	5 00
S. T. Skidmore	5 00
J. C. Spencer	25 00
John Sullivan	25 00
Mrs. M. Sternberger	3 00
H. R. Searles	10 00
H. D. Sedgwick	5 00
Mrs. H. G. Stevens	25 00
J. B. Slawson	10 00
S. S., St. James' Church, N. Y., through Rev. Cor's. B. Smith	21 00
Floyd Smith	5 00
James Stokes	10 00

St. Michael's Church, N. Y., Missionary Box $1 30
U. J. Smith 10 00
Charles F. Southmayd 10 00
Charles E. Strong 10 00
Seabury Hall, by Miss M. L. Frost 25 06
Mrs. Chas. S. Spencer 5 00
Mrs. N. Sands 5 00
Mrs. "S. W. E." 5 00
Mrs. Charles W. Smith 10 00

T

A. G. Thorp 25 00
Mrs. Wm. M. Tweed 20 00
J. H. Titus 10 00
P. C. Tiemann, $52, $77 .... 129 00
Hon. Daniel F. Tiemann 77 00
Mrs. M. A. Townsend 5 00
Mrs. L. E. Tinker 10 00
Miss Hattie A. Townsend 10 00
Mrs. T. G. Thomas 5 00
L. Turnure 25 00
Mrs. Jane M. Thorn 10 00
Samuel C. Thompson 10 00
S. D. Tompkins 20 00
George F. Thomae 5 00
Theodore Timpson 10 00
Montgomery H. Throop 5 00

U

J. W. Underhill 5 00
Mrs. Mary V. Underhill 5 00
M. Ulshoeffer 5 00
United States Express Co 25 00

V

A. Van Rensselaer 10 00
C. Van Santvoord 20 00
B. Van Auken 5 00

Mrs. A. Vanderpoel.................................... $50 00
H. C. Von Post, to make Mrs. Von Post a life member.. 100 00
C. H. Van Brunt....................................... 25 00
A. Voorhies... 10 00

W

Mrs. Thomas Watt's children, for Maggie's Gravestone... 5 00
W. Wilson & Co.. 10 00
E. P. Wheeler... 10 00
Thurlow Weed.. 10 00
Mrs. "W. B. I.".................................... 5 00
Mrs. J. Walker.. 5 00
Mrs. J. R. Wood....................................... 10 00
John Ward... 10 00
Gracie, Willie, Ellie and Nettie Whitlock............. 5 00
E. L. Winthrop.. 10 00
D. A. Wood.. 10 00
L. P. Williams.. 10 00
Thomas Watt... 100 00
Miss Ida A. Wesley.................................... 25 00
E. R. Ware.. 5 00
Mrs. Mary Watt.. 100 00
Wm. C. White.. 5 00
Mrs. "W. H. S.".................................... 5 00
Abram Wakeman... 25 00
Miss Williams... 5 00
Mrs. J. L. Wallack.................................... 5 00
Miss Mary C. Ware..................................... 4 00
"W. K. T."... 20 00
Rev. W. T. Wilson, Rector of the Church of the Mediator,
 South Yonkers, N. Y................................. 50 00
Wheeler & Wilson Manufacturing Co..................... 25 00
Thomas M. Wheeler..................................... 5 00
Henry C. Ward... 5 00
"W. M.".. 2 00
Timothy Whittemore.................................... 25 00
S. C. Williams.. 10 00
S. C. White... 5 00

Mrs. Mary W. Woodruff	$5 00
Samuel Willets	25 00
John D. Wolfe	500 00
John Warren	25 00
J. Butler Wright	10 00
Miss Ida Whittingham	5 00
Mrs. H. D. Wyman	100 00
Fred'k S. Winston	50 00
Mrs. Samuel Waterbury	3 00

Y

Alfred Youngs	10 00

Z

Mrs. Zabriskie and her Children, for Gravestone	6 00
Mrs. S. J. Zabriskie	50 00
Dr. I. Zacharie	5 00

———:o:———

THEO' LADIES' ASSOCIATION, FOR INFIRMARY.

Mrs. Slade	$10 00
Mrs. Ogden Hoffman's School	25 00
Mrs. David Leavitt, Great Barrington, Mass	50 00
"A Friend"	5 00
Proceeds of Festival at the Anniversary reception	300 00
Peter Cooper	100 00

———:o:———

CHRISTMAS.

Wm. M. Kingsland	$5 00
Children of Mrs. Thomas Watt, for Christmas Tree	10 00
Charlie and Eugene	2 00
Miss L. Chittenden	20 00

Cash	$4 96
Henry Eagle, U. S. N	3 00
Mrs. Geo. S. Stringfield	5 00
Horace Porter (Tree)	5 00
A Little Boy Eight Years Old	5 00
A Young Communicant	2 00
St. Mary's Church, Manhattanville, N. Y., Christmas Offering	15 00
Mrs. D. T. Brown	5 00
Mr. and Mrs. Wm. Alex'r Smith	10 00
Mrs. Thorne	5 00
"Some Friends," through Mrs. Forrester	1 50
Miss Tillinghast	10 00
Miss E. Low	10 00
Hon. D. S. Jackson	5 00
Mrs. Gustav Schwab	5 00
Emily and Lucy Schwab	3 75
Mrs. C. W. Whiley	5 00
Mrs. Fleming	1 00
"A Friend in St. Mary's Parish"	5 00
The Misses Stephens	10 00
Through Essie Shilton	80
Lucille M. Wilde	25
Wm. A. Davies	10 00
Horace and Mamie (Milwaukee)	2 00
Miss M. Sorrill, for tree	1 00
	$167 26

——:o:——

THANKSGIVING.

Mrs. H. C. Von Post	$5 00
Mrs. Jno. DeRuyter	5 00
Mrs. Field	10 00
P. C. Tiemann	5 00
Mr. and Mrs. Alex'r Smith	10 00
Miss E. L. Holmes	2 00
Mrs. Boyce	2 00

NAMES OF THOSE WHO HAVE PAID THE BOARD OF CHILDREN FOR CHARITY.

Mrs. W. J. Beebe..*Minnie.*
St. John's Church, Stamford, Ct............*Geo. and John Botts.*
Miss Hannah Lee................................*Lizzie Lawler.*
St. Peter's Church, Morristown, N. J............*Sarah Walton.*
Mrs. Eugene Langdon........................*James Kennedy.*

———:o:———

CHILDREN CLOTHED.

By Mrs. Beebe......................................*Minnie.*
" Miss Cooper..................................*Jennie Smith.*
" The Misses Tiemann.........................*Maggie Hill.*
" Miss Chittenden............................*Frances Bauer.*
" Mrs. Franklin...............................*Maggie Boyce.*
" Mrs. Schwab.................................*Robt. Oliver.*
" Miss Newbold...............................*Eliza Wright.*
" Ladies of St. Peter's Church, Morristown, N. J..*Sarah Walton.*
" Mrs. Dr. Jenkins..........................*Mary Matthews.*

———:o:———

DONATIONS IN CLOTHING, ETC.

MAY, 1870.
  Mrs. D. H. Field, 52 Silver Watch Chains.
  Unknown, 4 boxes of Soap.
  Children of the Sewing School of St. James Church, Boston Highlands, 17 Pillow Cases, 53 Under-garments for little children.
  From Bazaar, 1 box Miscellaneous Articles, 70 Vols. Miscellaneous Books, a number of yds. of Muslin and Cambric, 1 case of Crockery, 1 tub Miscellaneous Articles, 20 Pails, 1 Frame, 14 Pictures, 1 doz. Children's Aprons, 1 Skirt, 7 Boys' Bows, 2 Dolls, 1 pair Mittens, 1 Pincushion, 1 basket of Dolls.
  From St. Michael's Table, 1 Dress, 1 Sack, 6 Bibs, 6 pairs Drawers and 41 other articles.
  Mrs. E. R. Ware, 1 Swing for Girls.

MAY, 1870.
  Mr. Field, for Garden Seeds, $2.
  Lady,   do. $2.
  Mrs. Tiemann, 1 doz. Skipping Ropes.
  Mrs. W. P. Lee, 4 pairs Shoes.
  Miss Comstock, 1 Apron, 1 Pair Socks.

JUNE.
  Miss Steers, 30 Oranges, for the infants.
  From the Pupils of Miss Steers' School, Ice Cream for all the Children.
  From the Ladies of St. Michael's Church, Cake for all the Children.
  From Miss Peters, a Parcel of second-hand Clothing and Shoes.
  Mrs. Robert F. Ware and Mr. Geo. K. Sistare, Ice Cream, Strawberries and Cake for all the Children.

AUGUST.
  Mrs. Peters, Clothing.
  E. C. Benedict, Peaches for all.
  Acker, Merrall & Condit, half bushel Cranberries.
  Mrs. Wasson, Tea and Rice.
  Mrs. D. T. Brown, Boys' Clothing and three pairs of Shoes.
  F. S. Winston, A copy of the Psalms and Gospels in raised letters for Blind Minnie.
  Mrs. Tiemann, Wicker Chair.
  Miss Kones, Picture Books for the little ones.
  Miss Robbins, Cakes for the boys.
  P. C. Tiemann, Boys' Clothes.
  B. H. Field, five dollars for Plants.
  Mrs. Field, Peaches for all.
  Mrs. Jones, Picture and Ivy for the Parlor, and a quantity of Vegetables.

SEPTEMBER.
  Mrs. Tiemann, 2 bushels Pears.
  Mrs. A. E. Wise, Candy, Grapes and Ivy.
  Miss Frost, "Views from Nature," one vol.
  Miss Steers, School Books.
  Acker, Merrall & Condit, Ham.
  Miss Peters, Shoes and Clothing.

SEPTEMBER, 1870.
  Miss Cleveland, Engraving for the office.
  Miss Frost, Wax Doll.
  Mrs. Bromley, Fifty Cents towards Nursery Clock.

OCTOBER.
  Mrs. Field, Plants and Candy.
  Mrs. Fleming, Cakes for the Nursery.
  S. Coburn, Box of Laundry Soap.
  New York Bible and Prayer Book Society, 30 Prayer Books.
  D. Talmadge's Sons, through W. E. Lawrence, Bag of Rice.
  Mrs. Peters, Shoes, 4 Dresses and Clothing.
  Miss Tiemann, Ivy for the Parlor.
  Mr. P. C. Tiemann, Atlantic Magazines, and Appleton's Journal for 1870, and 3 Photographs for the office.
  Miss Cleveland, Engraving of Bishop Clark.
  Miss Chittenden, Hanging-basket with Plants.
  Nellie Rodenstein, 6 Dresses for the Nursery.
  Acker, Merrall & Condit, Dried Apples.
  John D. Wolfe, Candy for all the Children.
  Miss Lizzie Williams, 18 vols. for the Children's Library.
  F. S. Winston, W. J. Beebe, Thos. M. Peters, D.D., A. S. Hewitt, Thos. Monahan, Benj. H. Field, Jas. L. Harway, Wm. H. Fogg, Hugh Auchincloss, Charles T. Raynolds, A Friend, Cortlandt DePeyster Field, E. Einstein, Franklin C. Field, H. C. Von Post, W. B. Clerke, Wm. A. Smith, John McKesson, Montagnie Ward, Smith E. Lane, John D. Wolfe, a Piano Forte.

NOVEMBER.
  Mrs. Morehouse, 5 vols. for Library.
  Boys of Mrs. Steers' School, 6 Bats and 6 Balls.
  Nelly Ryerson, Toys and Picture Books.
  S. Coburn, Box Carbolic Soap and Box Fancy Soap.
  Mrs. Burns, 1 pair Shoes.
  Mrs. Peters, Shoes and Clothing.
  Mrs. Birdsall, 1 pair Stockings.
  Mrs. D. T. Brown, Boys' Clothing.
  Mrs. Atwill, 3 Under-garments, 1 Apron and 2 pairs Stockings, all new.

NOVEMBER, 1870.

Children of Mrs. Thomas Watt, 44 yards Canton Flannel, 43 yards dark Calico, 8 new Aprons and 2 Dresses.

Mrs. W. J. Beebe, 2 new Aprons, a barrel of Vegetables, and a Canary Bird for the Infirmary.

Emma Beebe, Apples and Candy for the Nursery.

John David Wolfe, 12 papers of Candy and 100 Mince Pies.

Harry Brown, Caramels.

R. Prior, 7 dozen Cakes.

Mrs. Isaac P. Martin, 6 Turkeys, a case of canned Tomatoes and a barrel of Apples.

Messrs. DuBois, Barringer and others, barrel of Apples, Nuts, Crackers and Cakes.

Mrs. Thomas Cock, 2 pairs knitted Stockings.

DECEMBER.

Mrs. Kirkland, 7 yards Calico.

Mrs. D. S. Jackson, Jr., Rubbers, 1 dozen Neckties and suit of Boy's Clothes.

Mrs. J. W. Miller, Canton Flannel.

Mrs. George Jones, 60 pairs Stockings.

Mr. Woodbury Langdon, 12 pairs new Shoes for the Boys.

Mrs. Franklin Edson, Frock and 36 pairs Woolen Stockings.

The Misses Edson, 12 pairs Woolen Stockings and 6 Neckties.

Mrs. Ira Brown, Pocket Handkerchiefs and Candy.

A Lady of St. Paul's Church, East Chester, N. Y., 10 yards Calico, 4 pairs knitted Stockings, 3 Flannel Skirts and 6 Shirts.

Freddie Ware, 3 Under-garments, 2 pairs Stockings and 2 Blankets.

Mrs. Wm. Alex. Smith, 12 yards Sheeting, 28 yards dark Calico and 23 yards Canton Flannel.

Miss Mills, Trinity Parish, Cloth Sack and 5 new Under-garments.

Mrs. Banker, 4 pairs Stockings and a suit of Boy's Clothes.

Through Mrs. Vogel, 6 pairs Shoes, 6 pairs Stockings, Handkerchiefs and Underclothes for the Ede and Guion boys.

Mrs. Lamborn, Manhattanville, 18 pairs Stockings, 6 pairs Shoes, 12 Caps and Hood, 12 Nets.

J. R. Terry, through Mrs. R. F. Ware, 10 Caps for boys.

Vanderlip & Taylor, through Mrs. R. F. Ware, a quantity of Worsted Goods.

DECEMBER, 1870.

POULTRY, EATABLES AND GROCERIES.

Luhrlng, Central Market, barrel of Vegetables.
Mrs. J. G. Keator, do.
Mr. W. P. Furniss, do.
Hiram Paulding, Jr., barrel of Apples.
Wm. Weyman Mali, do.
Andrew Smith, do.
Wm. M. Chamberlain, box of Oranges.
Acker, Merrall & Condit, large bag of Oranges.
Park & Tilford, box of Sugar and Rice.
W. E. T., box of Herrings, Codfish, Oatmeal and Apples.
E. K. Willard, Esq., Fort Washington, barrel of Flour, do. Sugar, do. Apples, do. Potatoes, 10 gallons Syrup, 103 lbs. Turkey.
Wm. S. Corwin & Co., 900 Broadway, through Mrs. Tiemann, a Ham and 2 Sides of Bacon.
Mrs. Tiemann, 100 lbs. Buckwheat.
Mrs. Gustav Schwab, Apples, Nuts and Candy.
Mrs. Isaac P. Martin, 100 Oranges, 100 filled Cornucopias.
A Member of St. Ann's Church for Deaf Mutes, a Turkey.
From Children of Mrs. Mark Allen, a Feast for the Nursery Children in honor of Mollie's Birthday, Poultry, Apples and Cakes.
Miss M. Louise White, Cakes, etc., for the Nursery.
John David Wolfe, 50 Mince Pies.
Mrs. Roberts, Carmansville, pair of Chickens.
Madame Thorne, Apples, Cakes, Hommony, etc.
Luie Lee, Materials for Plum Pudding.
Mrs. H. S. Gerry, large basket of Poultry, etc.
Mrs. J. W. Miller and others, large basket of Groceries.
Through Mrs. Sackett, Turkey and box of Crackers.
Mrs. E. A. Edgar, Turkey.
Mrs. R. W. Aborn, basket of Oranges.
Mrs. Mark Allen, basket of Cakes, Candy, Mince Pies, etc.
Mrs. Geo. Birdsall, box of Cakes.
Willet C. Ward & Co., box of Raisins, sack of Prunes, sack of Nuts, Figs, etc.

DECEMBER, 1870.

BOOKS, TOYS, ETC.

Miss Julia A. Low, box of Toys.
Mrs. Langdon, do.
Mrs. Colford Jones, do.
Mrs. E. A. Duyckinck, do.
Miss Augusta P. Slade, do.
Sylvie D., through Mrs. Forrester, do.
Some Friends, through Mrs. Forrester, do.
The Misses Stephens, 18 Dressed Dolls.
Miss Minnie Cole, 18 Crying Babies.
Miss Antoinette Tiemann, 6 Sleds.
Mrs. D. F. Tiemann, large basket of Toys and 12 Dressed Dolls.
Misses Julia and Martha Tiemann, 2 dozen Pictures of Birds, framed.
Young Ladies of College Hill Seminary, Poughkeepsie, large box of Toys and Clothing.
S. W. Johnson, through Mrs. R. F. Ware, 54 Toy Books.
John David Wolfe, Sled and Doll's Carriage.
Through T. R. Edson, 3 dozen Book Slates.
The Misses Brierly, 2 Muffs, 2 Dressed Dolls and other Toys.
Julius Schlueter, 5 Chromo-Lithographs and a large box of Gingerbread.
Mrs. Kirkland, Toys and Candy.
Mrs. Isaac P. Martin, box of Toys.
Freddie Ware, Candy for all the Children.
H. J. Cammann, Ornaments for the Christmas Tree.
Mr. Taylor, through Mrs. Tiemann, box of Toys.
Master Butler Fearing, box of Books.
Mrs. G. R. Jackson, Ornaments for the Christmas Tree.

MISCELLANEOUS.

Mrs. J. Pettigrew, 5 dozen pairs Knives and Forks.
Miss Wolfe, Music Rack.
J. Russell & Co., through Mrs. R. F. Ware, 6 dozen pairs Knives and Forks.
Mr. Karl Klauberg, through Mrs. R. F. Ware, 2 doz. pairs Scissors.
D. B. Bedell, through Mrs. Tiemann, 2 dozen Fancy Mugs.
Mr. Peter Cooper, Likeness of Mrs. Cooper.
Judge Betts, large Lithograph.

DECEMBER, 1870.
RECEIVED IN BAGS.
Groceries, Fruit and Nuts—124 *Bags.*

Mrs. T. P. Cummings; L. Turnure; Mrs. C. R. Green; Mr. Jas. Graham; Mrs. Mary R. Sanford; Mrs. Ogden Hoffman (4 bags); Mrs. Wm. A. Dooley; Unknown; Miss Israell; J. B. Churchill; C. Einstein; Miss Hannah Lee; P. R. Bonnett; Mrs. W. H. Wisner; Wm. Whitlock, Jr. (5 bags); Mrs. R. Upjohn; Mrs. John Pettigrew; Mrs. Von Post (2 bags); J. W. Pettit (2 bags); George Finnegan; Miss F. Cotheal; J. T. Metcalfe (4 bags); Mrs. W. C. Gilman; Mrs. Long; Unknown; Mrs. Charles Cole; Jos. M. Cooper; Jas. C. Fargo; Wm. M. Evarts; James J. Byron; Mrs. Silas Mason; Mrs. G. W. Ryerson; Mrs. Fink; Mrs. Kent; Mrs. Fellowes; Mrs. Swords; Mrs. Holmes; Mr. Wade; Allie Beebe; Mr. and Mrs. Charles E. Beebe (2 bags); Elias Wade; Mrs. John M. White; Mrs. More; Mrs. Wm. Tracy; H. C. Deckbam; Mrs. E. Anderson; G. Thompson; Mr. N. Chandler; Unknown (Rice); E. L. Pecke; A Friend; Wm. Daniels; J. H. Stephens; Mr. Wm. P. Lee (2 bags); J. W. Underhill; Mrs. P. Hanford; Miss M. Ottiwell; Mrs. J. H. Gillespie; Mr. N. Fisher; Geo. W. McCullum; Miss M. Acker; Mrs. Daniel Le Roy; Thos. Back; Albro & Polhemus (4 bags); Mrs. Hitchcock; American Merchants Union Express Co.; F. Hornby; Mrs. M. F. Jenkins (2 bags); Unknown (Oatmeal); A Friend (Oranges and Apples); John R. Platt; Mary Pondir; Mrs. F. Leiber; Mrs. D. H. Twiner; George J. Quackenboss; A. M. Ferris; George Jones; Unknown (Apples, 2 bags); C. V. A. Schuyler & Son (2 bags); Mrs. W. C. Emmett; Mr. J. B. Boyd; Miss Simpson; Elsie Tiemann; Carrie Pettit; Jas. Pettit; Mrs. D. S. Jackson, Jr.; H. Wagner; Mrs. Peters; Edmund Bachran; Mrs. W. P. Dixon; Mrs. Jackson, Harlem; Unknown, Harlem, (Ham, Figs, etc.); Miss M. E. Lockwood; Mr. Davison; Mrs. S. E. Parker; R. Skell & Co. (2 bags); Sunds H. Fish (2 bags); C. Anmann & Co.; Philip Dater & Co.; W. H. H. Beebe; Mrs. W. G. Ray; Mrs. W. W. Huntington.

Clothing—36 *Bags.*

Miss L. Clarkson; Mrs. Wm. M. Kingsland; Reginald H. Sayre; W. L. Cogswell; Mrs. Wm. M. Chamberlain; Unknown (2

DECEMBER, 1870.

dozen pairs Stockings and Scarfs); Jas. C. Fargo; J. A. Cone; L. Seixas; St. Ann's Sunday School, Morrisania (13 bags, principally Clothing and Toys); Miss F. Melville; Grace Guin (4 years old, through Mrs. Brittain); Mrs. Brittain; Mrs H. S. Gerry; Mrs. Nesbitt, Miss Jane A. Duncan; Mrs. R. W. Aborn; Mrs. W. B. Duncan; Clara Lall; Mrs. Heiser; Mrs. Wm. Tracy; Unknown (St. Andrews, Harlem); Unknown; R. H. Garner.

Candy and Cake—48 Bags.

Mrs. Edward Kearney; Mrs. Colford Jones; Mrs. G. W. Burnham; Mrs. Stewart; Mary Hitchcock; Mrs. Von Post (2 bags); E. Einstein; Miss E. J. Lynch; Miss Julia A. Low; Miss J. W. Quincy; Miss C. E. S. Stuyvesant; Fannie Stuyvesant; Elbridge Geary; Mrs. G. W. Livingston; Unknown; Mrs. A. Dodge; Miss K. Chase; Mrs. Sayre; Mrs. W. G. Ray (2 bags); Louis Johnson; A. Van Rensellaer; H. E. Handerson; Mrs. Sydney Webster; Mrs. R. F. Ware (2 bags); G. A. Seixas; Unknown, through Mrs. E. Wells Sackett (2 bags); Mrs. George Birdsall; Mrs. C. C. Adams; Mrs. J. H. Hinton; Mr. F. N. Johnson; Mr. A. L. Pell; C. W. Sandford; Mrs. S. K. Greene; Mrs. C. A. Sherman; F. W. Grear; The Misses Haddon; Mrs. Wm. Alex. Smith; Mrs. George Richmond; William Mitchell; J. C. Cockcroft; Miss Lucille M. Wilde; Miss Belle Ballantyne; Mrs. J. W. Miller; Mrs. H. W. Miller.

Toys and Miscellaneous Articles—25 Bags.

Mrs. N. P. Bailey; John Smarden; R. H. Arkenburgh; Mrs. E. A. Duyckinck; Mrs. R. S. Tucker; P. R. Bonnett; Thomas H. Faile; Emma Beebe and Nelly Ryerson; Mrs. J. G. Keator; Miss Keator; Miss M. Louise White's S. S. Class; Wm. A. Emory; Charles De Rham; Mrs. Kate Brown; Mrs. Daniel Le Roy; W. M. Fliess; Unknown; Mrs. Wm. Taylor; Miss E. G. Tackaberry; Little Madeleine Livingston; Mrs. Wm. B. Asten; Mrs. H. H. Crocker; Mrs. Edward Jones; Miss L. Brooks; Children of Seabury Hall, through Miss Frost.

Tea and Coffee—14 Bags.

Mrs. W. G. Ray; The Misses Furniss; S. D. Tompkins; Mrs. G. P. Gilman; A Friend; Beebe & Brothers; Smith & Noyse; Carter, Hornby & Co.; Wm. Scott & Sons (5 bags).

DECEMBER, 1870.
Meat and Poultry—10 *Bags.*
C. Robbins; Mrs. George R. Jackson; Unknown, through Mrs. Sackett, (Turkey and Mutton); Mr. Glover; John D. Fish; Wm. Pratt; Miss E. L. Holmes; Mrs. Peters; J. V. B. Bleecker; Mr. Alvord.

JANUARY, 1871.
Clara, Freddy, Susy and Helen Hinton, Christmas Parcel.
Mrs. L. A. Rodenstein, Basket of Clothing.
A Lady of St. Ann's Church, Wrapper for Mina.
Miss Helen Rudderow, 3 pairs Stockings.
Mrs. W. W. Huntington, parcel of Clothing.
Mrs. E. J. Bostwick, 2 pairs Stockings.
Mrs. William F. Morgan, Wrapper, 5 Dresses, 2 Cloaks and 3 Muffs.
Mrs. James Hall, 6 Calico Dresses and a large bag of Clothing.
Miss Nelly Rodenstein, 2 Dresses and 2 Sacks.
Mrs. Julius Tiemann, 5 pairs Stockings.
Mrs. James Tinker, box of Clothing.
Mrs. D. F. Tiemann, Bracket for the Parlor.
A Friend, through Mrs. W. J. B., Corner Bracket.
Freddy Ware, Bagatelle Board.
Miss E. S. Clapp, Parlor Thermometer.
J. Schonburg, 5 pounds of Candy.
H. Wagner, 36 pounds Beef.
Mrs. A. E. Wise, Candy for the Nursery.
P. C. Tiemann, 6 colored Engravings.
Elsie Tiemann, "Children's Friend" for 1871.
Addie Tiemann, "Infants' Magazine" for 1871.
Mr. J. D. Wolfe, 25 copies "Christian Soldier" for 1871 and 25 copies "Missionary Echo" for 1871.
May Peters, "Children's Magazine" for 1871.
Mrs. L. A. Rodenstein, Assistance in sewing (made 50 Aprons).
Mrs. Thomas Cock, Madame Rodenstein, Miss Antoinette Tiemann, Assistance in Knitting.

FEBRUARY.
Miss E. Pike, Flag for Boys and 2 Flannel Waists.
Miss Ferguson, 6 Calico Dresses, 6 Shirts, 3 pairs Stockings 15 yards Sheeting, 3 Spreads, 14 Under-garments, 2 Sacks.

FEBRUARY, 1871.

Unknown, Christmas bag of Clothing.
Mrs. P. C. Tiemann, 5 pairs Shoes, box of Clothing and Toys.
Mrs. T. M. Peters, 2 pairs Shoes.
Mrs. Rodenstein, 3 pairs knitted Stockings.
Miss Acker, Suit of Clothes.
Ladies' Society of St. Thomas' Church, 14 Dresses, 4 Flannel Sacks, 19 Flannel Skirts, 6 Aprons, 9 Under-garments
Mrs. D. T. Brown, Overcoat.
Mrs. Wm. Tracy, 7 pairs Knitted Stockings.
Edward M. Peters, Writing Case.
Mrs. P. C. Tiemann, "Atlantic Magazine" and "Every Saturday" for 1871.
Miss E. Heath, Apples and Oranges for all the Children.
Helping Hand Society of St. Ann's Church for Deaf Mutes, Assistance in Sewing, Making of 26 Aprons.
Mrs. L. A. Rodenstein, do., 22 Aprons.
Miss E. Pike, do., 17 Aprons.
The Misses Tiemann, do., 6 Shirts.
Mrs. D. F. Tiemann, 1 dozen Towels.

MARCH.

Elsie Tiemann, Ice Cream for all.
Mrs. D. F. Tiemann, a large box of Cakes, 6 Aprons, 2 dozen Pocket Handkerchiefs and 2 Looking-Glasses.
Freddy Ware, Candy for all.
Mr. F. Betts, through Mrs. R. F. Ware, Dictionary.
Mrs. M. L. Whitlock, Illuminated Text, framed.
Mrs. F. S. Church, 2 pairs knitted Stockings.
Mrs. Ogden Hoffman, 7 pairs knitted Stockings.
Nelly Ryerson and Emma Beebe, 20 framed Toy Pictures and a Feast of Candy and Cake for the Nursery.
Mrs. Birdsall, 2 Flower Pictures.
Mrs. R. M. Shaw, Parcel of Clothing.
Mrs. Rodenstein, 3 pairs knitted Stockings.
Helping Hand Society of St. Ann's Church for Deaf Mutes, Assistance in Sewing, making of 27 Aprons.
Miss E. Pike, do., 14 Aprons.
Mrs. Langdon, do., 14 Bibs.
Mrs. Fearing, do., 26 pair Pantaloons and 119 Sheets.

MARCH, 1871.

Miss Helen Rudderow, Assistance in Sewing, 6 Shirts.
Ladies of Christ Church, Watertown, Conn., do., 13 Aprons.
Miss Kate Williams, do., 6 Shirts.
Mrs. D. F. Tiemann, Jr., do., 6 Shirts.
St. Michael's Ant Hill, do., 2 pairs Sheets, 17 Table Napkins and 3 Aprons.

APRIL.

Acker, Merrall & Condit, 3 dozen Oranges and 3 dozen Lemons.
Mrs. D. F. Tiemann, 8 doz. Easter Eggs and box of Sand-soap.
Freddie M. Burr, 4 pairs Stockings, 9 Dresses, 3 Skirts, 1 pair Gloves, 1 Book, 1 Toy.
Bible-Class in Stamford, Conn., through Mrs. George L. Brown, 28 Aprons, 3 Under-garments.
Miss Antoinette Tiemann, 1 dozen Pocket-handkerchiefs and a quantity of Plants.
An Easter Offering from a Class of Little Girls belonging to St. Peter's Church, Morristown, N. J., 6 Aprons.
Mrs. Benj. H. Field, 26 yards Ingrain Carpeting and 1 piece Binding.
Mrs. Lamborn, 16 Hats.
Mary Wade, Emma Holiday, Maud Diak, Mary Voight, Ida Pool, Addy Myers, Sarah Armstrong, Mary Waldron, Ida Sickles, Ann Lauritz, Ella Saunders, Maggie Mulligan, Ann Roundtree, Sarah Zider, Bella Gordon, Lena Garland, Clara Norris, Mony Ellis, Maud Doake, Jennie Blair, Ida Timpson, Ida Wilson, Ella Kamp, Phebe Willis, Josephine Krouse and Mary Norris, members of the Industrial School of the Bp. Wainwright Memorial Church, 5 yds. Plaid, 5 yds. DeLaine, 30 Garments.
Mrs. Thos. F. Cock, 4 pairs knitted Stockings.
Miss Peters, Ernest Bolte, Mr. and Mrs. P. C. Tiemann, Dr. Brown, Francis A. Drouty, Miss Brierly, Mrs. Silas Mason, Mrs. D. F. Tiemann, Trees, Plants, Shrubs, Vines and Sod.
Jas. Pettit, Mr. Cowan, Robert Prior, several loads Manure for garden.
Ladies' Employment Society of the Church of the Incarnation, Assistance in Sewing, making of 43 Aprons.
Miss Gerry, do., 14 Bibs.
House of Industry, do., 36 pairs Pantaloons and 30 Aprons.

APRIL, 1871.
  Mrs. A. V. Williams, Assistance in Sewing, 8 Shirts.
  Mrs. Brown and Miss Rudderow, do., 8 Shirts.
  St. Michael's Ant Hill, do., 7 Shirts, 35 Towels, 1 dozen Pocket-handkerchiefs.
  Ladies' Benevolent Society of St. Mark's Church, do., 85 Sheets, 48 Shirts, 14 Bibs, 12 Pillow-cases.

PRAYERS

TO BE USED BY THE FRIENDS OF

"The Sheltering Arms."

ALMIGHTY and most merciful Father, whose well beloved Son, our Saviour, did welcome the young children to His arms and bless them, look with pity, we beseech Thee, upon these little ones committed to our care, that, being shielded from temptation and delivered from evil, they may glorify Thy holy name, and finally, by Thy mercy, obtain everlasting life, through Jesus Christ, our Lord. AMEN.

OH, Lord God and Heavenly Father! infinite in love and full of mercy, send down thine Holy Spirit, as upon all friendless children and orphans, so especially upon these little ones, whom Thou hast given into our keeping, grant that the old Adam in these children may be so buried, that the new man may be raised up in them.

Grant that all sinful affections may die in them, and that all things belonging to the Spirit may live and grow in them.

Grant that they may have power and strength to have victory, and to triumph against the devil, the world, and the flesh.

Grant that, being dedicated to Thee, they may also be endued with heavenly virtues, and everlastingly rewarded, through Thy mercy, O blessed Lord God, who dost live and govern all things, world without end. AMEN.

Founded in 1864.
THE SHELTERING ARMS,
10th Avenue and 129th Street.

"The Sheltering Arms."

EIGHTH ANNUAL REPORT.

NEW YORK,
1872.

Incorporated October, 1864.

New York:
E. WELLS SACKETT & BRO., STATIONERS, AND BOOK & JOB PRINTERS,
56 & 58 WILLIAM STREET.

Officers of "The Sheltering Arms."

PRESIDENT.
REV. THOMAS M. PETERS, D. D.............Address, Broadway, cor. 99th St.

VICE-PRESIDENTS
FRED'K S. WINSTON..144 Broadway
WM. ALEX. SMITH..40 Wall Street.
WM. J. BEEBE..104 Wall Street.

SECRETARY.
PETER C. TIEMANN..Manhattanville.

TREASURER
WOODBURY G. LANGDON.......................................719 Fifth Avenue.

VISITOR.
RT. REV. H. POTTER, D. D., D. C. L., LL. D..............38 East 22d Street.

TRUSTEES.
HENRY J. CAMMANN..8 Wall Street.
HERMANN C. VON POST...2 Bowling Green.
BENJ. H. FIELD..127 Water Street.
D. TILDEN BROWN, M. D..Manhattanville.
WM. D. CLERKE...25 Broad Street.
WM. H. FOGG...32 Burling Slip.
THOS. WATT..605 Fifth Avenue.
WM. P. LEE...326 Fifth Avenue.
WM. M. KINGSLAND..116 Fifth Avenue.
REV. H. E. MONTGOMERY, D. D...............................209 Madison Avenue.
FRANKLIN EDSON...19 Whitehall Street.
CHARLES E. STRONG..68 Wall Street.
ABRAM S. HEWITT..9 Lexington Avenue.
E. WELLS SACKETT..56 and 58 William Street.
REV. E. GAY, JR...Stony Point, Rockland Co.

PHYSICIAN.
L. A. RODENSTEIN, M. D..Manhattanville.

CONSULTING PHYSICIAN.
ABRAHAM JACOBI, M. D...110 West 34th Street.

OPHTHALMIC SURGEON.
THOMAS H. POOLEY..209 West 34th Street

Ladies' Association of "The Sheltering Arms."

VICE-PRESIDENT.
MRS. WM. P. LEE...... ....326 Fifth Avenue.

SECRETARY.
MISS M. CHAUNCEY................................53 West 36th Street.

TREASURER.
MRS. B. F. CORLIES...................................39 Nassau Street.

ACTING TREASURER.
MISS M. A. COOPER..................................17 Burling Slip.

MEMBERS.

Mrs. R. W. ABORN.....43 West 39th St.
Miss S. E. KITCHEN...121 West 49th St.
" S. B. NEWBY....314 West 28th St.
" L. PETERS...Ddw'y, cor. 112th St.
" F. COTHEAL....26 Univ'lty Place.
" J. A. TIEMANN.....Manhattanville.
" LIZZIE HOLMES....123 Fifth Ave.
Mrs. JOHN DE RUYTER.75 Madison Ave.
Miss KATE BELL......20 West 20th St.
Miss HOFFMAN........Cornwall, N. Y.
Mrs. A. S. HEWITT....9 Lexington Ave.
Miss MONTGOMERY....209 Madison Ave.
Mrs. G. B. DRAPER.5th Av. c. 130th St.
Miss G. REED, cor. 38th St. & Park Ave.
" CRITTENDEN...Inwood, N. Y. City.
" J. WILLIAMS..Yonkers, West'r Co.
Mrs. E. W. SACKETT.....54 W. 127th St.
Miss AUGUSTA SLADE....5 East 38th St.
" WILSON........127 West 48th St.
Mrs. R. F. WARE......138 W. 36th St.

Mrs. E. KENNY.........Staten Island.
Miss S. F. RICHMOND...Manhattanville.
" C. B. ARNOLD....279 Madison Av.
" WOLFE..Madison Av. cor. 24th St.
Mrs. J. MUNRO........14 West 30th St.
" I. P. MARTIN...Fort Wash'n, N. Y.
Miss SCOTT............40 East 41st St.
" H. BEACH ......220 Second Ave.
Mrs. J. L. LEIB.......Yonkers, N. Y.
" P. V. DU FLON.....35 W. 27th St.
" M. I. WHITLOCK..Gt. Barr'n, Mass.
" F. T. WHITING.Gt. Barring'o, Mass.
Miss A. SIMPSON..Manhattanville, N. Y.
Mrs. A. M. KEATOR....Manhattanville.
" H. E. DUNCAN...Matteawan, N. Y.
Miss CARTER........153 Lexington Ave.
Mrs. A. MESIER.Wappinger's Falls,N.Y.
Miss McCURDY........10 East 14th St.
" G. H. WILDES....Riverdale, N. Y.
" M. SPAULDING....Riverdale, N. Y.

OBJECTS OF THE INSTITUTION.

"THE SHELTERING ARMS" was opened October 6, 1864, for the reception of homeless children, for whom no other institution provides.

The classes of children received are as follows :

1st. The blind and deaf mutes, until the age at which they become entitled to admission at the Asylums especially devoted to such unfortunates.

2d. Crippled children, past hope of cure, and therefore no longer retained in ordinary hospitals.

3d. Children of poor parents, obliged on account of sickness to enter a hospital, and who commit their children for a season to our charge, with the expectation, upon recovery, of reclaiming their own.

4th. Children rendered temporarily homeless by fire or other accident.

5th. Children whose home has been broken up by the intemperance or desertion of father or mother. In such cases, the remaining parent pays according to ability a small sum monthly.

6th. Children abandoned by both parents, brought to us by friends or relatives unable to find immediately a proper home, and yet unwilling to lose control of the children or to place them beyond their reach.

Children placed at "THE SHELTERING ARMS" are not surrendered to the Institution, but are held subject to the order of parents and relations.

All the children of sufficient age attend the school of the Institution, where they receive a common education. The larger girls are also trained to household work. The children attend St. Mary's Protestant Episcopal Church, and are under the pastoral care of the Rev. T. M. Peters.

REPORT

OF THE

Board of Trustees,

MAY, 1872.

EIGHT years have passed since "THE SHELTERING ARMS" began its preparations to receive various classes of homeless children not otherwise provided for.

From May 1, 1871, to April 30, 1872, there have been 285 applications for the admission of children, of whom 85 only have been received. Seventy-eight have been discharged. The average number present throughout the year has been 134.

There are now in the Cottages 135 beds, in the Infirmary five, and in the Hospital ten. The last fifteen we desire to hold vacant, leaving our utmost accommodation 135, although we have at times run up to one hundred and forty, which is really a great many more than ought to be distributed in four families.

Even with this crowding, however, we have refused admission to two hundred, or seventy per cent. of the calls at our door.

The health of the children has been generally good, and the cases of illness light. Varioloid appeared in the winter, but went no further than the little patient of four years old first attacked. We have had ten girls taken with scarlet fever in its mildest form. The children's eyes have given some trouble, although but a few have been seriously affected.

If some kind friend would build us covered piazzas, on

which the little children might exercise during the winter, leaving for a part of each day the confined air of their playrooms, the general health of the two Nursery Cottages would undoubtedly be benefited.

We cannot be too thankful for having consulted the physician rather than the treasury, in purchasing a year ago, upon the recommendation of a Special Committee, the isolated Hospital. It is unhappily true that we are still in debt for it, but happily also true that by being able to remove at once from the Cottages every case of infectious disease, we were preserved from extensive contagion, and have not a single death to attribute to its presence. Better to labor for years under that debt than to add one to the number of our graves. Of the seventy-eight discharged, but one has been in obedience to the inexorable demand of death—Jeanie Tompkins, the feeble little girl of four years, who died in September last.

The religious and moral condition of the children calls for our devout gratitude to Him who has sent us women who have proved the best of mothers to our families and teachers in our school. "I never saw so many children together," says the experienced lady in charge, "with so little disobedience, so little lying, so little quarreling, and so much good feeling." "I won't," said another of the ladies, "is an expression entirely unknown among our children; one never hears it." This state of things is to be attributed in great degree to the division of the children into families, thus bringing a comparatively small number together under one motherly care. Especial praise is due to the heads of the Mrs. PETER COOPER Cottage for larger girls, and the JOHN D. WOLFE Cottage for larger boys. Their care in the religious training of their children has been rewarded by the endeavor on the part of many to follow that Christ held up to them as their example. Eight of the older children are preparing for confirmation at the next visitation of the Bishop.

The Trustees gratefully acknowledge their obligation to the lady in charge, whose selection of persons for the various positions in the House, and whose vigilant superintendence have lightened their own work. They also make this public acknowledgment of the services gratuitously rendered by Dr. RODENSTEIN, Physician, and Dr. POOLEY, Oculist, to the Institution. The diseases of the past winter and spring have made large demands for attention, which has been freely and daily given.

The Rev. Mr. ADAMS, Rector of the neighboring Church of St. Mary, has our thanks for the kind interest manifested by him in the children, and his readiness in placing the Church, whenever wanted, at our disposal.

The Trustees also gratefully record their appreciation of the aid given by the LADIES' ASSOCIATION in adding to the receipts, both for the building fund and for current expenses, as well as in editing the monthly paper.

To all our many friends who constantly and cheerfully send the willing offering and speak the encouraging word, the work we do must be our most fitting return of thanks.

So far as means have been placed at their disposal, the Trustees have followed out with but slight variation the plan originally proposed. The departure from the rule intended has been in receiving a larger proportion of children entirely free of charge. A year ago there were in the Cottages ninety inmates whose friends paid nothing for their support. The average payment for board had fallen off from $24.50 for each child in 1865, to $12.19 in 1871. Consequently the very large sum of $17,000 must be made up in other ways; and as the endowment fund at interest amounted to only $1,000, yielding annually $76, nearly the whole of the $17,000, the cost of the children to the Trustees, must be met by the gifts of the charitable.

The result has been that our free beds prove too many for our means, and we come to the close of our financial year with the treasury in arrears. In order to restore the equilibrium of our budget, measures have been recently adopted which will produce their effect upon the year which we are now entering.

The first looks to the support of a child by individuals or Churches. One additional bed has been endowed by a gift of $2,000, and the expense of seventeen others has been guaranteed by individual subscribers.

By enlarging the monthly paper to receive advertisements, that useful little messenger will cease to be a charge upon the treasury.

The third measure aims at increasing the amount received for board. This has been commenced by going over our list of children with a view to ascertaining, so far as possible, the ability of parents or other relatives, and requiring them, where able, to pay a monthly sum for board. The changes already made will more than double the receipts from this source the coming year.

The expectation at the time of our incorporation was that one-half the outlay of the Institution would be balanced by receipts for board. Our past experience would indicate that in giving the especial relief for which we were organized, so large a proportion as an average of one half-pay for each child is more than can ever be realized. At the same time we are of opinion that without greatly stinting the measure of succor which we now give, the income from this source can be increased to one-fourth, possibly to one-third of the annual expenses. We have received in frequent cases, entirely without pay, families of three, four, and even more children, suddenly rendered homeless, with the intention of keeping them a few months until the great emergency should pass by. In several instances the breaking up of home has proved permanent, and the children have remained years on our hands.

It would probably be for the benefit of the children themselves, when the household is never likely to be re-established, were we to make arrangements for placing them with respectable families often applying for girls, sometimes for boys. Our growing conviction is, that, even with the advantages of our Cottage system, we can offer but an imperfect substitute for the true family with father as well as mother, and in which the association of the children one with the other is lifelong instead of being, as with us, generally transient.

Unfortunately, parents seldom share in the belief that it is better to place their children permanently out of their hands, than to trust to the relief afforded by institutions like our own. Parties inquiring for children to adopt or rear are always unwilling to receive those whom at any moment they may be required to surrender. A few months since a mother, with the shadow of a human hope, but no earthly prospect of gathering her three children once more into a home, was advised to give one of the boys to a family in the central part of New York State, wishing to adopt it. "They may take it," said the mother, an American woman, "but I cannot sign away my own flesh and blood." Who could require it? Not a father. "Then let the children go to the Almshouse," said another who heard the story; they were her children, not *his*. She would not do it—any wretched shelter of squalidness, but not its dreaded doors.

Could we harden our heart and nerve our tongue to say to every mother of our non-paying children, "that child must go out from here," few of them would find so good a shelter as even the Almshouse offers. They might be removed, but it would be to wretched homes in the City, thick with the seeds of disease, where their tattered clothing would unfit them for appearance at the Public School. They leave us to grow up in ignorance and vice.

Were "THE SHELTERING ARMS" established for the benefit of parents, our line of action might be different. Our single aim from the beginning has been to save the children from destruction. Therefore, in every instance where it is for them peril without, safety here, we desire to give ready welcome.

For support we trust to Him who said, "it is not the will of your Father which is in heaven that one of these little ones should perish," and, "whosoever shall do the will of my Father which is in heaven, the same is my brother, and sister, and mother."

In obedience to the necessities of our situation we have, nevertheless, as has been stated, inquired into the condition and abilities of the friends of our children with various results. One sent from one of the Chapels of St. George's Church was unable to pay anything. "Let that child remain;" said one of the Trustees, "and I will be responsible to the treasury for its support." Of course, that child stays with us. A sweet spoken girl made a call at the House to prove the impossibility, at least for the present, of paying more than $3 for a cripple kept at an expense to us of $18 per month. She pleaded earnestly, and concluded thus: "If you send M * * * home, mamma will die." The result may be readily guessed. That child remains. In December last application was made for a boy whose father, a working man, had just met with an accident which sent him to the Hospital for four months. Of course, that child must be received even with no expectation of payment.

We might multiply similar examples. It would require very stern people to stand at our threshold and meet such visitors with the words, "you cannot come in;" or to go through the wards with the ledger in hand and say, "nothing paid—you must go."

Very stern people, not being of the sort who take hold of public charities for the sake of doing good, the probability is that we shall never have a front door to shut itself in the face of troubled fathers and sad mothers who can neither give nor honestly promise.

Of course, we feel ourselves bound in prudence and justice to give relief only to the extent of our means, and having cut down the number of our free beds from ninety to seventy-five, must, if necessary, reduce them still further, and raise the rates a dollar or two monthly for any who do pay.

This is our action under necessity. As our endowment increases and larger gifts flow in, we expect, as formerly, to receive according to the exigencies of the case, entirely regardless of what any applicant can pay.

Another change made during the year past is to place the applications from Clergymen for members of their own flocks among the first to be attended to, ranking the Clergy in this respect with the officers of "THE SHELTERING ARMS" and the givers of large sums. This we do for two reasons: One, because the City Clergy need every aid in taking care of the immense burden of poor thrown upon them; and the second, because we find the Clergy generally better informed regarding cases which they send us than others who, quite as often as otherwise, know nothing at all of the merits or needs, but apply in behalf of some friend who has asked their intercession. We have thus departed from our former usage of taking applicants in order as their names stood upon the Register, and now receive those whom we think most benefited by the favor.

We are sometimes asked if we could not support the same number of children on a less expenditure.

We reply, that although the cost of each child is less with us than in the average of well-appointed institutions, we could reduce our expenses by four measures which no person familiar with "THE SHELTERING ARMS" and the appearance of its inmates would consent to adopt.

We might break down our partition walls, throwing all our Cottages into one great building, and dispensing with the services of three of our assistants.

We could close the Infirmary for Cripples, the seed of our proposed Innocents' Hospital, and discharge the nurse.

We could reverse our policy of the past year, which has been to improve the quality of the children's food. But then we might be laying the foundation for future infirmity.

We could reduce our bill for clothing if we were willing

to step down to the level of a large Institution for children, of which a visitor lately remarked that only one-eighth of its inmates could be dressed fit to appear outside the gates. The spirit of a growing child cannot be more effectually crushed than by thus marking its inferiority. Our children are clad in such a manner that neither in the street, nor at School, nor in Church, they need feel ashamed of the comparison with others.

If we were indulging costly fancies we could not, under present circumstances, decline to lay them aside. Yet we cannot put in practice either of the four measures named without changing the character of the Institution, or injuring physically, morally, or spiritually, those whom we desire to train as healthy, high-toned, conscientious men and women, Americans and Christians.

Think, after all, dear friends, with how little money it is done. Nineteen thousand dollars, a sum spent in the support of many a family in New York, is the annual cost in food, clothing, and education, for the hundred and fifty persons under our roof. The toys, and trifles, and luxuries of many a rich man's child, would pay the entire charges of one of those whom we are striving to save.

As a memorial of dear children no longer with you, make one of our's your ward. Add your name to the list of those whose endowment or annual gift offers a bed free to some child of need.

To each donor or subscriber of large sums or small, we would say, find one among your friends to add a sum like to your gift, and thus our means for doing good will be easily doubled.

In these efforts to strengthen our present foundations, we would bear in mind that our work, if well begun, is yet only begun. Seventy per cent. of applications rejected stimulates our desire to procure our country home. There the gifts of faith and love shall build Cottages and create happiness, and prepare usefulness for little ones whom the

Providence of God has driven out, not that they should perish, but that we might build them a Zoar; that selfish humanity both in them and us might learn to glow with the Divine life; that we might feed at once them, and Christ, and ourself.

The Trustees would not close their Report without recording their sense of the greatness of the loss which, upon the eve of the Annual Meeting, has fallen upon this Charity and the Church.

By the death of John D. Wolfe "THE SHELTERING ARMS" has lost its early, constant, and generous friend. The remembrance of his many words of cheer is our possession still. The memory of his frequent and pleasant visits will linger in the Cottage which he built, until the youth who gladly welcomed that friendly face are gone out from us into active life.

Blessed be God who has not left the earth in darkness, but is ever present in those who love His name, and speak His words, and do His deeds.

THOMAS M. PETERS,
President.

THE SHELTERING ARMS in Account with J. S. BREATH, Treasurer.

1871.				DR.
May 1—	To	Balance old Account...................		$ 76 18
	"	Expenditure on New Buildings..........		3,549 71
	"	" for Bread.................		1,909 12
	"	" " Meat and Fish...........		1,723 11
	"	" " Milk...................		1,841 44
	"	" " Groceries and Vegetables.		1,957 93
	"	" " Fuel...................		1,102 40
	"	" " Gas....................		363 40
to	"	" " Water, Express & Carfare.		214 63
	"	" " Wages and Labor........		3,209 75
	"	" " Insurance...............		281 17
	"	" " Interest................		189 33
	"	" " Household Material......		2,150 80
	"	" " Printing................		1,311 35
	"	" " Stamps and Stationery...		326 08
	"	" " Salaries and Collection...		1,854 18
	"	" " Church Sittings.........		250 00
1872.	"	" " Repairs................		885 89
April 30—	"	" " Sundries................		80 80
		Balance to new acc't...........		178 76
				$23,456 03

1871.				CR.
May 1—	By balance of Bazaar Fund, through			
1872.		Mr. W. A. Smith, Treasurer..		$ 201 71
May 1—	"	Cash from Comptroller of City.		672 00
	"	" " " of State...		1,136 00
to	"	" Annual Subscriptions and		
		Paper..................		845 90
	"	" Special for Christmas.....		171 10
	"	" Received for Board........		1,753 46
April 30—	"	" Donations................		10,975 66
		Loans..............		7,700 00
				$23,456 03
1872.				
May 1—	By Balance on hand......................			$178 76

NEW YORK, June 3, 1872.

At a meeting of the Finance Committee of "The Sheltering Arms," the account of the Treasurer for the year ending April 30th, 1872, showing a balance on hand of $178.76, was examined and found correct.

    H. C. VON POST,
    WILLIAM H. FOGG, } *Auditing Committee.*
    WM. B. CLERKE,

FOUNDERS OF A COTTAGE BY THE GIFT OF FIVE THOUSAND DOLLARS.

Mrs. Peter Cooper (1869).
Mr. John D. Wolfe (1869).

---:o:---

ENDOWMENT OF BEDS.

By resolution of the Board of Trustees, passed on the 27th day of March, 1871, it was decided to accept endowments of beds at the rate of $1,000, the nomination of the occupant to remain in the donor for life ; or of $2,000, with right of nomination in perpetuity ; and that all sums so received be invested, and the interest only be applied to the support of The Sheltering Arms.

NAMES OF PERSONS ENDOWING BEDS.

1871.
   Mrs. Henry Salisbury............................ $1,000 00
1872.
   In memory of little Alice......................... 2,000 00

---:o:---

PATRONS OF THE SHELTERING ARMS, BY THE PAYMENT IN ONE YEAR OF FIVE HUNDRED DOLLARS.

1866.
   Frederick Hubbard, Robert B. Minturn, John D. Wolfe.
1867.
   Mrs. H. Rose.
1868.
   Loring Andrews, W. L. Andrews, James Punnett, Rev. T. M. Peters, D.D., H. C. Von Post, Thomas Ward, M.D., Mrs. James Punnett, Mrs. T. M. Peters.
1869.
   Frederick DePeyster, Thomas Garner, Azel Graham, C. C. Haight. Mrs. H. D. Wyman, Mrs. Steers, Mrs. Thomas Ward, Mrs. H. D. Aldrich.

1870.
Stewart Brown.
1871.
Mrs. George Kemp.
1872.
Mrs. Ann Fortune, Mrs. Eugene Langdon.

——:o:——

LIFE MEMBERS, BY THE PAYMENT IN ONE YEAR OF ONE HUNDRED DOLLARS.

1865.
Wm. J. Beebe, Chas. E. Beebe, John Caswell, Thomas H. Faile, B. H. Field, W. H. Fogg, W. A. Haines, Rev. R. S. Howland, D.D., George Merritt, Rev. W. A. Muhlenberg, D.D., Adam Norrie, Gideon Pott, Lizzie Punnett, Herman D. Aldrich, Wm. Alex. Smith, W. K. Kitchen, S. S. Wyckoff, Miss Montgomery, Miss Jenkins.

1866.
Stewart Brown, Simeon Draper, Frederick G. Foster, Horace Gray, Jr., W. C. Gilman, Franklin F. Randolph, Mrs. Catherine L. Spencer, Mrs. Martin E. Greene, Thos. W. Ogden, Rev. S. H. Tyng, Jr., Rev. Thomas Gallaudet, D.D., A. Cooper, Miss Kate Norwood, Miss Louise Cooper, Miss Nesbitt, Miss Amory, Miss Daxter, Miss Carrie T. Lawrence, Miss Chauncey, Miss M. E. Snow, John A. McKimm, Louis F. Therasson, C. T. Whittingham, Reverdy Estelle, Henry A. Oakley, Mrs. Henry A. Oakley.

1867.
W. Armstrong, Jay Cooke, Mrs. Frederick De Peyster, D. B. Fayerweather, Robt. J. Livingston, J. W. Minturn, Mrs. J. B. Kissam, Miss Steers, "W. B. R.," A friend.

1868.
Mrs. S. C. Baring, Edward Jones, Rev. H. E. Montgomery, D.D., Mrs. Mary Watt, Mrs. Laura L. Wallen, W. B., Mrs. Edward Jones.

1869.
Wm. H. Aspinwall, Wm. M. Kingsland, Arthur Kimber, A. A. Low, Edwin C. Litchfield, Wm. P. Lee, Wm. Weyman Mall, Levi P. Morton, Wm. P. Furniss, David Stewart, Horace Williams, Miss Drake, Miss J. Van Horne, Rev. E. A. Washburn, D.D., Richard W. Weston, Miss Fanny Austin.

1870.
Mrs. R. T. Auchmuty, F. A. Peters, S. D. Babcock, Mrs. T. H. Hubbard, Rufus Hatch, Charles P. Kirkland, Allan McLane, Richard Mortimer, Royal Phelps, W. C. Rhinelander, B. Schlesinger, Alex. T. Stewart, Wm. Niblo, Joseph Sampson, Mrs. Wm. L. Tweed, Mrs. D. T. Brown, Miss Ferguson.

1871.
J. A. Bostwick, John Bloodgood, Miss L. Peters, Cortlandt Field Bishop, A. J. Peters, Peter C. Tiemann, Thomas Watt, Peter Cooper, Mrs. H. C. Von Post, Miss Newberry, Miss Iselin, H. W. T. Mali, James Pott, Mrs. Sylvanus Reed, Wm. R. Peters, John P. Peters, Andrew Peters.

1872.
Albert G. Thorp, Jr., Ida P. Pirsson, Isaac P. Martin, Edward Cooper, A. S. Hewitt, Woodbury G. Langdon, Miss C. E. Wolbert, Mrs. S. J. Zabriskie, Charles Place, James F. DePeyster, Madame C. Mears, A. Bierstadt, Miss C. L. Wolfe.

ANNUAL SUBSCRIBERS.

Mrs. Aaron Arnold	$5 00
Mrs. D. B. Allen	5 00
C. F. Alvord	5 00
Mrs. Hugh Auchincloss	10 00
Miss Arnold	10 00
Mrs. R. W. Aborn	5 00
Mrs. J. H. V. Arnold	10 00
Mrs. William Alsop	5 00

Mrs. James Brooks	$5 00
Miss Hattie T. Bryce	5 00
D. B. Bedell	5 00
Mrs. C. C. Baldwin	5 00
Mrs. J. J. Coddington	5 00
William Cooper	10 00
Charles W. Cooper	10 00
George E. Cooper	5 00
Mrs. H. Colt	5 00
Miss M. Cunard	5 00
Mrs. Colden	5 00
Miss E. M. Cotheal	5 00
Miss F. Cotheal	2 00
Miss M. J. Corlies	5 00
Mrs. Samuel Colman	5 00
Mrs. W. P. Dixon	10 00
W. H. Draper, M.D.	10 00
Miss Emily Emmet	3 00
Mrs. J. L. Englehardt	5 00
Mrs. Fitzgerald	10 00
Mrs. H. T. Gerry	5 00
Miss Gerry	5 00
Miss M. Glover	5 00
" " donation	10 00
Miss M. M. Gandy	5 00
J. Milton Goetchius	5 00
Miss Ann J. Garner	10 00
Mrs. Azel Graham	5 00
Mrs. C. F. Heywood	5 00
Miss Emily Hollingsworth	5 00
W. B. Hoffman	5 00
Mrs. S. Hinton	10 00
Mrs. Ogden Hoffman	5 00
Miss M. C. Hoffman	3 00
Miss V. S. Hoffman	3 00
Mrs. P. Hanford	5 00
Mrs. H. H. Holly	5 00
Miss M. A. Jones	5 00
Miss M. S. Jones	5 00

Mrs. George Keyes	$5 00
Mrs. J. G. Kentor	5 00
Mrs. Edward Kearny	10 00
Mrs. Kalbfleisch	5 00
Mrs. J. L. Leib	5 00
Mrs. A. N. Lawrence	5 00
Miss S. Lawrence	3 00
Mrs. H. A. Lydocker	5 00
Mrs. N. Lawrence	5 00
Miss E. Low	10 00
Mrs. Wm. P. Lee	5 00
Mrs. John Munro	5 00
Mrs. Charles E. Milnor	20 00
Miss Montgomery	3 00
Mrs. Theodore Moran	5 00
Mrs. Henry Meigs, Jr	5 00
Mrs. E. L. Molineux	5 00
Mrs. H. McKim	5 00
Mrs. J. T. Metcalfe	10 00
Mrs. A. B. Morrell	5 00
Mrs. B. McEvers	5 00
Miss M. S. Mortimer	3 00
Miss S. L. McCurdy	5 00
Mrs. Charles Palmer	5 00
Mrs. A. M. Pell	5 00
Mrs. J. J. Phelps	10 00
Mrs. J. W. Quincey	3 00
Mrs. D. E. Ritter	2 00
Mrs. L. A. Rodenstein	5 00
Mrs. Wm. Alexander Smith	5 00
Mrs. E. Shedden	5 00
Miss Augusta Slade	5 00
Mrs. Gustav Schwab	10 00
Mrs. A. T. Sackett	10 00
Mrs. Edwin Stoughton	5 00
John Sullivan	5 00
Mrs. D. F. Tiemann	5 00
Miss Martha Tiemann	5 00
Mrs. Theodore Timpson	5 00

Miss Katherine P. Tracy	$5 00
Mrs. Richard Vose	5 00
Mrs. H. C. Von Post	10 00
Miss C. Van Wyck	5 00
Miss H. K. Wilkes	5 00
" " donation	10 00
Hamilton F. Webster	5 00
Mrs. Ann Walter	25 00
William Whitlock, Jr	10 00
Mrs. S. H. Whitlock	5 00
Miss Wilkes	5 00
Miss Grace Wilkes	5 00
Mrs. W. H. Wisner	10 00
Miss M. A. Wisner	5 00
J. O. Ward	5 00
Mrs. C. S. Weyman	5 00
Mrs. R. Woodworth	5 00
Mrs. Samuel Waterbury	3 00

LEGION OF ONE DOLLAR SUBSCRIBERS.

COMPANY 1.

KITTIE JACKSON, Mrs. Olliffe, Mrs. Stacey, Miss Stacey, Anna L. Petit, George P. Stringfield, A. V. Williams, Lillie Graham, Grace Jackson, Willie Bleakley, John Somerville, Minnie Somerville, Andrew Jackson, Arthur Davis............. $14 00

COMPANY 2.

JULIA T. PETERS, B. F. Tiemann, Ruth Tiemann, Elsie C. Tiemann, Paul E. Tiemann, Minnie Ferguson, Andrew Peters, W. L. Sanford, William C. Peters, J. P. Ellicott, E. D. Peters, G. H. Peters, A. J. Peters, Harrie Sheridan, Irving Kitchell, Emma Thurston, Lizzie Williams, Mary Tully, Clara Yenni...... $19 00

COMPANY 5.

HENRIETTA M. BRIERLY, Mrs. D. Cutter, C. A. Thompson, Mrs. E Lange, Mrs. L. Schüll, Annie J. Brierly, M. W. Brown, Francis Pounden, Mary I. Graham, Wm. Yeandle, Mrs. F. A. Utter, Wm. L. Sanford, Agnes Lall, Bertha Schedler.......... $14 00

SCATTERING.

Ebby Hicks, Rev. W W. Olssen, Miss Mary McKee, Mrs. J. Mildeberger, Miss Susie Gifford, Miss Sherrill, Frank Lowerre, Hugh S. Dickey, Jr., "N. A. Y. or Z.," Mrs. J. G. Baldwin, Little Sylvie, Miss Annie Mixen, Geo. H. Butler, Miss M. Sorrill, Miss M. Scoville, Mrs. Mary Haskell, Mrs. Johnson, Mrs. Lilly Willson, Mrs. G. M. Merwin, Miss Holmes, Mrs. Lamborn, Miss Nannie Meire, Miss Annie Ten Eyck, Miss Mary Talmage, St. Michael's Church Missionary box, "H.A.H.".................... $26 00

DONATIONS.

A.

Alms Box..	$20 34
"A. R. & Co."...	10 00
"A. H. M."..	5 00
An American living abroad, through Mrs. Jno. A. Marsh,	50 00
Mrs. J. S. Abecasis...................................	10 00
Arnold, Constable & Co., through Mrs Tiemann.........	10 00
Mrs. Arthur Amory....................................	10 00
J. W. Alsop..	25 00
J. B. Alexander.......................................	25 00
Mrs. Richard Alsop...................................	8 00
D. H. Arnold..	20 00
American Merchants' Union Express Co...............	25 00
Lloyd Aspinwall.......................................	10 00
William H. Aspinwall.................................	50 00
"A. R. B."..	2 00
Mrs. W. C. Arthur.....................................	5 00
"A. H. S."..	5 00

B.

Mrs. E. R. Bell	$5 50
Mrs. W. J. Beebe, for one year's board, Minnie	96 00
Stewart Brown	100 00
" " Infirmary	100 00
Mrs. M. A. Bery	5 00
Baptismal Fee	20 00
Mrs. Richard Bayley	2 00
Mrs. E. A. Bull	5 00
J. Barclay	5 00
H. A. Burr	10 00
Mrs. P. R. Donnett	5 00
Miss E. M. Baldwin	5 00
Mrs. A. Boody	5 00
Mr. and Mrs. Jno. H. Boynton	20 00
P. Bruner	5 00
C. Butler	5 00
Samuel Bonnell, Jr	5 00
Mrs. N. P. Bailey	10 00
Mrs. Brown, through Miss Wilkes	10 00
W. T. Blodgett	10 00
Sylvanus Bedell	5 00
W. B. Bishop	2 00
William Betts	10 00
Mrs. Seely Brown	5 00
Edward A. Boyd	10 00
G. W. Bruce	50 00
George Bell	10 00
Miss C. B. Bell	25 00
Miss Mary Benkard	50 00
Gordon Knox Bell, one month old	5 44
Mrs. L. F. Battelle	5 00
Mrs. J. R. Boyd	5 00
Mrs Edward Baldwin	5 00
Mrs. C. P. Burdett	4 00
Baker & Kitchen	10 00
Mrs. H. H. Bean	2 00
Miss C. E. Boardman, through Mrs. Whiting	5 00

W. F. Beekman	$5 00
Miss J. Brinckerhoff	10 00
M. G. Baldwin	10 00
Mrs. G. W. Burnham	5 00
G. Banyer	10 00
Mrs. Stephen Brush	5 00
Mrs. W. N. Beach	5 00
George Bernard, D. D. S.	5 00
Mrs. W. Barton	10 00
J. H. Beekman	5 00
Mrs. W. G. Breese	5 00
A. Bierstadt. A Painting by him in aid of the Bazaar, sold by M. Knoedler (net)	225 00
J. V. B. Bleecker, U. S. N.	5 00
Cornelius Bogart	25 00
Miss J. M. Boardman	5 00
W. Blackstone	5 00
Thomas Barron	50 00
James Baker	5 00
Williamson Bacon	10 00
C. Braker, Jr.	10 00
Balance from Bazaar, through W. Alexander Smith	201 71
Beadleston, Price & Woertz	25 00
J. L. Brownell & Brother	10 00
Bequest of Mrs. Ann Fortune, through Miss Angeline Simpson, Executrix	500 00

C.

Cash $1, 5, 5, 10, 5, 5, 10, 5, 2, 5, 5, 5	63 00
" $2, 25, 50, 5, 25, 5, 1, 5, 2, 5, 2	127 00
" $10, 5, 25, 10, 5, 20, 10, 5, 1, 1, 5	97 00
" $10, 5, 25, 10	50 00
Edward Cooper	100 00
Coleman House	5 00
George A. Clark & Brother	10 00
George Carlisle	5 00
Miss E. H. Chew	5 00
J. S. Cox	10 00

Mrs. C. L. Case	$5 00
Charles M. Congreve	10 00
Charles E. Carryl	5 00
Rev. Lyman Cobb	5 00
J. S. Cushman	5 00
Sanford Cobb	5 00
Mrs. Chas. F. Chickering	5 00
W. L. Cogswell	10 00
Legrand B. Cannon	10 00
Mrs. F. W. Coggill	10 00
Comptroller of N. Y. City	672 00
Cash through Chas. E. Strong	10 00
R. S. Clark	25 00
T. C. Chardavoyne, $5, $5	10 00
Peter Cooper Golden Wedding Fund, for shoes	50 00
Mrs. J. A. Cone	10 00
Mrs. William Cohen	2 00
T. G. Churchill	5 00
Mrs. "C. K. S."	5 00
Miss Cowman	2 00
J. J. Clark	10 00
Mrs. L. Clarkson	5 00
Mrs. Martha E. Coles	10 00
John J. Cisco	25 00
George Chesterman	25 00
Mrs. A. Chandler	5 00
Mrs. J. B. Church	5 00
M. & H. Clarkson	25 00
W. L. Chamberlain	10 00
W. A. Camp	10 00
Comptroller State of N. Y.	1,136 20
J. Colles	5 00
Mrs. William Campbell	2 00
Mrs. Elie Charlier	5 00
Christ Church, Poughkeepsie, Rev. P. K. Cady, D. D., Rector, of which $24.41 from the Young Ladies of Cottage Hill Seminary	34 41
J. A. Cisco	5 00
Mrs. S. E. Coleman	5 00

D.

U. J. Dudley	$5 00
P. Ditmar	5 00
Russel Dart	5 00
John Downey	5 00
Theodore M. Davis	25 00
"D. W. B."	20 00
Mrs. J. F. Delanier	5 00
"D. A. W."	10 00
E. Delafield, M. D.	10 00
J. H. Diggles	5 00
C. J. DeWitt	10 00
Edward DeWitt	10 00
Henry Delafield	5 00
Charles DeRham	5 00
Mrs. David Dows	25 00
E. A. Duyckinck	5 00
Mrs. W. A. Dooley	5 00
Mrs. A. Denilson	5 00
James F. De Peyster, to make him a Life Member	100 00
Mrs. W. B. Dinsmore	20 00
"D. H."	20 00

E.

William M. Evarts	20 00
Pupils of Mrs. Earle's School, Rye, N. Y.	6 00
Endowment Fund Interest	77 00
"E. A. Q."	5 00
Mrs. Everdell	2 00
Mrs. H. Edgar	5 00
S. J. Egleston	5 00
Mrs. Ann R. Edwards	5 00
Little Edie	3 50
Mrs. Wm. C. Emmet	5 00
Little Edie, Easter Offering	2 50
S. C. Evans	5 00
E. Elsworth	10 00
Henry Elsworth	10 00
James Emott	10 00

"E. S."	$5 00
Richard S. Ely	10 00
Easter Offering of a member of Christ Church, Rye, N. Y.	5 00
Easter Offering, "chiefly in memoriam" of Christ Church, Watertown, Connecticut, Rev. W. H. Lewis, D.D., Rector.	44 80
Minnie and Lulie's Lent-Box, " " "	6 00

F.

A Friend, through W. Alexander Smith	35 00
A Friend in Sing Sing	5 00
C. G. Francklyn	10 00
William M. Fliess	10 00
A. Morton Ferris	10 00
"F. S."	10 00
Miss F	25 00
Mrs. F	25 00
Fair held by Bertie and Harry Thorp, for the benefit of the sick Children	116 20
W. W. Fessenden	5 00
A. Goodrich Fay	25 00
C. B. Foote	10 00
Thomas H. Faile	100 00
J. D. Fish	20 00
Josiah M. Fiske	10 00
Cash, Friend	5 00
E. L. Ferry	10 00
J. P. Girard Foster	20 00
Friend, through Mrs. R. L. Cutting	25 00
William Forrester	4 00
James C. Fargo	25 00
Charles L. Frost	25 00
D. V. H. Floyd	5 00
H. W. Ford	15 00
Fair held by Ida L. Pirsson, with Contributions from Mrs. R. L. Phillips, Mrs. F. T. Luqueer, Miss Minnie Lee, Mrs. J. P. Pirsson, Miss Susie Scott, Miss Flora Thompson, Miss Lizzie Eames	100 00
William B. Fletcher	10 00

G.

G. G. Gray	$20 00
A. Gilsey	5 00
Mrs. H. H. Garner	5 00
J. H. Gautier	25 00
M. A. Grosvenor	25 00
C. T. Gostenhofer	25 00
Mrs. J. C. Gray	10 00
Mrs. Isaac Gibson	2 00
Mrs. W. T. Garner	5 00
"G. B."	5 00
Peter Gilsey	10 00

H.

Abraham S. Hewitt	100 00
Mrs. T. H. Hubbard ('71, $10—'72, $10)	20 00
G. G. Howland	10 00
Thomas Holland	5 00
C. F. A. Hinrichs	5 00
A. O. Headley	10 00
Mrs. W. T. Hicks	5 00
George A. Hearn	15 00
Mrs. A. Heywood	10 00
Rev. S. Hollingsworth, Port Chester, Children's Missionary Box	4 44
M. M. Hendricks	10 00
L. H. Holmes	5 00
O. P. Hoe	5 00
Mrs. M. Hartley	10 00
Mrs. S. C. Herring	10 00
P. S. Halstead	5 00
H. Hudson Holly	5 00
"H. A. C."	8 00
Cash, "H."	10 00
P. H. Holt	5 00
S. V. Hoffman	10 00
Mrs. F. Hendricks	5 00
Mrs. J. Hendricks	5 00
John A. Hardenburgh	10 00

N. P. Hosack	$5 00
J. M. Hare	5 00
V. G. Hall	25 00
F. C. Havemeyer	10 00
Mrs. Peter S. Hoe	10 00
Misses Hadden	10 00
"H. A. C.," through H. J. Cammann	20 00
Mrs. Thomas J. Hoyt	5 00
William P. Howell	5 00
Howe Machine Co	25 00
J. T. Harris	5 00
Mrs. E. W. Holbrook	5 00
F. Hornby	10 00

I.

Mrs. Ann S. Ireland	5 00
Mrs. J. A. Iselin	5 00
Frederick E. Ives	10 00
Miss M. Inglis	10 00
Adrian Iselin	50 00
Richard Irvin	25 00

J.

"J. H. V. C."	10 00
Mrs. Colford Jones	25 00
" " " Infirmary	15 00
Mrs. M. Mason Jones	20 00
" " " Infirmary	5 00
Miss Katie H. Jackson	3 50
"J. A. H."	5 00
Mrs. W. L. Jenkins	10 00
"J. L. S."	10 00
Hon. D. S. Jackson	5 00
"J. H. R."	7 00
"J. T. S."	5 00
W. M. Johnson	10 00
Lewis C. Jones	5 00
F. M. Jones	10 00
Mrs. Geo. R. Jackson	5 00

"J. L. R."	$50 00
Louis Johnson	2 00
George Jones	25 00
Mrs. "J. G. L."	10 00
Miss Jones	5 00
Mrs. "J. Q. A."	5 00

K.

Mrs. Edward N. Kent	5 00
Mrs. George Kent	10 00
Edward King $10, $5	15 00
Mrs. L. Kip	5 00
Wm. M. Kingsland	20 00
W. M. Kingsland, to support a child one year	138 00
Mrs. J. P. Kernochan	20 00
Isaac L. Kip, M.D.	25 00
William W. Kip	10 00
Mrs. E. Keteltas	10 00
Thomas B. Kerr	10 00
Mrs. P. R. Kearny	5 00
Coleman E. Kissam	5 00
J. Knower	10 00
Edward Kearny	5 00
Peter V. King	10 00

L.

Mrs. Eugene Langdon, for Infirmary	500 00
Woodbury G. Langdon, for Infirmary	100 00
" " " to support a child one year	138 00
Mrs. Dr. Lieber	5 00
Miss M. E. Lockwood	10 00
Ladies' Committee of the Church of the Incarnation, through Mrs. Archibald	3 00
William K. Lothrop	5 00
Mrs. Joseph Lawrence	5 00
Miss Isabella Lawrence	10 00
Mrs. F. Leland	5 00
Mrs. Job Long	5 00
F. R. Lee	5 00

P. Lorillard & Co.	25 00
Mrs. T. J. Leslie.	5 00
Walter Langdon.	10 00
J. T. Lea.	5 00
Rev. W. Langford, St. John's Church, Yonkers.	5 00
Cyrus H. Loutrel.	5 00
Mrs. R. E. Livingston.	10 00
Mrs. H. A. Lydecker.	5 00
Miss Julia A. Low.	20 00
Mrs. G. W. Livingston.	5 00
R. J. Livingston.	25 00
E. H. Ludlow.	10 00
Daniel Le Roy.	5 00
William Lottimer.	20 00
Edward Livingston.	10 00
Mrs. W. H. Lee, B. F.	10 00
Cyrus J. Lawrence.	10 00
Mrs. C. S. Little.	5 00

M.

Mrs. John W. Minturn.	20 00
Isaac P. Martin, $50, $50.	100 00
P. McMartin.	10 00
Albert McNulty.	5 00
Thomas H. Messenger.	5 00
John H. McKim.	25 00
Thomas McMullen.	5 00
Mrs. John McKesson.	5 00
William Mackay.	10 00
William Mackey.	10 00
Charles Morgan.	10 00
Mrs. Minturn.	10 00
Rutson Maury.	5 00
Samuel F. B. Morse.	5 00
Mrs. Martin.	5 00
Mrs. A. B. Marks.	5 00
Mrs. Peter Morris.	5 00
"M. M."	10 00
A. P. Man.	10 00

Member of St. Thomas' Church	$50 00
Member of St. Ann's Church, N. Y., through Rev. Dr. Gallaudet	5 00
John D. Mairs, through Mr. C. Edson	10 00
Mrs. E. Marthens	5 00
Master Roland Molineux	1 03
Thomas Morrell	10 00
William Weyman Mall	25 00
Zophar Mills	5 00
G. W. McCollum	10 00
Mrs. J. A. Munsell	5 00
Henry M. Morris	10 00
Mrs. "M. A. C. R."	10 00
Miss L. E. Morgan	5 00
John Mortimer, Jr	10 00
George Merritt	100 00
"Lucy Morton, In Memoriam"	20 00
Mrs. S. E. Morse, Jr., Maimy and Lily Morse	10 00
Madame C. Mears, through Mrs. R. F. Ware, proceeds of Concert at her house, for Infirmary	384 70
James Moir	5 00
J. R. Maurice	25 00
"M. H. T."	2 00
James Maurice	15 00
"J. M."	5 00
William C. Moore	5 00
Henry L. Morris	10 00
Mrs. Abm. Mesier	2 00

N.

William Niblo, 1871, $25, '72, $25	50 00
Adam Norrie	125 00
George F. Nesbitt	10 00
H. D. Noyes	5 00
N. Y. Condensed Milk Company	25 00
Mrs. S. P. Nash	5 00
H. W. Niemann	5 00

O.

Thomas Owen	10 00
Mrs. E. H. Owen	5 00
Oswald Ottendorfer	10 00
Joseph Ogden	5 00
C. V. B. Ostrander	20 00
Offering of Zion Church, Wappinger's Falls, N. Y., through Mrs. Abm. Mesier	33 00

P.

Penfold, Chatfield & Co.	25 00
S. N. Pike	10 00
Mrs. J. S. W. Parkin	3 00
John E. Parsons	10 00
Park & Tilford	25 00
William R. Powell	5 00
Miss Mary S. Pondir	20 00
Mrs. C. A. Peabody	10 00
J. K. Pell	5 00
Levi Pawling	5 00
Mrs. C. L. Perkins	10 00
Mortimer Porter	5 00
Mrs. G. W. Pell	10 00
Mrs. J. J. Pettit	5 00
Cortlandt Palmer	10 00
William Paul	5 00
Mrs. John Pettigrew	50 00
A Parishoner of St. John's Church, Woodside, Newark, N. J., through Rev. Samuel Hall	5 00
Samuel R. Platt	10 00
Through Rev. H. C. Potter, D.D.	5 00
Francis Pott	10 00
Charles Place, for support of a child, through Mrs. E. W. Sackett	100 00
Mrs. G. C. Peters	5 00

Q.

Mrs. M. M. Quackenbos	10 00
Mrs. G. P. Quackenbos	3 00

R.

John A. Robinson	$20 00
Mrs. Wolcott Richards, $5, $10	15 00
Rutton & Bonn	20 00
Edward C. Richards	10 00
Mrs. E. Robbins	5 00
William Remsen	5 00
J. A. Roosevelt	25 00
Richardson, Boynton & Co	25 00
Thomas T. Read	30 00
Rent received	30 00
H. L. Rogers	5 00
T. W. Riley	10 00
Chandler Robbins	10 00
Mrs. M. P. Read	10 00
W. C. Rhinelander	25 00
Lewis M. Rutherford	10 00
C. B. Ransom	10 00
J. Reese	5 00
Alfred Roe	10 00
Samuel Raynor	5 00
Mrs. Winthrop G. Ray	5 00
William A. Ross	5 00
William Redmond, Jr	10 00
C. T. Raynolds	10 00

S.

Miss Senrab	10 00
Shoes sold	6 80
Mrs. J. T. Soutter	5 00
E. Wells Sackett, Infirmary	50 00
Mrs. George K. Sistare	5 00
Hamilton R. Searles	5 00
St. Chrysostom's Chapel Offering at Children's Service, through Rev. Thomas H. Sill	20 69
Gustav Schwab	50 00
St. Michael's Church, N. Y	14 65
Charles G. Smull & Co	10 00
Charles F. Sanford	50 00

Miss Armide Smith	$5 00
Mrs. J. Schmelzel	5 00
Caleb Swan	10 00
Wm. Alexander Smith	100 00
John Sneden	20 00
B. Schlesinger	20 00
James Rufus Smith	10 00
Mrs. W. W. Sherman	50 00
Caleb T. Smith	20 00
James L. Schieffelin	10 00
Charles E. Strong	25 00
Mrs. J. T. Soutter	50 00
Mrs. M. Sternberger	3 00
Mrs. H. Stuyvesant	5 00
Mrs. J. Sonneborn	5 00
B. L. Solomon	5 00
E. H. Schermerhorn	10 00
Alfred Schermerhorn	25 00
Mrs. Catherine L. Spencer	100 00
Charles H. Smith	10 00
R. Seaman	15 00
Miss Scott	5 00
Mrs. James G. Stacey	10 00
Frederick Schuchhardt	10 00
Mrs. J. W. Soutback	5 00
Stamford Manufacturing Co	10 00
Mrs. W. H. Swift	5 00
William H. Scott	25 00
J. B. Slawson	10 00
David Stewart	50 00
W. C. Schermerhorn	5 00
Mrs. Charles A. Sherman	5 00
Miss "S. E. W."	10 00
A. V. H. Stuyvesant	20 00
Mrs. A. V. H. Stuyvesant	20 00
Miss M. D. Smith	5 00
Miss Julia Seymour	10 00
S. T. Skidmore	5 00
Mrs. H. G. Stevens	25 00

T. J. Searles.........................	$10 00
Robert Soutter......................	25 00
Floyd Smith.........................	5 00
William N. Seymour..................	5 00
C. W. Sandford......................	5 00
U. J. Smith.........................	5 00
Mrs. C. Smith.......................	5 00
Samuel S. Sands.....................	10 00
C. F. Southmayd.....................	10 00
Mrs. Wilhelm Schaus.................	25 00
S. S. of St. Michael's Church, N. Y.—Pearl Gatherers.....	6 71
" " " " Household of Faith.	3 98

" " " " Christmas Offering.

Class S....... 2 30	
" P....... 4 80	
" A....... 5 38	
" J....... 2 01	
" V....... 0 75	
	15 24
S. S. St. Mary's Church, N. Y., through Rev. C. C. Adams.	15 00
S. S. Children of St. George's Church, Astoria, L. I......	42 53
S. S. of St. James' Church, Great Barrington, Mass., Rev. H. Olmstead, D.D., Rector.......................	18 72
Missionary S. S., Canon City, Minnesota, through Rev. Frank Millspaugh..................:..............	3 00
S. S. St. James's Church, New London, Conn., of which $1.28 is the Easter Offering of an Infant Class, through Rev. R. A. Hallam, D.D...........................	10 00

S. S. of Calvary Church, N. Y., through Mr. James Pott, Superintendent, viz :

Children of Humility......	5 25	
Young Christian Racers...	10 00	
Little Followers of Jesus...	4 24	
Children of Hope.........	1 25	
Children of the Temple....	4 75	
Children of Zion..........	10 00	
Bible Class..............	17 00	
Tender Branches.........	7 00	
Little Pilgrims...........	5 60	
Soldiers of Christ.........	5 00	

Pillars of the Temple.....$10 00
Little Travelers.......... 4 32
Pearl Gatherers.......... 7 00
Pathfinders.............. 5 00
Not Specified............ 6 13
───── $102 54

S. S. of the Church of the Holy Apostles, Christmas Offering, through Rev. Dr. Landy....................... 30 44

T.

J. Nelson Tappan.. 5 00
A. G. Thorp, Jr... 25 00
Miss Julia Tiemann, Sale of Wax Flowers............. 10 00
Mrs. D. H. Turner....................................... 10 00
Mrs. John Townshend.................................... 5 00
"T. B. R.".. 5 00
James H. Titus.. 10 00
Peter C. Tiemann.. 50 00
Mrs. J. M. Thorn.. 10 00
Mrs. James Tinker....................................... 10 00
Mrs. Mary A. Townsend................................... 10 00
Thank Offering on the first Anniversary of the Baptism of
 "A. M. H.".. 5 00
Miss Hattie A. Townsend................................. 10 00
Mrs. William K. Thorn................................... 20 00
S. C. Thompson.. 10 00
Mrs. T. G. Thomas....................................... 5 00
Miss Ruth Tompkins...................................... 5 00
Montgomery H. Throop.................................... 5 00

U.

John W. Underhill....................................... 5 00
Mrs. James W. Underhill................................. 10 00
M. Ulshoeffer... 5 00
United States Express Company........................... 25 00

V.

Mrs. F. L. Vultee....................................... 10 00
Mrs. Abm. Voorhies...................................... 10 00

Thomas Vernon	$5 00
T. A. Vyse, Jr	25 00
Alexander Van Rensselaer	5 00
J. V. Vanwoert	5 00
Madame de Vangrigneuse	10 00
C. Van Santvoord	10 00
Mrs. A. Vanderpoel	50 00
J. Van Norden	5 00
C. H. Van Brunt	25 00
J. Van Schaick	10 00

W.

Ross W. Wood	5 00
F. H. N. Whiting	5 00
D. W. C. Wheeler	25 00
Mrs. J. E. Wylie	5 00
Mrs. G. G. Williams	5 00
Miss C. E. Wolbert, New Rochelle, N. Y., and her pupils: Anita Evans, Nellie V. C. Phelps, Kittie Wright, Nellie Fowler, for the Infirmary	125 00
E. P. Wheeler	5 00
Thurlow Weed	10 00
P. R. Warner	2 00
Mrs. Henry Weil	5 00
Mrs. Joseph Walker	5 00
A. S. Webb	5 00
Mrs. James R. Wood	10 00
Mrs W. G. Ward	5 00
Geo. William Wright	10 00
Mrs. Elijah Ward	50 00
E. L. Winthrop	10 00
Horace Williams, Clinton, Iowa	100 00
Miss Ida A. Wesley	25 00
William C. White	5 00
Master J. R. Walter, 2d	5 00
Miss Beatrice Walter	5 00
S. Williams	2 00
E. K. Willard	50 00
Gracie, Ellie, and Nettie Whitlock	5 00

Miss C. L. R. White...	$5 00
S. C. Williams...	10 00
T. Whittemore...	10 00
T. M. Wheeler...	5 00
Samuel Willets...	25 00
H. C. Ward...	5 00
Miss Ida Whittingham...	5 00
Miss Catharine L. Wolfe, through Rev. Dr. H. C. Potter...	100 00
Thomas Watt...	200 00
W. Wilson & Co...	5 00
William A. Whitbeck...	10 00

Y.

Mrs. D. T. Youngs...	5 00
Alfred Youngs...	10 00

Z.

Mrs. S. J. Zabriskie...	100 00

——:o:——

THANKSGIVING.

Mrs. B. H. Field...	5 00
Mr. William Alexander Smith...	5 00
Mrs. William Alexander Smith...	5 00

——:o:——

CHRISTMAS.

William M. Kingsland...	5 00
Miss S. E. Kitchen...	10 00
Mrs. Jane L. Swift...	5 00
Mrs. W. A. Smith...	10 00
Mrs. Thorne...	10 00
Mrs. Forrester...	4 00
Little Sylvie...	1 00
Mrs. Johnson...	1 00
Mrs. Kirkland...	0 50

E. Thorne	$0 60
Miss Low	10 00
Mrs. Ralph Mead, Jr	5 00
Miss A. Tiemann	5 00
Hon. D. S. Jackson	5 00
Mrs. D. T. Drown	5 00
Henry Eagle, U. S. N.	2 00
Williamson Bacon	10 00
Frederick De Peyster	25 00
Miss Churchill	5 00
Horace Porter	5 00
Mrs. M. A. Dory	5 00
Misses Stephens	10 00
J. Schlueter	10 00
J. A. Robinson	5 00
"H. A. H."	1 00
H. Wagner	5 00
Miss M. Sorrill	1 00
George A. Clark and brother	10 00
Miss Ann S. Ireland, instead of filling Bag	4 00

OTHER DONATIONS, FOR SPECIAL PURPOSES.

Crib and Railing for Infirmary.

Mrs. Eugene Langdon	25 00

Water Cooler.

Miss. R. W. Tompkins	5 00

For the Festival, May, 1871.

"M. F. H."	20 00
Mrs. Colford Jones	5 00
Mr. F. Goodridge	5 00
Miss Cooper	5 00
Miss Peters	5 00

For Children's Book-Case.

Townsend & Davis	25 00

To Take the Children to See the California "Big Tree."

Benj. H. Field	5 50

To Purchase Furniture.

Mrs. D. W. Bishop, Miss Mary De Peyster, Mrs. C. De P. Field, Miss Julia Rhinelander, Miss I. Jones............ $20 00

For Fresh Air.

Mrs. S. J. Zabriskie...................................	5 00
Miss Zabriskie...	1 00
"A. T. B."..	5 00
Mrs. D. F. Tiemann....................................	1 00
Anonymous...	1 00
Mrs. Cock..	1 00
Mrs. Brown..	1 00
John D. Wolfe...	100 00
George F. Irwin.......................................	2 00
Woodbury G. Langdon..................................	2 00
Mrs. Keator...	1 00
Charles Place...	1 00
R. F. Mason...	1 00
D. M. Geiffen..	1 00
Charlie Place Sackett.................................	1 00
Children's Friend.....................................	5 00

For Prizes at School Examination.

Rev. Dr. Peters.......................................	10 00

For Uniforms.

Woodbury G. Langdon, for four Boys...................	20 00
Mrs. W. A. Smith......................................	5 00
Master J. L. Kernochan................................	5 00
Miss Kate Kernochan...................................	5 00
Mrs. Keator—Lenten Savings...........................	5 00
W. H. Raynor, through Mrs. R. F. Ware................	10 00

For Bedsteads and Bedding.

Mrs. D. F. Tiemann, for one Child.....................	14 00
Woodbury G. Langdon, for two Children................	28 00
Mrs. McKee, for one Child.............................	14 00
Miss Maria Ogden, for one Child.......................	14 00
Ella, George and Julia Coggill, for one Child.........	15 00
Mr. and Mrs. A. McNulty, " "	14 00
" " " for outfit of occupant of do.	6 00

"M. N. M.," another Bed for another Baby............ $15 00
Miss Caroline E. Wolbert and her pupils, Anita Evans,
    Nellie V. C. Phelps, Kittie Wright, Nellie Fowler, Tommy
    Evans, Edie Burrill, for two Beds.................. 28 00

To Give Mary (one of our former Pupils, too feeble for
            hard work) a Musical Education.
"T. M."... 12 00
"W. C."... 10 00
"H. A."... 5 00
"A Friend."... 35 00
"A Friend."... 2 00
"A Friend."... 1 00

——:0:——

FREE BEDS SUPPORTED.

By Salisbury Endowment....................... *Henry Stracke.*
" Little Alice   " .... *Emma Stracke.*

By Payment of $138 for One Year.

By John F. Carey....................... *Samuel Holmes.*
" Mrs. John F. Carey.................... *Fannie Holmes.*
" St. Michael's Church.................. *Katy Adkins.*
" Wm. Alexander Smith................... *Jennie Clifford.*
" E. Wells Sackett...................... *Frank Talmadge.*
" Charles Place......................... *George Bromley.*
" William H. Fogg....................... *Oscar Stracke.*
" Franklin Edson........................ *Francis Weaver.*
" Wm. M. Kingsland...................... *Edith Bromley.*
" Mrs. Frederick Goodridge.............. *Ida Holmes.*
" Wm. B. Clerke......................... *Edward Dwyer.*
" Peter C. Tiemann...................... *Elizabeth McEwen.*
" Woodbury G. Langdon................... *Walter Sarrington.*
" Wm. J. Beebe.......................... *Annie Smith.*
" H. C. Von Post........................ *Amelia Clark.*
" John Benjamin......................... *Maggie Foster.*
" Ladies of St. Peter's Church, Morristown, N. J.. *Sarah Walton.*

CHILDREN CLOTHED.

By Miss Cooper..*Jennie Smith*.
" The Misses Tiemann.........................*Maggie Hill.*
" Miss Chittenden.............................*Frances Bauer.*
" Mrs. Schwab ....*Robert Oliver.*
" Miss Cammann..............................*Olive Du Bois.*
" Mrs. Woolsey................................*Bella Foster.*
" Ladies of St. George's Church, Schenectady....*Annie Stewart.*

———:o:———

DONATIONS IN CLOTHING, ETC.

MAY, 1871.

   N. Y. Bible and Prayer-book Society, 25 Prayer-books.
   Mrs. L. A. Rodenstein, 8 Aprons, 2 pairs Knit Stockings.
   Dr. Rodenstein, Drum.
   Madame Rodenstein, 1 pair Knit Stockings.
   Mrs. Lamborn, 5 yards Plaid, 5 yards Delaine.
   Mrs. T. M. Peters, 4 pairs Shoes.
   Mrs. Mark Allen, 3 Dresses, 3 Aprons, basket of Cakes.
   Mrs. Cole, 5 Dresses, 1 Jacket, 1 pair Shoes.
   Mrs. D. T. Brown, 1 suit Boy's Clothes.
   Young Ladies of Mrs. Ogden Hoffman's School, 14 Dresses, 13 Aprons, 9 pairs Knit Socks, 20 Handkerchiefs, 5 Garments, 2 Pillow-cases.
   Mrs. Ware, Bath-tub for Infirmary.
   Woodbury G. Langdon, Wall-pocket.
   Cortlandt Field Bishop, Engraving of Gen. Grant.
   Mr. R. B. Coleman, Parcel of Clothing.
   Acker, Merrill & Condit, 6 lbs. Coffee, 28 lbs. Ham.
   Mrs. M. E. Bauer, a Feast of Cake and Strawberries for the Nursery.
   Mrs. C. L. Spencer, Mrs. Colford Jones, Mrs. D. F. Tiemann, Miss S. B. Schieffelin, Messrs. J. F. Depeyster, B. H. Field, Wm. P. Lee, Woodbury G. Langdon, 29 yards Brussel Carpet for the parlor.
   Helping Hand Society of St. Ann's Church, Assistance in Sewing, Making of 20 Aprons.
   St. Michael's Ant-hill, do., 43 Towels, 2 Aprons.

MAY, 1871.

DONATIONS FOR THE FESTIVAL, RECEIVED BY THE LADIES' ASSOCIATION.

Fancy Articles.

Mrs. Sackett, Mrs. D. F. Tiemann, Mrs. De Ruyter, Mrs. Wm. P. Lee, Mrs. Corlies, Mrs. Williams, Mrs. R. F. Ware, Mr. Hall, Mr. Squier, Mr. Sprague, Managers of N. Y. Boarding House Association for Working Women, Young Ladies of Mrs. Reed's School, Miss K. Cotheal, Miss A. Tiemann, Miss Julia Tiemann, Miss Snow, Mrs. Noble, Miss Chauncey, Miss Henrietta Brierly.

Refreshments.

Mrs. W. Kingsland, Mrs. Wm. Tracy, Mrs. De Ruyter, Mrs. S. F. B. Morse, Mrs. R. Aborn, Mrs. Holmes, Mrs. Sackett, Mrs. R. F. Ware, Mrs. D. F. Tiemann, Mrs. T. M. Peters, Miss Kate Bell, Miss J. Cotheal, Miss E. Dick.

Flowers.

Mrs. D. F. Tiemann, Mrs. P. C. Tiemann, Miss Cooper, Miss Bessie Peters, Mr. Walter Reid, through Mrs. Ware.

JUNE, 1871.

John David Wolfe. 10 Copies Illustrated Christian Weekly for a year.

R. H. Prior, Box of Macaroni.

E. Maginnis, 2 pet Rabbits.

Miss M. Tiemann, House for the Rabbits.

Mrs. B. H. Field, Wicker Carriage for Mina, and a Stove for the Infirmary.

Mrs. P. C. Tiemann, Clock.

Thos. & Wm. Powell, Oranges, Cakes, Pineapples, Sardines, etc., for the Children's Pic-Nic at Mount Morris Square.

J. H. Draper, Likeness of Simeon Draper.

Ladies of St. Michael's Church, large quantity of Lemonade.

Mrs. Cammann, 6 framed Prints.

Alice Luka Sewing Society of St. James' Church, Great Barrington, Box of Clothing and 5 worsted Balls.

Miss Matilda Cammann, 4 Calico Dresses, 8 Garments and 1 pair Stockings.

Mrs. T. M. Peters, Parcel of Clothing.

JUNE, 1871.
  Ladies of St. Luke's Church, Mattcawan, N. Y., Assistance in Sewing, making of 35 Aprons.
  Mrs. Eliza Lee, do., 24 Pillow Cases.
  Ladies of St. John's Church, Watertown, Conn., do., 24 Aprons and 20 Bibs.

JULY, 1871.
  J. F. Cary, Parcel of Clothing and Magazines.
  Miss Mary Talmadge, Raspberries for the Nursery.
  Mrs. Archibald, Parcel of Canvas, Berlin-wool and Clothing.
  Mrs. R. F. Ware, Parcel of Clothing.
  Miss Heiser, Cake, Fruit and Flowers.
  A Friend, a Chair and Toys for the Nursery.
  Young Ladies of Mrs. Earle's School, Rye, N. Y., 16 Aprons, 10 Shirts, 3 Dresses, 1 pair Pantaloons, 1 Hood, 1 dozen Handkerchiefs, 1 dozen Towels, 4 Flannel Shirts, 10 Baby's Garments, 7 pairs Stockings.
  St. Michael's Ant-hill, Assistance in Sewing, making of 5 Shirts, 12 Handkerchiefs, 7 Aprons, 8 Pillow-cases.
  Mrs. Rodenstein, Do., making of 15 Aprons.

AUGUST, 1871.
  St. John's Cove Sunday School, Stamford, Conn., Parcel of New Clothing and 2 Scrap Books.
  Mrs. D. T. Brown, 4 pairs Boy's Socks.
  F. Schack, Esq., Materials for 24 Aprons and 26 Shirts.
  Mrs. A. G. Dunn and friends, making up do.
  George F. C. Thompson, Parcel of Clothing.
  Mrs. D. F. Tiemann, Peaches for all.
  Edward E. Brown, 1,000 Envelopes.
  Nellie Rodenstein, 8 pair knitted Cotton Stockings.

SEPTEMBER, 1871.
  Mrs. A. E. Wise, Cakes for the Nursery.
  Mrs. D. W. Foster, 2 Baskets of Pears.
  Miss E. Williames, Toy Carriage.
  Mrs. D. F. Tiemann, Box of Beef-stock.
  Mrs. Kentor, Parcel of Clothing.
  Nelly Rodenstein, 8 new White Aprons.
  Miss Cleveland, Rocking Chair.

SEPTEMBER, 1871.
  Mrs. W. W. Huntington, Baby-jumper.
  Mrs. Peters, Parcel of Clothing.
  Mrs. P. C. Tiemann, Mrs. Willard, Plants and Shrubs.
  From the Officers of the Company, through Mr. E. Wells Sackett, Trip for all the Children old enough to enjoy it, in the "Sylvan Glen."

OCTOBER, 1871.
  Children of Grace Church, White Plains, Box of new Articles, 6 Night Gowns, 5 Dresses, 6 Waists, 15 Undergarments, 4 White Dresses, 3 White Sacks, 7 Flannel Skirts.
  "M. N. M.," 3 pairs Knitted Socks.
  Mrs. D. T. Brown, 2 Boy's Suits.
  Mrs. W. B. Hoffman, 8 White Skirts, 6 White Dresses, 9 pairs Drawers, 2 Girl's Suits, 2 pairs Woolen Leggins, 4 Hats, 3 pairs Shoes, 2 Linen Aprons, 6 pairs Stockings, 2 Flannel Sacks.
  Mrs. William Tracy, 6 pairs knitted Cotton Stockings.
  Mrs. P. C. Tiemann, "Alone in London," for the Library.
  Mrs. Peters, Clothing.
  Emily and Lucy Schwab, Cakes for all the Children.
  S. Coburn, 3 dozen Cakes Soap.
  A Friend, Clothing.
  B. L. Sherman, through Mr. E. W. Sackett, Barrel of Sugar.

NOVEMBER, 1871.
  From the Officers, through Mr. E. Wells Sackett, Admission to the American Institute Fair, for all the Children old enough to enjoy it.
  Rev. Chas. E. Phelps, New Brunswick, N. J., 5 bags Turnips.
  Mrs. P. C. Tiemann, Box of Clothing.
  Miss Antoinette Tiemann, 12 pairs Knitted Stockings.
  Mrs. D. F. Tiemann, 3 pairs Knitted Stockings, 1 bag of Flour.
  N. Y. Bible and Prayer-Book Society, through Mr. Jas. Pott, 52 Prayer Books.
  Mrs. Brown, 12 Flannel Shirts.
  Mrs. Lamborn, 9 Hats, 1 dozen pairs Gloves.
  Mrs. D. T. Brown, 1 Wrapper.
  Mrs. L. A. Rodenstein, Assistance in Sewing, making 15 Aprons.

NOVEMBER, 1871.
  Miss Sherrill, do., 5 Flannel Shirts.
  St. Andrew's Sewing School, do., 7 Skirts and 7 Shirts.

FOR THANKSGIVING.

John D. Wolfe, 100 Mince Pies.
J. B. Churchill, Pair of Chickens.
R. Prior, Basket of Cakes, large quantity of Rolls, 2 Pies, Celery.
Hiram Paulding, Jr., Barrel of Apples.
Mrs. D. F. Tiemann, large Basket of New Year's Cakes.
Levi P. Morton, 4 Turkeys.

DECEMBER, 1871.
  Mrs. B. H. Field, Chestnut Washstand and Table.
  Miss F. Cotheal, Velvet Hat.
  Miss H. Swords, 2 Knitted Shirts.
  Miss Scott, Papers and Patchwork.
  Mrs. J. W. Munro, 22 Gingham Aprons.
  American Bible Society, 50 Bibles.
  Miss M. Talmadge, 2 pairs Stockings.
  Anonymous, Parcel of Clothing.
  Mrs. Goodridge Fay, through Mrs. Vogel, 20 yards Canton Flannel, 18½ yards Grey Flannel.
  C. G. Gunther's Sons, 6 Hats for Girls, 2 Muffs, 2 Boas.
  Mr. Wm. Taylor, Box of Toys and Ornaments for Tree.
  Messrs. Lord & Taylor, through Mrs. D. F. Tiemann, 10 pieces Dress Goods, containing 60 yards.
  Acker, Merrall & Condit, bag of Lemons.
  Mrs. Brown, 10 Flannel Shirts.
  Anonymous, Dissected Picture.
  Mrs. Einstein, 2 jars Jelly.
  Miss De Peyster, 40 yards Calico.
  Mrs. Kentor, barrel of Vegetables.
  A Friend, through Mrs. Forrester, 8 yards Shirting.
  Mrs. Kernochan, box of Candy.
  Mr. F. S. Winston, 36 New Volumes for the Library.
  Mr. R. Prior, 150 Rolls.
  The Misses Stephens, 2½ dozen Dressed Dolls.
  Little Bennie S. and Hannah M. Cooke, 5 Cups and Saucers, 5 Plates, 5 Spoons, 5 Knives and Forks, for five new children at "The Sheltering Arms," and a parcel of Toys.

DECEMBER, 1871.
- J. D. Wolfe, 50 Mince Pies.
- Robert MacDonald, 4 Turkeys.
- S. Coburn & Co., 1 gross Honey Soap.
- E. K. Willard, 4 Turkeys, Barrel of Flour, do. Potatoes, do. Apples, 2 bags Sugar, 2 bags Tea, 10 lbs. Butter, quantity of Toys and Cakes.
- Miss L. Chittenden, Toys for Frances and William Bauer.
- Mrs. E. R. Bell, Toys for the Lyons children.
- The Misses Tiemann, Toys for Maggie Hill, and 14 boxes of Candy for the Sewing-Class.
- Mrs. R. M. Shaw, 2 bags Hominy, 2 Geese, 1 Turkey.
- Sunday School of the Church of the Reconciliation, 20 lbs. Candy.
- Andrew Smith, 2 parcels of Slates, and 6 Baskets.
- George W. Read, Crate of Chickens.
- Mrs. F. L. Vulté, box of Groceries and Canned Peaches.
- Mrs. A. M. Kalbfleisch, box of Poultry.
- Miss Slade, box of Books, etc.
- Mr. Terhune, Chair and Toys.
- Harry Brown, Rocking Horse.
- St. Luke's Association of Grace Parish, through Mrs. Vogel, Shoes for the Ede and Guion boys, and a pair of Boots for Horace.
- J. R. Terry, through Mrs. Ware, 6 Caps.
- S. W. Johnson, through Mrs. Ware, 6 dozen Toy-books, and a package of Little Delights.
- Vonkellar & Allen, through Mrs. Ware, 10 yards Cloth, in Remnants.
- Mr. Thompson, 3 barrels Vegetables.
- Mrs. Mark Allen, Box of Provisions.
- Mrs. Brower, Ham and Provisions.
- Woodbury G. Langdon, 1 dozen Merino Shirts, 2 dozen Towels, 1 dozen pairs Stockings, Toys and Candy.
- Mrs. Vernon Brown, parcel Boy's Clothing.
- Mrs. Morse, parcel of Toys and Scarfs.
- Mrs. D. F. Tiemann, 3 pairs Skates, 1 Sled and Toys.
- Major James E. Montgomery, 1 dozen Rubber Balls, 2 large Photographs of "Farragut" and "Sheridan's Ride."
- Mrs. J. W. Miller, Candy and Clothing.

DECEMBER, 1871.
  Anonymous, Half-barrel Flour.
  Anonymous, Half-bushel Potatoes.
  "From a poor Friend," box of Potatoes and a pair of Shoes.
  " M.," parcel of Clothing.
  Levi Pawling, 1 box Raisins and 1 bag Nuts.

CHRISTMAS BAGS.

The whole number of Bags received was 338, acknowledged below under the three heads "Provisions," "Clothing," "Miscellaneous."

Some of the bags contained a variety of articles, and accordingly are classified according to the principles of plurality voting. Many of the names upon the bags were defaced and a few obliterated before reaching the House. Great pains were taken to preserve and decypher names, with the following result:

Provisions—215 *Bags.*

Mrs. A. Boody ; Miss M. E. Lockwood ; James Moir ; Miss Louie Lee ; Master Miller ; J. H. Brower ; George Walt (2 bags) ; J. Banshee ; Arnold, Sturgis & Co. ; Smith & Noyes ; William J. Beebe ; A. M. Ferris ; H. J. Dickey ; Mrs. J. G. Keator ; a Friend of Wm. M. Kingsland ; Mrs. W. H. Riblet ; Miss Grace Stebbins ; J. Banshee & Co. ; Chandler Robbins ; Edith L. Draper ; Edward King ; A. Polhemus, Jr. ; Mrs. F. H. Delano ; Mrs. L. H. Holmes ; Mrs. Frances Lieber ; Mrs. Timpson ; Mrs. Phil. R. Kearney ; Mrs. R. F. Ware ; Joseph M. Cooper ; Mrs. H. V. Ryder ; Charles De Rham ; Mrs. H. B. Clarkson ; Mrs. Mary Johnson ; P. Dator & Co. ; B. P. Davis ; W. B. Hunter & Co. ; Beebe & Brother ; Mrs. Peter Winney ; William Pennoyer ; Hamilton Webster ; Mrs. James Brooks ; Thomas Owen ; A Friend ; Mrs. E. E. Anderson ; Mrs. J. R. Platt ; Miss L. E. Morgan ; Mrs. Cammann ; Mrs. C. A. Cammann ; Gen. Sandford ; Mrs. Ludlum ; Mrs. C. L. Case ; Mrs. Fitzgerald ; Mrs. G. L. Brown ; Edward A. Boyd ; Mrs. John M. White ; Mrs. J. C. Homeyard ; Mrs. P. R. Bonnett ; R. D. Coleman & Co. ; Miss E. M. Cotheal ; Mrs. G. W. Livingston ; T. P. Cummings ; Mrs. Wm. H. Wisner ; Mrs. J. R. Boyd ; Samuel Holmes ; Mrs. Pettigrew ; John A. Stevens ; Andrew Smith ; Mrs. Lynch ; Children of Daniel Le Roy ; William M. Evarts ; J. J. Petit ; Mrs. De Ruyter ; Mrs. Schwab ; Charlie Place Sackett ; Mrs. G. W.

DECEMBER, 1871.

Ryerson ; Mrs. W. B. Hoffman ; James Pettit ; Mrs. R. M. Shaw ; J. H. V. Cockcroft ; Mrs. Gourand ; Mrs. Brower ; Mrs. G. R. Jackson ; W. S. Corwin & Co. (2 bags) ; Mrs. Peters ; Henry J. Barbey ; W. L. Chamberlain ; Mrs. E. A. Bull ; J. D. Fish & Co. (2 bags) ; Mrs. L. Simpson ; Mrs. C. S. Fontaine ; C. Ammann & Co. (2 bags) ; Mrs. G. F. Gilman ; Misses Furniss ; Mrs. Sarah A. Barclay ; Amy H. Draper ; Mrs. C. S. Little ; Mrs. C. R. Green ; Mrs. N. Sands ; Mrs. Wm. H. Whitney ; Mrs. Tiemann ; Mrs. J. W. Quincy ; Edward R. Bell (4 bags) ; R. W. Bootman ; A Friend ; B. W. Griswold ; John Pyne ; C. Einstein ; A. McNulty ; Mrs. Allen ; De W. C. Wheeler ; Mrs. Edward Boyd ; Mrs. Thomas Watt's children (12 bags) ; G. M. Griffin ; Jacob Reese ; Mrs. P. Handford ; Wm. C. Emmet ; Miss E. J. Lynch ; Katy Ruckel ; Mrs. Samuel Lawrence ; Mrs. A. Scholl ; Miss M. F. Jenkins ; Miss Jones ; Mrs. G. K. Sistare ; Mrs. R. B. Minturn, Jr. ; H. D. Sedgwick ; Mrs. T. B. Newby ; E. L. Ludlow ; Mrs. Gerry ; Mrs. Clapp ; Mrs. Lewis A. Sayre ; Mrs. Baldwin (2 bags) ; Miss Hadden ; Miss Einstein ; C. C. Haight ; Mrs. J. T. Metcalfe (2 bags) ; Miss Deming ; John A. Prigge ; John K. French ; Mrs. A. Chandler ; Mrs. R. Jones ; Charles G. Small & Co. ; C. V. A. Schuyler & Son (3 bags) ; Miss Mary Ottiwell ; J. B. Slawson ; Mrs. F. C. Salisbury ; Mrs. Sudlman ; Doyle & Hueston ; Mrs. Place ; Mrs. Sackett ; Miss Bertie Ryerson ; Mrs. C. C. Adams ; Mrs. D. F. Tiemann ; Mrs. E. R. Cole ; Mrs. Von Post (3 bags) ; E. P. Wheeler ; Mrs. Swift ; Mrs. B. Moore ; Mrs. Alvord ; Mrs. Edward Leavitt ; Masters Draper ; Mrs. Snow ; Mrs. Hamilton ; Mrs. A. Dennison ; Miss Snow ; William Perkins ; Mrs. Turner ; Bowerman Bro. ; Miss E. M. Olcott ; Mrs. B. H. Field ; Mrs. Beecher ; Mrs. F. L. Vulté ; Mrs. E. Edgar ; Misses McGunigle ; Mrs. Jones ; Mrs. Birdsall ; Anonymous (9 bags) ; Baby Carrie ; Mrs. E. Kent ; Miss F. Cotheal (2 bags) ; Mrs. D. M. Fitch ; Rev. Dr. Montgomery.

Clothing—56 Bags.

Mrs. C. K. Alvord ; Mrs. H. D. Wyman ; Mrs. Seixas ; Master and Misses Ward; Miss Hutchings; Mrs. V. H. Brown; Mrs. W. T. Garner ; Mrs. Cambridge Livingston ; Mr. Terhune ; Mrs. Gerry ; Miss Ida Whittingham ; Mrs. Read and Mrs. Starkweather ; Mrs.

DECEMBER, 1871.

P. A. Morgan ; P. S. Halstead ; Mrs. Eliz. Britton ; Mrs. L. Clarkson ; Miss R. M. Jones ; T. R. Jackson ; Mrs. L. A. Jones ; Mrs. S. P. Nash ; Mrs. Catherine Pell ; Mrs. F. W. Coggill ; Mrs. Minturn ; J. Montgomery Hare ; Cove Mission Sunday School, Stamford, Ct. ; Mrs. Lawrence ; Mrs. Lamborn ; Mrs. L. B. Martin ; Miss M. Aldrich ; Four little Girls, through Mrs. H. H. Garner ; May Brower ; Miss Read ; Miss M. E. Horner ; Miss Julia Pierrepont ; Miss Bell (3 bags) ; Mrs. Cohen ; Mrs. Morse ; Mrs. W. P. Lee ; J. F. Kernochan ; Maggie Somerville ; Miss Wolfe (2 bags) ; Freddie M. Burr ; Miss A. M. Cammann ; John H Morris ; Mrs. Cammann (2 bags) ; Miss E. J. Lynch ; George Jones ; Miss Jones ; Mrs. J. Hadden ; Mrs. Marcus Beach ; Mrs. Stephen Williams ; Mrs. Paran Stevens.

Miscellaneous—67 Bags.

Freddie Ware ; Master Jay ; Mrs. A. B. Marses ; Miss Simpson ; Miss Lawrence ; Mrs. Clapp : G. A. Hearn ; Miss Ida Pirsson ; L. C. Jones ; Misses Lillie, Sallie and Mina Macy (2 bags) ; Kitty Everdell and Brothers ; Mrs. C. S. Weyman, "from Harry and Isabel ;" Mrs. Lee ; Miss McKee ; Miss Ellen H. Cotheal ; Hattie and Sadie Holly ; K. and M. F. Cotheal ; H. H. Holly ; Lulu and Mabel Van Rensselaer ; B. Schlesinger ; Mrs. Augustus Embury ; Mary Hitchcock ; Harry Salisbury ; George W. Smith ; D. W. Hoffmann ; Thomas H. Faile (3 bags) ; Mrs. M. Hartley ; Mrs. S. E. Morse ; Mrs. Colden ; Anonymous (10 bags) ; Abraham Wakeman ; Miss Dater (2 bags) ; Ida and Florence ; Thos. J. S. W. Parkins ; Mrs. Brower ; Master Joseph M. White ; Misses Wilkes ; W. H. Lewis, Jr. ; Miss Wolfe ; E. A. Duyckinck ; Master Kernochan ; Mrs. Wm. Barton ; Mrs. Wolcott Richards ; Mrs. J. W. Miller ; Mrs. Hitchcock ; D. B. Bedell ; William Furniss ; Miss Bertie Ryerson ; Nellie Ryerson ; E. L. Ludlow ; Mrs. J. B. Church ; Little Madeleine ; Miss M. H. Lawrence ; Miss M. Hutchings and Miss A. Reed.

JANUARY, 1872.

Mr. J. B. Churchill, Lamb.
Mrs. Little, 10 dozen Cakes.
Stone & Osborn, 2 barrels Apples.
Mr. R. Prior, Rolls.

JANUARY, 1872.
  Miss A. Paulding, Parcel of Clothing.
  Through Mrs. H. C. Von Post, 10 pairs Stockings.
  Mrs. Julius Tiemann, Parcel of Clothing.
  Mrs. J. B. Hickson, Dress.
  Mrs. R. D. Laurence, Suit of Boy's Clothes, 1 pair of Shoes.
  Mrs. Lall, 6 pairs Stockings.
  Miss A. H. Garner, Christmas bag of Woolen Goods.
  Mrs. D. F. Tiemann, 2 pairs Stockings.
  Miss Helen Rudderow, 4 pairs Stockings.
  Miss Delle Balentine, Christmas bag of Nuts, Candy, etc.
  Master John Kemble, Scrap-Book for the boys.
  Master Edward Kemble, Books, etc., for the girls.
  Mr. J. D. Wolfe, Candy and Illustrated Papers.
  Mrs. Brown, Parcel of Boy's Clothes, Roll of Old Linen, and 8 pairs new Stockings.
  Mr. W. G. Langdon, Chromo-lithographs of "Launching the Life-boat," "Sunset on the Coast," 3 "Views in Central Park" and 8 Photographs.
  Mrs. F. T. Whiting, Parcel of Clothing.
  Mrs. M. L. Whitlock, Books and Stockings.
  Willard P. Whitlock, Scrap-Book.
  Ladies of St. Luke's Church, Matteawan, Assistance in Sewing, making 41 Aprons.
  Sewing School of St. Andrew's Church, Harlem, do. do., 7 Garments.

FEBRUARY, 1872.
  Mrs. Huntington, Parcel of Clothing.
  Mrs. Commodore Livingston, through Mrs. Washburn, 6 pairs Stockings.
  Rev. Dr. Peters, 8 Bird-houses, 20 dozen Tea-biscuits, and 12 dozen Jumbles.
  Mrs. Burgoyne, 2 Parcels of Clothing.
  Mrs. Matthew P. Read, 6 pairs Stockings.
  Mrs. Peters, Parcel of Clothing.
  Miss "J. B.," 4 gross Gilt Buttons.
  Elsie Tiemann, Children's Friend, 1872.
  Addie Tiemann, Infant's Magazine, 1872.
  May Peters, Children's Magazine, 1872.

FEBRUARY, 1872.
    Rev. Dr. Carter, Parcel of Clothing.
    Miss Augusta Slade, 1 Dress, Chocolate, Toys and Oranges for the sick children.
    Miss Kate B. Bell, 4 new Mattresses, 4 new Pillows, 4 new Blankets, Flowers and Oranges.
    Miss Helen Rudderow, 2 pairs Stockings.
    Miss Halser, Parcel of Clothing.
    Mrs. Treharne, Assistance in Sewing, making 3 Dresses and 14 Bibs.
    St. Michael's Ant-hill, do, do., 3 Aprons.

MARCH, 1872.
    Sewing Society of the Church of the Mediator, Kingsbridge, 9 Dresses, 7 Flannel Skirts.
    Mrs. Coddington, Parcel of Clothing.
    Through Mrs. Brown, 3 pairs Stockings.
    Mrs. Peters, Parcel of Clothing.
    Mrs. Graham, Photograph of Mr. Azel Graham.
    Mrs. S. P. Nash, Parcel of Clothing.
    Miss Gerry, 12 pairs Knitted Stockings.
    Mrs. Loyall Farragut, 10 Shirts, 18 Undergarments, 4 Dresses, 4 Wrappers.
    Mrs. Cary, Scrap-Book.
    Mrs. P. C. Tiemann, Parcel of Clothing.
    Mrs. D. F. Tiemann, 11 dozen Eggs, 1 pair Stockings.
    W. S. Corwin & Co., through Mrs. Tiemann, 2 Hams.
    Acker, Merrall & Condit, 15 dozen Eggs, 6 dozen Lemons.
    R. Prior, 10 dozen Rolls.
    An Easter Offering from the Ladies of the "Guild" Christ Church, Riverdale, New York, 40 Aprons.
    Mrs. L. A. Rodenstein, Assistance in Sewing, making 24 Aprons.
    Bible Class of St. John's Church, Stamford, Ct., do. do., 30 Aprons.
    Ladies of St. Luke's Church, Matteawan, N. Y., do. do., 53 Aprons.
    Helping Hand Society of St. Ann's Church, New York, do. do., 27 Aprons.
    St. Michael's Ant-hill, do. do., 7 Aprons.
    Miss Sherrill, do. do., 6 Dresses.

MARCH, 1872.
- Lenten Work of Mrs. Hitchcock's S. S. Class, St. Peter's Church, Morristown, N. J., 7 Aprons.
- Mrs. C. C. Adams, Ball of Kite-cord.
- Mrs. O. B. Potter, Oranges, Tea, Beans, and 22 jars Jelly.

APRIL, 1872.
- Messrs. Lord & Taylor, through Mrs. D. F. Tiemann, 12 remnants, containing 40 yards of Calico.
- St. James' Class of St. Chrysostom's S. S., Eggs and Oranges, "To build up Katy Brooks."
- Mrs. D. F. Tiemann, Ham.
- Mrs. T. M. Peters, Parcel of Clothing.
- Easter Gift from Mrs. H. H. Beard, 6 new Garments.
- Ladies of the Church of the Good Shepherd, Hartford, Conn., 12 Night-Dresses.
- Rev. Dr. Peters, Cake, and 10 dozen Tea-Biscuit.
- Mrs. Richard Bayley, Hall-stove and Fixtures.
- Mrs. M. L. Whitlock, 2 pairs Stockings.
- Messrs. Pott, Young & Co., Parcel of Children's Books, and 8 Colored Engravings.
- Mr. W. G. Langdon, Chromo-lithographs of "Easter Morning," and "In and Out."
- Mrs. D. S. Jackson, Parcel of Clothing.
- Mr. Lyle, 3 dozen Straw Hats.
- St. Michael's Ant-hill, Assistance in Sewing, making 6 Aprons and 6 Towels.
- Helping Hand Society of St. Ann's Church, do. do., 26 Aprons.
- St. Mark's Benevolent Society, do. do., 94 Pillow-Cases and 55 Sheets.

Founded in 1864.
THE SHELTERING ARMS,
10th Avenue and 129th Street.

"The Sheltering Arms."

NINTH ANNUAL REPORT.

NEW YORK,
1873.

Incorporated October, 1864.

New York:
E. WELLS SACKETT & BRO., STATIONERS, AND BOOK AND JOB PRINTERS,
56 & 58 WILLIAM STREET, CORNER PINE.

Officers of "The Sheltering Arms."

VISITOR.
RT. REV. H. POTTER, D. D., D. C. L., LL. D.......Address, 88 East 22d Street.

PRESIDENT.
REV. THOMAS M. PETERS, D. D....................Broadway cor. 99th St.

VICE-PRESIDENTS.
FRED'K S. WINSTON..................................144 Broadway.
WM. ALEX. SMITH..................................40 Wall Street.
WM. J. BEEBE......................................104 Wall Street.

SECRETARY.
PETER C. TIEMANN..................................Manhattanville.

TREASURER.
WOODBURY G. LANGDON..............................719 Fifth Avenue.

MANAGERS.
HENRY J. CAMMANN..................................8 Wall Street.
HERMANN C. VON POST...............................2 Bowling Green.
BENJ. H. FIELD....................................127 Water Street.
D. TILDEN BROWN, M. D.............................Manhattanville.
WM. B. CLERKE.....................................25 Broad Street.
WM. H. FOGG.......................................32 Burling Slip.
THOS. WATT..606 Fifth Avenue.
WM. P. LEE..326 Fifth Avenue.
WM. M. KINGSLAND..................................116 Fifth Avenue.
REV. H. E. MONTGOMERY, D. D.......................209 Madison Avenue.
FRANKLIN EDSON....................................19 Whitehall Street.
CHARLES E. STRONG.................................68 Wall Street.
ABRAM S. HEWITT...................................9 Lexington Avenue.
E. WELLS SACKETT..................................56 and 58 William Street.
REV. E. GAY, JR...................................Tomkins' Cove, Rockland Co.

PHYSICIAN.
L. A. RODENSTEIN, M. D............................Manhattanville.

CONSULTING PHYSICIAN.
ABRAHAM JACOBI, M. D..............................110 West 34th Street.

OPHTHALMIC SURGEON.
THOMAS H. POOLEY..................................209 West 34th Street.

Ladies' Association of "The Sheltering Arms."

―:o:―

Vice-President.

MRS. WM. P. LEE..................................326 Fifth Avenue.

Secretary.

MISS M. CHAUNCEY.............................53 West 36th Street.

Treasurer.

MRS. B. F. CORLIES..............................39 Nassau Street.

Members.

Mrs. R. W. ABORN........19 Fifth Av.
" HITCHCOCK......Morristown, N. J.
Miss S. B. NEWBY.....314 West 28th St.
" L. PETERS....Bdw'y, cor. 101st St.
" F. COTHEAL.......26 Univ'lty Place.
" J. A. TIEMANN....Manhattanville.
" LIZZIE HOLMES......123 Fifth Ave.
Mrs. JOHN DE RUYTER..75 Madison Ave.
Miss KATE BELL........20 West 20th St.
" HOFFMAN..........Cornwall, N. Y.
Mrs. A. S. HEWITT....9 Lexington Ave.
Miss MONTGOMERY.....209 Madison Ave.
Mrs. G. B. DRAPER..5th Av. c. 130th St.
Miss G. REED,........6 East 53d Street.
" CRITTENDEN....Inwood, N. Y. City.
" J. WILLIAMS...Yonkers, West'r Co.
Mrs. E. W. SACKETT...54 West 127th St.
Miss AUGUSTA SLADE....5 East 38th St.
Mrs. TALBOYS..........2 West 16th St.
" R. F. WARE.......136 W. 36th St.

Mrs. MORRISON........10 East 54th St.
Miss S. S. RICHMOND..Manhattanville.
" C. B. ARNOLD...279 Madison Av.
" WOLFE..Madison Av. cor. 24th St.
Mrs. J. MUNRO........14 West 36th St.
" I. P. MARTIN..Fort Wash'n, N. Y.
Miss SCOTT..........40 East 41st St.
" H. BRACH.......226 Second Ave.
Mrs. J. L. LEIB......106 East 58th St.
" F. C. WITHERS..218 West 22d St.
" M. L. WHITLOCK, Gt.Barr'n, Mass.
" F. T. WOITING,   "   "
Miss A. SIMPSON, Manhattanville, N.Y.
Mrs. A. M. KEATOR...Manhattanville.
" H. E. DUNCAN..Matteawan, N.Y.
Miss CARTER......153 Lexington Ave.
Mrs. A. MESIER, Wappingers Falls, N.Y.
Miss MCCURDY ......10 East 14th St.
" G. H. WILDES...Riverdale, N. Y.
" M. SPAULDING..Riverdale, N. Y.

OBJECTS OF THE ASSOCIATION.

"THE SHELTERING ARMS" was opened October 6, 1864, for the reception of homeless children, for whom no other institution provides.

The classes of children received are as follows:

1st. The blind and deaf mutes, until the age at which they become entitled to admission at the Asylums especially devoted to such unfortunates.

2d. Crippled children, past hope of cure, and therefore no longer retained in ordinary hospitals.

3d. Children of poor parents, obliged on account of sickness to enter a hospital, and who commit their children for a season to our charge, with the expectation, upon recovery, of reclaiming their own.

4th. Children rendered temporarily homeless by fire or other accident.

5th. Children whose home has been broken up by the intemperance or desertion of father or mother. In such cases, the remaining parent pays, according to ability, a small sum monthly.

6th. Children abandoned by both parents, brought to us by friends or relatives unable to find immediately a proper home, and yet unwilling to lose control of the children or to place them beyond their reach.

Children placed at "THE SHELTERING ARMS" are not surrendered to the Institution, but are held subject to the order of parents and relations.

All the children of sufficient age attend the school of the Institution, where they receive a common education. The larger girls are also trained to household work. The children attend St. Mary's Protestant Episcopal Church, and are under the pastoral care of the Rev. T. M. Peters, D.D.

REPORT

OF THE

Board of Trustees,

MAY, 1873.

THE Trustees of "THE SHELTERING ARMS" with thankful hearts present to their friends and the public this their ninth Annual Report. Through the manifold mercies of our Heavenly Father the past year has been one of unusual prosperity. It was entered upon under some disadvantages, and as to individual members of the incorporation with some misgivings. Owing to the diminution of one half in the amount received for board, and the increase in the number of children, the current expenses had exceeded the income, so that the commencement of a new year left a deficit in that department of the finances. There was besides a debt for the purchase of the Infirmary and for many additions and improvements which it had been found necessary to make upon the Cottages, School House and grounds. At the date of the Semi-Annual Report of 1871, Nov. 1st, the whole indebtedness was over $15,000. The past eighteen months have seen it reduced to $4,500, besides paying within that time upwards of $1,400, interest on loans, meeting every expense of the Institution, and with the Treasury holding at the closing of the year's account a sufficient sum in hand to insure the payment of all the May bills.

This result is owing to faith and brave work on the part of all the friends of our charity. A few timid voices said;

"You have too many inmates, send them away." The Trustees proposed another course and replied: "We cannot steel our hearts to apply such remedy, but good friend, take you a child, and you, and you, and pay its charges and let it stay where God has led it, and it is being trained for usefulness and heaven." Many a friend cheerfully accepted the burden, and thus in the course of the past eighteen months patrons have been found for forty-one beds at a cost of $138 each per year.

The next resort was to the parents and friends of the children. They were told: "THE SHELTERING ARMS is running behind in its expenses, we will not send your little homeless ones away, but we want you to pay all that you can possibly spare towards their support." A ready compliance with this reasonable request increased the average amount received from 25 to 50 cents a week for each child; gradually adding to the receipts from that source until they doubled, becoming equal to the average amount paid for each child during the first two years after the opening in Bloomingdale.

Thus faith and brave work have received God's blessing and triumphed, although obliged for a time to seek shelter in the abode of Patience and watch the result. Not a child was sent away, no parent's heart grieved, no family oppressed.

The Trustees went further than to retain all their liabilities. They assumed another, and announced in their last Annual Report that, for reasons there given, applications from clergymen for members of their own flocks should rank among the first to be attended to. This resolution has been kept and for twelve months no such application has been declined or for more than a week postponed.

The clergy have retaliated to be sure and done us many a good turn, but while the expenses of each child commence at entrance, the contributions of churches are necessarily slower in their appearance. We therefore assumed an immediate liability in the prospect of a future partial reimbursement, in some cases yet to come.

While the Trustees appear before the public with a more cheerful financial exhibit than last year, they send out with this statement the same call to energetic work, because after May they have nothing in hand for the current expenses of the barren Summer months, and because they intend this year to pay off the $4,500 now owing, in addition to daily support, and because they have another gold-consuming proposition to make, which will appear before the report closes.

Of those in whose behalf are all these labors, the children, the Institution has since April, 1872, sheltered always from 130 to 140. The applications during the year were 258, of whom 65, or one-quarter, were received, and 193, or three-quarters, refused, in almost every case solely for lack of room.

Not a child has died during the year, and two only have been seriously ill. The infirmary was emptied of patients last Summer and has seldom since that time been in requisition, except as a convenient lodging place when the cottages are overcrowded.

Dr. Rodenstein and Dr. Pooley have continued their valuable and voluntary services, giving to the children all the attendance required, and deserve and receive our warmest thanks.

The Trustees desire publicly to acknowledge the kindness of the Rev. C. C. Adams, Rector of St. Mary's Church, who has, as heretofore, manifested a constant interest in the welfare of the children and has offered his Church, whenever wanted, for our use.

The Ladies' Association merits most honorable mention. To their charity is to be attributed in good degree the improvement in both financial condition and prospect. To increased collections they have added also the promise to enlarge their gifts, until every one of the thirty-four children of the Ladies' Cottage is supported without drawing upon the general receipts of the Treasury.

A Committee appointed from the Ladies' Association has assisted in editing the monthly paper. By this means the care of its preparation is lightened.

The insertion of paid advertisements relieves the Treasury to a large extent of printing bills, and the mailing being done at the Institution, only the postage stamps have to be provided. For not over $500 a year, we now send out monthly thirty-four hundred of these messengers, once costing us not far from $2,000 per annum, and well worth to us even that expenditure.

The beneficial effects of the cottage system are more and more evident in the general good behavior of the children, in the interest taken in their evening gatherings around the family table for devotion and instruction and amusement, and also especially in their attention to those things which belong to the immortal life.

Last June three of the Wolfe Cottage boys and five of the Cooper Cottage girls were at their own earnest desire confirmed and admitted to the communion, and have continued faithful to their profession. In addition to the instruction of the Pastor and the resident ladies, volunteers from neighboring churches visit the Institution on Sundays and gather the children in classes for catechetical and Bible lessons. Few Sunday Schools are more thoroughly taught or so fruitful in result.

Large praise is also due to the Mothers of the Cottages, and to the Head of the House, for the satisfactory condition physically and morally of those committed to their charge.

Regarding the School, still under the instruction of the Misses Cleveland, the Trustees also report with pride that it is thorough and efficient, providing for the boys and girls such an education as will be useful in the condition of life from which they are taken and to which they will return. The School accommodations are insufficient for the number of children, consequently two of the eldest, and twenty or more of the youngest inmates have been sent to the neighbouring public school.

A play-room apart from the Cottages will be built the coming summer. We shall then be able to adopt the best preventive against the return of the eye troubles of the winter of 1871-2, by emptying each day and thoroughly airing every room of all the cottages.

Each year of added experience contributes to carrying out more effectually our original design of offering shelter to those in the sorest need, and whose parents and friends, on the down-hill slant from comfort into adversity, find their chief cause of anguish in the impossibility of retaining home privileges for their children. We may not make public all the tales of woe which both sadden and stimulate us in our labors. But if you run over our record you will read honorable names. Scan the faces of our children, especially of the girls, and many a feature and expression bears indisputable testimony to refined and gentle parentage.

We have them now, three, four, and even six of one household, covered from the storm, while the parents in tears of joy go forth, to re-erect out of the shattered remnants of the past the sacred temple of home. The relief thus rendered and evident is the great spring of our rejoicing.

Dwellers in prosperous homes, spare us the pains of again reporting that where we open our arms to one, we must turn our back upon three. Build us other cottages, that when the storm of life wrecks your hopes and lays your roof-tree low, here your offspring may find unfailing shelter in the arms of Christ. May there soon be other glad days in our history like that of which our little paper lately made mention. A Christian lady sent for the President of "THE SHELTERING ARMS" by note and, upon his calling, stated that it had been her intention to leave by will money for the Institution, but as she learned from our publications that more room was needed she had decided to give while she lived. Drawing unostentatiously from her pocket a small roll of bills she handed them, five thousand dollars, to the President, leaving the disposition entirely to the Trustees. Thus is added to the list of our Founders a name which it is forbidden here to repeat.

A legacy of $1,000 has been received from the estate of Thomas C. Moore.

The will of the late Mrs. Jas. P. Van Horne contains a legacy not yet received, and the exact amount of which is not yet ascertained. There is therefore made in this year's report no further mention of the gift, excepting that it will place another name among the Founders.

The Trustees have adopted at recent meetings two resolutions, one of which takes these and all future legacies out of the fund disposable for current expenses, devoting them to enlarging the accommodation or endowing beds. The other resolution appropriates not only what has been already received or is expected, but also a great many thousand dollars more for which we rely on God and Christians. This second resolution contemplates the erection of the long proposed Innocents' Hospital for permanently crippled children.

"THE SHELTERING ARMS" when projected was announced as intended to offer a Home to children, for whom no other Institution provides. Under the head of "Objects of the Institution," printed with each annual report, the second named is "Crippled Children past hope of cure and therefore no longer retained in ordinary hospitals."

Our first annual report in 1865, says: "Incurables and hopeless cripples have from the beginning formed part of our household." To-day we repeat those words as applying to the whole eight years of interval.

In our annual reports of '69 and '70 it was declared that

upon the completion of our new cottages the next step onward should be the erection of the Innocents' Hospital for permanent cripples. A year ago we referred to our Infirmary as the seed of our proposed Innocents' Hospital for Cripples. The readers of the little paper have been often reminded that the day would come when we should ask once more for large gifts, and that the object of the new solicitation would be the Innocents' Hospital to which we might transfer the cripples from our cottages, and into which might be gathered many who, in the tenement houses of this and neighboring cities, suffer for the want of gentle treatment and languish in default of nourishing food.

The Trustees of "THE SHELTERING ARMS" are now ready to receive those gifts and lay the foundation stone of this new building.

It is well, perhaps, that in the providence of God this commencement has been thus long delayed. Three years of experience in the cottages, with constant thought given to the subject, prepare us to do what otherwise might have been immaturely entered upon.

We know to-day precisely what is wanted and propose, retaining our cottage system, to gather three families of cripples.

Instead of being placed like the cottages for sound children side by side, with wash-room, dining-room, play-room, and dormitory in different stories. We propose arranging our new building in four stories, kitchen and store-rooms below, and on each of the other three floors a wash-room, play-room, dining-room and dormitory for a family of 25 or 30, each family with distinct head as at present, and having all the required accommodations complete on one floor.

From 75 to 90 crippled children can then be received and the aggregate of the inmates increased to about 220.

The circumstances under which the present cottages were erected admitted of no delay and the Trustees were accordingly compelled to go forward, even with the certainty of incurring a heavy debt.

They propose to build the Innocents' Hospital only as the funds are contributed, suspending the work and delaying its completion as the appropriations for this especial purpose may be for the time consumed.

The Trustees propose to make the Innocents' Hospital memorial in its character, the gifts of the triumphant in heaven to the sufferers upon earth. They ask therefore of parents gifts in memory of their own little ones who have early gone to the land of freedom and rest. The name of the departed, thus commemorated, it is proposed to inscribe upon marble slabs around the sides of the little chapel in which the inmates of the Hospital will join in daily prayer and praise. The supplications and thanksgivings of the living will arise from the midst of the memories of the departed.

Such briefly is the plan of the Trustees as at present developed, and for the accomplishment of the purpose they ask to-day for prompt and abundant gifts.

Blessing His holy name who has hitherto helped them, the Trustees in prayer and confidence await His signal to move on.

THOMAS M. PETERS,
President of the Board of Trustees.

May 12, 1872.

TREASURER'S ANNUAL REPORT.

THE SHELTERING ARMS in account with

Cr.   WOODBURY G. LANGDON, *Treasurer.*

May 1. 1872.	Cash,	Balance of Old Account..............	$178 76
	"	Income of Endowment, Interest, Insurance, etc......................	309 42
	"	Estate of Thos. C. Moore............	965 83
	"	Comptroller of City.................	5,000 00
to	"	Board at Sheltering Arms............	2,997 00
	"	Advertising*........................	840 09
	"	Annual Subscriptions and Subscriptions to support a child during one year...	3,101 58
May 1.	"	Donations...........................	15,616 66
1873.	"	Special for Christmas................	79 99
			$29,089 33

Dr.

May 1.	To Expenditure on New Buildings,	$64 78	
	" Bread............................	2,477 22	
	" Meat and Fish...................	1,726 23	
	" Milk.............................	1,083 74	
	" Groceries........................	1,826 94	
	" Fuel.............................	752 73	
	" Gas..............................	378 30	
	" Express, Car-fare & Sundries..	313 93	
	" Wages...........................	2,488 50	
	" Labor............................	119 93	
	" Insurance........................	406 11	
	" Interest..........................	1,404 55	
	" Household Material.............	475 92	
	" Printing*........................	1,704 15	
	" Stamps and Stationery..........	498 31	
	" Salaries and Collection.........	1,796 61	
	" Church Sittings.................	250 00	
	" Repairs..........................	1,215 88	
	" Clothing.........................	1,318 76	
	" Payments on account of Loans.	8,200 00	
	" Balance on hand................	586 74	
			$29,089 33

E. A. O. E.   *May* 10, 1873.

WOODBURY G. LANGDON, *Treas.*

NEW YORK, June 3, 1873.

At a meeting of the Finance Committee of "The Sheltering Arms," the account of the Treasurer for the year ending April 30th, 1873, showing a balance on hand of $586 74, was examined and found correct.

H. C. VON POST,
WILLIAM H. FOGG, } *Auditing Committee.*
WM. B. CLERKE,

---

* $110 00 should be deducted from amount of Printing.

FOUNDERS OF A COTTAGE BY THE GIFT OF FIVE THOUSAND DOLLARS.

Mrs. Peter Cooper (1869).
Mr. John D. Wolfe (1869).
Mrs. Wm. P. Furniss (1873).

---:o:---

ENDOWMENT OF BEDS.

By resolution of the Board of Trustees, passed on the 27th day of March, 1871, it was decided to accept endowments of beds at the rate of $1,000, the nomination of the occupant to remain in the donor for life; or of $2,000, with right of nomination in perpetuity; and that all sums so received be invested and the interest only be applied to the support of The Sheltering Arms.

NAMES OF PERSONS ENDOWING BEDS.

1871.
  Mrs. Henry Salisbury $1,000 00
1872.
  In memory of little Alice 2,000 00

---:o:---

PATRONS OF THE SHELTERING ARMS, BY THE PAYMENT IN ONE YEAR OF FIVE HUNDRED DOLLARS.

1866.
  Frederick Hubbard, Robert B. Minturn, John D. Wolfe.
1867.
  Mrs. H. Rose.
1868.
  Loring Andrews, W. L. Andrews, James Punnett, Rev. T. M. Peters, D.D., H. C. Von Post, Thomas Ward, M.D., Mrs. James Punnett, Mrs. T. M. Peters.
1869.
  Frederick DePeyster, Thomas Garner, Azel Graham, C. C. Haight. Mrs. H. D. Wyman, Mrs. Steers, Mrs. Thomas Ward, Mrs. H. D. Aldrich.

1870.
Stewart Brown.
1871.
Mrs. George Kemp.
1872.
Mrs. Ann Fortune, Mrs. Eugene Langdon.
1873.
Madame C. Mears.
Thomas C. Moore.

———:o:———

LIFE MEMBERS, BY THE PAYMENT IN ONE YEAR OF ONE HUNDRED DOLLARS

1865.
Wm. J. Beebe, Chas. E. Beebe, John Caswell, Thomas H. Falle, B. H. Field, W. H. Fogg, W. A. Haines, Rev. R. S. Howland, D.D., George Merritt, Rev. W. A. Muhlenberg, D.D., Adam Norrie, Gideon Pott, Lizzie Punnett, Herman D. Aldrich, Wm. Alex. Smith, W. K. Kitchen, S. S. Wyckoff, Miss Montgomery, Miss Jenkins.

1866.
Stewart Brown, Simeon Draper, Frederick G. Foster, Horace Gray, Jr., W. C. Gilman, Franklin F. Randolph, Mrs. Catherine L. Spencer, Mrs. Martin E. Greene, Thos. W. Ogden, Rev. S. H. Tyng, Jr., Rev. Thomas Gallaudet, D.D., A. Cooper, Miss Kate Norwood, Miss Louise Cooper, Miss Nesbitt, Miss Amory, Miss Baxter, Miss Carrie T. Lawrence, Miss Chauncey, Miss M. E. Snow, John A. McKimm, Louie F. Therasson, C. T. Whittingham, Reverdy Estelle, Henry A. Oakley, Mrs. Henry A. Oakley.

1867.
W. Armstrong, Jay Cooke, Mrs. Frederick De Peyster, D. B. Fayerweather, Robt. J. Livingston, J. W. Minturn, Mrs. J. B. Kissam, Miss Steers, "W. B. R.," A friend.

1868.
Mrs. S. C. Baring, Edward Jones, Rev. H. E. Montgomery, D.D., Mrs. Mary Watt, Mrs. Laura L. Wullen, W. B., Mrs. Edward Jones.

1869.
 Wm. H. Aspinwall, Wm. M. Kingsland, Arthur Kimber, A. A. Low, Edwin C. Litchfield, Wm. P. Lee, Wm. Weyman Mall, Levi P. Morton, Wm. P. Furniss, David Stewart, Horace Williams, Miss Drake, Miss J. Van Horne, Rev. E. A. Washburn, D. D., Richard W. Weston, Miss Fanny Austin.

1870.
 Mrs. R. T. Auchmuty, F. A. Peters, S. D. Babcock, Mrs. T. H. Hubbard, Rufus Hatch, Charles P. Kirkland, Allan McLane, Richard Mortimer, Royal Phelps, W. C. Rhinelander, B. Schlesinger, Alex. T. Stewart, Wm. Niblo, Joseph Samson, Mrs. Wm. L. Tweed, Mrs. D. T. Brown, Miss Ferguson.

1871.
 J. A. Bostwick, John Bloodgood, Miss. L. Peters, Cortlandt Field Bishop, A. J. Peters, Peter C. Tiemann, Thomas Watt, Peter Cooper, Mrs. H. C. Von Post, Miss Newberry, Miss Iselin, H. W. T. Mall, James Pott, Mrs. Sylvanus Reed, Wm. R. Peters, John Peters, Andrew Beters.

1872.
 Albert G. Thorp, Jr., Ida P. Prisson, Isaac P. Martin, Edward Cooper, A. S. Hewitt, Woodbury G. Langdon, Miss. C. E. Wolbert, Mrs. S. J. Zabriskie, Charles Place, James F. De Peyster, Madame C. Moars, A. Bierstadt, Miss. L. Wolfe.

1873.
 Franklin Edson, Wm. B. Clerke, Mrs. Colford Jones, E. Wells Sackett, A Friend at Scarborough, Geo. W. Carleton, Miss Julia Watt, Mrs. Hannah Slade, J. Van Schaick, Mrs. John Pettigrew, Henry H. Thorp, John Benjamin, John Carey, Jr., Mrs. Jno. Carey, Jr., Mrs. F. Goodridge, Miss M. G. Pinckney, Edward Clark, Mrs. D. F. Tiemann, Miss Penfold, Rev. W. D. Walker, Mrs. Edward Cooper, Rev. C. T. Ward.

FREE BEDS SUPPORTED.

By Salisbury Endowment .... *Henry Stracke.*
" Little Alice   "   .... *Susan Ross.*

BY PAYMENTS OF $138 FOR ONE YEAR.

By E. Wells Sackett......................... *Ernest Ratzman.*
" Charles Place........................... *Edwin Holmes.*
" Wm. M. Kingsland...................... *Frank Wells.*
" Wm. B. Clerke......... .... *Michael Nelson.*
" H. C. Von Post............................... *John Otto.*
" John Benjamin........................... *Annie Wootten.*
" John Carey, Jr........................... *Samuel Holmes.*
" Mrs. John Carey, Jr...................... *Fannie Holmes.*
" Mr. and Mrs. John Carey, Jr...... .... *James Holmes.*
" Geo. W. Carleton .... *Margaret Ross.*
" Thomas Watt......................... *Fredk. Sarrington.*
" Grace Church,   I............................ *Louis Ede.*
"   "   II............. .... *Charles Ede.*
"   "   III....................... *Robert Guion.*
"   "   IV......................... *Ed. Guion.*
" St. Michael's Church........................ *Katy Adkins.*
" St. Peter's, Morristown................... *Sarah Walton.*
" Wm. A. Smith............................ *Jane Clifford.*
" Wm. J. Beebe............................ *Annie Smith.*
" Children of Thos. Watt...... .... *Pauline Baker.*
" Peter C. Tiemann....................... *Elizabeth McEwen.*
" Mrs. Colford Jones ... . *Horace Ede.*
" Woodbury G. Langdon................. *Walter Sarrington.*
" William H. Fogg............................ *Oscar Stracke.*
" Mrs. Frederick Goodridge .... *Ida Holmes.*
" Franklin Edson........................ *Frances Weaver.*
" Horace Williams . ... *Leonard Butler.*

LADIES' ASSOCIATION.

By Mrs. Hannah Slade,   I......... . ... *Lily Barker.*
" Mrs. John Pettigrew,   II.................. *Emma Stracke.*

By Miss Kate Bell,   III.....................Annie Stuart.
                     IV.....................Caroline Otto.
                     V......................Jennie Jacobus.
                     VI.....................Clara Ratzman.
                     VII....................Minnie Merritt.
                     VIII...................Fanny Caveron.
                     IX.....................Margaret O'Rourke.
                     X......................Alexander Smith.
                     XI.....................John Reib.
                     XII....................Sydney Butler.
                     XIII...................Ellen Christy.

---:o:---

CHILDREN CLOTHED.

By Miss Cooper..................................Jennie Smith.
" Mrs. Schwab..................................Harry Merritt.
" Miss Cammann................................Olive Du Bois.

DONATIONS.

May, 1872.

T. W. Gale....................................	$10 00
L. R. Greene..................................	25 00
Mrs. F. H. Delano.............................	20 00
F. Wigand & Co................................	10 00
Mrs. N. Sands.................................	5 00
Peter Marié...................................	10 00
Harding, Colby & Co...........................	10 00
Little Minnie W., on her fifth birthday, pennies saved during the year for the "poor little girls,"	2 80
J. A. Marshall................................	5 00
Coleman House.................................	5 00
Wheeler & Wilson Manufacturing Co.............	20 00
Mrs. Jno. Carey, support of child six months..	69 00
For the Lambs.................................	2 00
A. V. Blake...................................	5 00
E. L. Ludlow..................................	10 00

K., D. & Co.	$5 00
Jas. A. Alexander	20 00
Jas. F. Cox	25 00
St. Ann's Church, N. Y., per Rev. Dr. Gallaudet,	4 00
Cash, H. M.	25 00
Mrs. O. B. Potter	25 00
Cash	5 00
Jacob Hays, 2d	15 00
Mrs. J. W. Thorne	5 00
Jno. Carey, Jr., support of child for six months,	69 00
Miss A. M. Barnes	10 00
Alexander Major	10 00
Cash	1 00
Mrs. Richard Hoffmann	2 00
John Galller	5 00
Jno. A. Robinson	20 00
Jno. Benjamin, per Rev. S. Cook, monthly subscription for support of child	11 50
Mrs. J. L. Sutherland	5 00
S. D. Tompkins	20 00
S. S. St. Michael's Church, N. Y., Class A	3 56
Class B	1 04
Class E	1 41
Class F	75
Class H	1 29
Class I	1 78
Class J	2 00
Class O	1 39
Class P	3 00
Class S	97
Class T	2 13
Class V	2 25
Mrs. H. D. Wyman	50 00
Mrs. Archibald Watt	100 00
Mrs. Chas. Wall	5 00
Mrs. George Bell	5 00
Mrs. J. C. Hamilton	5 00
Miss M. G. Hamilton	3 00
Miss Cornelia Davis	5 00

Misses Renshaw	$10 00
Mrs. C. W. Hall	5 00
Mrs. E. E. Anderson	5 00
Master Horace Porter	5 00
A Friend	10 00
Miss Charlotte Smith	5 00
J. H. V. C	10 00
The Misses Ripley	5 00
Miss M. E. Hornor, through Sister Ellen	10 00
Miss E. H. Chew	5 00
Mrs. E. A. Bull	5 00
T. B. Bleecker, Jr	2 00
Mrs. S. N. Pike	5 00
Mrs. C. Munzinger	5 00
Frank E. Kernochan	5 00
C. D. Dickey	20 00
Mrs. H. H. Little	1 00
Chas. Smith	5 00
Mrs. B. F. Corlies	5 00
Rev. S. G. Hitchcock	2 00
Dennistoun & Co	25 00
Wilson G. Hunt	5 00
H. D. Sedgwick	5 00
W. G. Creamer	5 00
Geo. A. Clark	5 00
Mrs. W. F. Mott	5 00
Helen R. Perkins	10 00
H. A. Wyckoff	20 00

June.

L. M. Clark	5 00
Geo. K. Sistare	5 00
Geo. Carlisle	5 00
O. M. Bogart	5 00
Mrs. S. Tousey	5 00
Mrs. Chas. S. Spencer	20 00
Mrs. Geo. H. Purser	10 00
R. W. Forbes	5 00
G. G. Howland	10 00
Alice S. Luka	3 00

A. S. Hewitt	$100	00
Edward Cooper	100	00
Mr. and Mrs. John Townshend	10	00
Lewis Curtis	10	00
Mrs. W. T. Hicks	5	00
Fair of Ladies Association	163	91
Mrs. F. Goodridge, support of a child for six months	69	00
Larry Timpson's Savings Bank	2	00
Mrs. W. J. Deebe, for Minnie	48	00
Chas. E. Carryll	5	00
P. McMartin	10	00
Mrs. G. G. Williams	5	00
A. Limbert	5	00
Mrs. W. A. Tillinghast	5	00
S. S. Church of the Mediator, South Yonkers	50	00

July.

H. C. Von Post, support of a child for one year	138	00
Mrs. D. for mending shoes	2	25
Children's Missionary Box, Portchester	2	00
Mrs. R. H. Foote	5	00
Mrs. Chas. A. Jackson	5	00
Mrs. F. L. Vulte	10	00
R. H. Macy	5	00
J. O. Bartholimew	5	00
Miss S. Hill	1	00
G. Schreiber	1	00
M. D.	1	00
Stanton Blake	10	00
P. C. Tiemann, support of a child for one year	138	00
Hon. Thos. W. Clerke	10	00
Mrs. Eliza A. Davis	1	00
Wm. Alex. Smith, support of a child for one year	138	00
W. J. Deebe, support of a child for one year	138	00
Horace Williams	50	00
Rev. C. E. Phelps	10	00
S. S. Zion Church, Wappinger's Falls, through Mrs. A. Mesier	20	00
Cash	1	00

W. H. Fogg, support of a child for one year	$138 00
Franklin Edson, support of a child for one year	138 00
Wm. B. Clerke, support of a child for one year	138 00
J. I. Adams	5 00
E. P. Wheeler	15 00
Chas. Kneeland	25 00
S. J. Fatman	1 00
J. F	1 00
P. W. G	1 00
H. B. & Bros	1 00
Mrs. L. F. Auger	1 00
Jno. Taylor's Son	1 00
S. H. Edgar	1 00
No Name	1 00
Through Rev. Samuel Cooke	1 00
Stewart Brown	100 00
L. Lincoln	1 00
Mrs. F. W. Lockwood	1 00
Wm. Heath	5 00
W. A. Haines	10 00

Legion Co. 5—One Dollar Each.

Henrietta M. Brierly, A. J. Brierly, Mrs. C. D. Etting, Mrs. Moloney, Mrs. E. Lange, M. T. Graham, Miss. C. A. Thompson, Mrs. Henry Wood, Mrs. J. Brower, Bertha Schedler, W. L. Sanford, John Mowatt, Harry Grimm, Francis Pounden	14 00

August.

Mrs. Colford Jones, support of a child during one year	138 00
Jno. Benjamin, support of a child during two months	23 00
J. B. O	50 00
Mr. and Mrs. John Carey, Jr., support of a child during six months	69 00
J. Schwab	50 00
F. C. Withers	25 00
Peter Cooper	50 00
W. W. Mall	25 00

Ladies of St. Peter's Church, Morristown, New Jersey...	$25 00
Hon. Wm. L. Learned...	25 00
E. Wells Sackett, support of a child during one year...	138 00
Adam Norrie...	75 00

September.

Cash...	2 00
A Friend at Scarborough, through W. M. Kingsland...	100 00
Mrs. M. A. Reeder...	5 00
Mrs. James Brooks...	5 00
J. H. Riker...	5 00
Rutten & Bonn...	20 00

October.

Mrs. N. Rhinelander...	5 00
Cash...	2 00
Thomas Holland...	10 00
O. P. Dorman...	5 00
Cash...	2 00
J. H. Purdy...	5 00
Jas. S. Cox...	10 00
J. L. Brownell...	5 00
Thos. McMullen...	5 00
C. G. Smull & Co...	10 00
Mrs. J. E. Wylie...	5 00
C. J. Lawrence...	10 00
J. H. McKim...	25 00
C. H. Mallory & Co...	10 00
W. C. Prime...	15 00
Mrs. J. P. Townsend...	10 00
W H. Lothrop...	5 00
A. Rusch & Co...	10 00
S. B. Collins...	5 00
M. Ulshoeffer...	5 00
A. O. Headly...	10 00
C. F. A. Hinrichs...	5 00
Douglas Robinson...	10 00
Cash...	5 00

Thurlow Weed	$10 00
Charles G. Franklyn	25 00
Floyd Smith	5 00
Cash	5 00
Mrs. Geo. W. Powers	10 00
C. Meyer	10 00
J. W. C. Leveridge	10 00
Mrs. W. B. Ireland	5 00
Arthur J. Peabody	10 00
Mrs. G. W. Burnham	5 00
W. Wilson & Co.	10 00
Miss Armide Smith	5 00
R. H. Arkenbergh	5 00
O. Ottendorfer	10 00
Mrs. C. L. Crary	5 00
Mrs. J. S. W. Parkin	3 00
H. G. Stebbins	10 00
Mrs. W. P. Talboys	5 00
E. C. Richards	10 00
M. G. Baldwin	10 00
Cash	5 00
John Sneden	20 00
Griswold Gray	20 00
L. L. W.	1 00
Miss Sallie K. Miller	1 00
Mrs. A. E. Guthrie	2 00
Rev. S. Cox, D. D.	1 25
St. Michael's Church, N. Y.	11 52
Mrs. W. L. Jenkins	10 00
Geo. W. Carleton, support of a child during one year	138 00
Mrs. Gerry, annual subscription	5 00
Miss Gerry	5 00
Savings of Louise T. King	3 00
C. M. Congreve	10 00
P. R. Warren	5 00
Mrs. J. P. Schemerhorn	5 00
C. T.	10 00
H. Well	3 00

A. H. S.	$5 00
F. Vilmar	10 00
Wm. Purdy	5 00
Mrs. Cambridge Livingston	10 00
Ida May Frost	25 00
Jas. Barclay	5 00

November.

Mrs. A. S. Webb	5 00
Mrs. Jas. Walker	5 00
Mrs. E. Robbins	5 00
Mrs. Catharine Wilkins	50 00
Wm. M. Fleiss	10 00
Cash	10 00
J. A. Hearn	5 00
Mrs. E. H. Nichols	5 00
Mrs. A. Haywood	5 00
George Brooks	5 00
Mrs. A. S. Scholle	5 00
J. A. Bostwick	100 00
S. H. Edgar, Treasurer S. R. R. Co.	25 00
St. Michael's Church, N. Y.	2 00
Miss Sherrill	1 00
Mrs. John J. Brandegee	5 00
St. Thomas' Church	45 00
Miss Chittenden, four months support of Emily Chapman	46 00
S. S. Zion Church, Wappinger's Falls, through Mrs. Mesier	33 00
Townsend & Davis	7 10
Mrs. D. H. Turner	10 00
M. M. Hendricks	10 00
J. S. Cushman	5 00
Wm. R. Stewart	10 00
Mrs. John Townshend	5 00
Miss May Townshend	1 00
J. I. S.	5 00
Wm. W. Thompson	10 00
Jno. E. Parsons	10 00
Peter Gilsey	10 00

A. M. Ferris	$5 00
Jas. Rufus Smith	10 00
John Downey	5 00
Mrs. C. C. Baldwin, annual subscription	10 00
Mrs. Zeno Secor	10 00
Peter Naylor	5 00
Andrew Gilsey	5 00
Mrs. Mary Mason Jones	10 00
W. H. Caswell	10 00
H. A. Burr	10 00
W. Mackay, 20 w. 31	10 00
W. Mackay, 27 w. 19	10 00
Miss Isabella Lawrence	10 00
Mrs. J. Lawrence	5 00
Mrs. M. Hartley	10 00
Mrs. J. W. Drexel	10 00
Mrs. F. U. Johnston	5 00
Chas. E. Milnor, annual subscription	10 00
Dr. Jas. R. Wood	10 00
Jno. Benjamin, three months' support of a child,	34 50
Mrs. Oswald Ottendorfer, through Mrs. R. F. Ware	25 00
Mrs. P. R. Bonnett	5 00
Adrian Iselin	50 00
Mrs. W. G. Ward	5 00
Chas. Morgan	10 00
Mrs. Lewis C. Jones	5 00
Mrs. Frank Work	10 00
Mrs. H. S. Leavitt	10 00
Sanford Cobb	5 00
J. F. Daly	5 00
Dolly's Fair, by children of Mr. Thos. Watt	150 00
Mrs. Richard Vose, annual subscription	5 00
Board of Chas. Haubeil, through Miss Susan O. Hoffman	5 00
Mrs. Abraham Voorhees, annual subscription	5 00
Cash	40 00
Miss E. M. Baldwin	5 00
E. Renshaw Jones	25 00

Geo. Wm. Wright	$5 00
W. B. Bend	10 00
Theodore M. Davis	25 00
Cash	1 00
Cash	5 00
Rutson Maury	5 00
Mrs. J. S. Low	5 00
J. G. McDonald	10 00
John Pondir	20 00
Mrs. H. H. Garner	5 00
I. C	10 00
F. M. Jones	10 00
Park & Tilford	25 00
Cash	5 00

December.

Mrs. H. A. Hurlbut	5 00
Mr. & Mrs. J. H. Livingston	10 00
F. Henriques	10 00
F. S. Winston	25 00
Mrs. J. H. V. Arnold	10 00
Thomas Owen	5 00
Mrs. John Martin, Jr	7 00
Alfred Youngs	10 00
Mrs. A. Boody	5 00
B. Johnson & Sons	5 00
Robt. V. McKim	25 00
F. Sturges	10 00
Mrs. Jno. Carey, Jr., support of Samuel Holmes, 6 months	69 00
Jno. Carey, Jr., support of Fanny Holmes 6 mos.	69 00
Mr. & Mrs. Jno. Carey, Jr., support of Jane Holmes 6 months	69 00
Mrs. Jas. W. Underhill, annual subscription	10 00
Arnold, Constable & Co., through Mrs. D. F. Tiemann	10 00
Mrs. B. L. Solomon	5 00
Mrs. Helen Stuyvesant	10 00
F. R. Lee	5 00
Mrs. M. M. Quackenboss	10 00

D. W. B.	$20 00
Miss F.	25 00
Messrs. F.	25 00
E. H. Schermerhorn	10 00
Wm. Remsen	5 00
F. G. Churchill	5 00
R. T. W.	10 00
W. R. Powell	5 00
Mrs. C. F. Chickering	5 00
Mr. & Mrs. J. H. Boynton	20 00
Emily V. Clark	50 00
M. A. Grosvenor	5 00
Mrs. W. S. Gurnee	10 00
Martin E. Greene	10 00
Mrs. R. R. Crosby	5 00
J. F. D. Lanier	5 00
J. K. Jones	10 00
Chas. Butler	10 00
Ed. F. Brown	5 00
Miss Susan O. Hoffman, to board of Chas. Haubeil,	5 00
Coleman E. Kissam	5 00
Jas. H. Titus	10 00
Mr. & Mrs. Peter Morris	10 00
Cash	2 00
W. L. Cogswell	10 00
A. P. Man	10 00
Cash	10 00
A. H. M.	5 00
Mrs. Phœnix	5 00
Mrs. W. T. Garner	10 00
S. M. Barclay	10 00
J. L. Barclay	10 00
C. T. Gostenhofer	50 00
Wm. Heath	5 00
Dan'l T. Hoag	5 00
Robt. Seaman	10 00
Madame Mears, through Mrs. R. F. Ware, concert for Infirmary	539 25
D. A. W.	10 00

Mrs. S. C. Herring	$10	00
C. F. Sanford	50	00
Mrs. Jas. Scott	5	00
R. S. Clark	25	00
Cash	25	00
Mrs. T. Dwight	25	00
J. A. Roosevelt	25	00
"The Peter Cooper Golden Wedding Fund," for shoes	50	00
Mrs. E. Smith	5	00
Richardson, Boynton & Co	25	00
Mrs. Smith	5	00
Walter Langdon	10	00
D. V. Floyd	5	00
J. Thorne	10	00
Joseph Hall	5	00
Mrs. E. H. Owen	5	00
Cash, A. H., Jr	5	00
J. L. Riker	50	00
"St. George's" Church, Astoria	60	62
Mrs. Henry Meigs, subscription for 1873	5	00
Mrs. T. T. Sturges, Jr	5	00
Stephen Johnson	10	00
Messrs. Van Buren	15	00
Mrs. Wm. Alsop	5	00
Wm. M. Evarts	10	00
Miss Florence Melville	1	00
Cash	2	00
Mrs. P. S. Halsted	5	00
A. V. R	5	00
H. Hudson Holly	5	00
Mrs. J. V. V. W	5	00
Millie E. Wright, 6½ years old, deceased, per J. D. Wright	25	00
Peter Cooper	100	00
J. Montgomery Hare	10	00
Mrs. Chas. Place, through Mrs. Sackett, support of Child	38	00
Miss A. J. Garner	10	00

Horace Williams, Clinton, Iowa	$100 00
Miss M. G. Pinkney	100 00
Mrs. J. G. Stacey	4 00
Frederic De Peyster	25 00
Miss M. W. Stacey	4 00
Geo. A. Clark & Co	15 00
A member of St. Ann's Church, N. Y., through Rev. Dr. Gallaudet	5 00
Christmas offering, S. S. Ch. Holy Apostles, Rev. J. P. Lundy, rector	31 40
Christmas offering, S. S. Ch. St. Mary's, Manhattanville, through Rev. C. C. Adams	15 00
Christmas offering, S. S. St. Michael's Church, N. Y., through Rev. T. M. Peters, Class A	4 28
Class B	1 50
Class H	2 24
Class S	1 94
Class J	2 20
Class O	1 91
Class V	1 52
Infant Class St. James S. S., New London, Conn., through Rev. M. Duff, asst. rector	3 00
Mrs. Ed. Kearney, annual subscription	10 00
Thos. S. Read, annual subscription	20 00
Mrs. Theodore Timpson	5 00
Mrs. Jno. A. D. Robinson	5 00
Miss Ellie B. Robinson	5 00
Mrs. Haslett McKim	5 00
Mrs. Geo. Richmond	2 00
J. Q. of Liverpool, through Mrs. Ed. Kearney	10 00

January, 1873.

Miss Emily Jones, subscription for 1873	50 00
James Maurice	20 00
Mrs. K. P. Billings	5 00
Mrs. W. B. Bishop	5 00
E. B. Van Winkle	5 00
Mrs. A. M. Minturn	20 00
J. S. Abecusis	10 00
Wm. Betts	10 00

Mrs. C. A. Peabody............................	$10 00
Sale of Picture, per Rev. H. E. Montgomery.....	125 00
St. Michael's S. S., N. Y., Class P..............	2 96
Mrs. E. Martheus.............................	5 00
H. A. H......................................	2 00
Mrs. Seely Brown.............................	5 00
Cyrus Loutrel Sniffin...........................	5 00
Cyrus H. Loutrel..............................	5 00
Miss Ida A. Wesley...........................	25 00
Mrs. Cash....................................	5 00
Mrs. F. Browning.............................	5 00
Mrs. R. E. Livingston..........................	10 00
Mrs. A. Arnold...............................	10 00
Cash...	10 00
E. Delafield, M. D............................	5 00
M. L. Potter..................................	25 00
Mrs. Jane Mary Thorn.........................	10 00
Mrs. J. W. Southack..........................	5 00
Cash...	50 00
Mrs. G. B. McClellan..........................	10 00
Mrs. W. H. Swift.............................	5 00
Edward Matthews.............................	50 00
Arthur Armory................................	10 00
Edward A. Boyd..............................	10 00
W. H. Scott...................................	10 00
J. B. Alexander...............................	25 00
Jas. W. Alsop.................................	25 00
G. W. B......................................	50 00
Stamford Manufacturing Co.....................	10 00
S. K. Satterlee................................	5 00
J. J. Althaus..................................	5 00
Mrs. Cash....................................	5 00
Singer Manufacturing Co.......................	20 00
William C. White.............................	5 00
C. F. Alvord..................................	5 00
Mrs. J. C. Gray...............................	10 00
Mrs. C. F. Alvord.............................	5 00
George Bell...................................	10 00
John T. Daly..................................	20 00

J. K. Pell	$5 00
Edward Baldwin	5 00
Ole B. Swachs	10 00
R. S. Ely	10 00
Mrs. R. L. Cutting, Jr	10 00
T. A. Vyse, Jr.	25 00
Mrs. J. R. Boyd	5 00
Mrs. Ann Walter, annual subscription	25 00
Master J. R. Walter	5 00
Levi Pawling	5 00
Cash	5 00
C. J. DeWitt	10 00
C. B. Foote	5 00
Mrs. Minturn	25 00
Beatrice Walter	5 00
Mrs. W. A. Smith, annual subscription	5 00
Mrs. Joseph Grafton	50 00
Mrs. Geo. F. Gilman	5 00
Zopher Mills	5 00
W. W. Parkin	10 00
Mrs. C. E. Perkins	5 00
F. P. P.	5 00
Cash	1 00
J. D. Fish	10 00
Mrs. C. L. Perkins	5 00
F. G.	5 00
Mrs. S. J. Egleston	10 00
W. A. Ross	5 00
J. L. Bogart	25 00
Henry Delafield	5 00
Geo. W. McCullum	10 00
Joseph Ogden	5 00
W. S. Abbott	10 00
C. V. D. Ostrander	10 00
S. V. Hoffman	10 00
Kitchen & Co.	50 00
David Stewart	50 00
Mrs. J. Bishop	25 00
Mrs. Rufus F. Andrews	2 00

Mrs. J. A. Munsell	$5 00
H. M. Morris	10 00
Mrs. A. J. Garner	10 00
E. Hendricks	5 00
Mrs. U. Hendricks	5 00
J. Bach	5 00
Jno. W. Underhill	5 00
Oliver W. Barnes	5 00
Mrs. B. P. Howe	10 00
Miss Mary E. McKee	5 00
Thomas H. Falle, through Miss Penfold	100 00
Miss. E. Low, annual subscription	5 00
K. Cotheal, annual subscription	5 00
F. Cotheal, annual subscription	3 00
Hugh Thompson Dickey, Jr., annual subscription	1 00
Miss Helen Beach, annual subscription	3 00
Miss M. S. Jones, annual subscription	5 00
Mrs. J. C. Hull, annual subscription	3 00
Hamilton Webster, annual subscription	5 00
Miss Arnold, annual subscription	10 00
Miss E. L. Holmes, annual subscription	3 00
Mrs. E. Shedden, annual subscription	5 00
Miss M. Sorrill, annual subscription	2 00
Mrs. M. S. Mortimer, annual subscription	3 00
Mrs. D. F. Tiemann, annual subscription	5 00
Miss. A. A. Tiemann, annual subscription	3 00
Miss M. C. Tiemann, annual subscription	5 00
Mrs. L. A. Rodenstein annual subscription	5 00
D. B. Bedell, annual subscription	5 00
Miss Henrietta Cooper	5 00
Mr. Wayte	10 00
Mrs. R. W. Aborn	5 00
M. T. Spaulding, Christmas bag	5 00
Mrs. Rice, Christmas bag	3 00
Mrs. I. W.	3 00
February.	
Mrs. H. H. Bean	1 00
Alms Box	3 00

Mrs. H. E. Sprague	$5 00
Cash	1 00
Mrs. Pierre Lorillard	20 00
Mrs. M. M. Livingston	5 00
Mrs. J. D. Fitch	5 00
Dr. J. D. Fitch	5 00
Mrs. M. A. C. R.	10 00
Mrs. W. E. Chisholm	10 00
Mrs. B. Schlesinger	20 00
Miss M. A. Townsend	10 00
W. C. Schermerhorn	10 00
Edward Clark	100 00
J. A. Hardenbergh	10 00
W. H. Draper, M. D.	10 00
A little boy's silver dollar	1 15
R. M. B.	10 00
C. Van Santvoord	10 00
Cash	5 00
E. A. Quintard	10 00
Chas. Kneeland, through W. A. Smith	50 00
R. J.	2 00
Miss S. O. Hoffmann, toward support of C. Haubeil	5 00
C. T. Reynolds	10 00
Mrs. H. Colt	5 00
Mrs. Richard Alsop	10 00
D. H. Arnold	10 00
Mrs. Chas. Lamson	10 00
Miss Julia A. Low, annual subscription	10 00
N. P. Hosack	5 00
D. H.	20 00
C. De Rham	10 00
Mrs. Benjamin F. Carver	10 00
Miss J. Penfold	25 00
Edmund Penfold	25 00
William H. Penfold	25 00
E. N. Mead, D. D.	5 00
Rev. J. H. Houghton, support of Lilly Dillon	10 00
Mrs. D. R. Lambuorn	1 00

Ladies of St. Peter's Church, Morristown, New Jersey, support of Sarah Walton.............	$25 00
Arthur W. Parsons...........................	10 00
Mrs. R. Woodworth..........................	10 00
Mrs. S. H. Carpenter	5 00
Mrs. U. Cadwell.............................	10 00
T. K. Fraser................................	5 00
Jesse Seligman..............................	10 00
Mrs. Colford Jones..........................	50 00
H. I. B.....................................	25 00
Mrs. Jane Kerr..............................	5 00
Mrs. John Kerr..............................	5 00
Mrs. F. Chandler	5 00
J. A. Benedict..............................	5 00
C. W. S....................................	10 00
Miss H. A. Townsend........................	10 00
H. W. F....................................	5 00
Mrs. C. A. Sherman	5 00
Mrs. W. H. Walter...........................	5 00
Miss M. R. Prime............................	5 00
Cash..	5 00
Mrs. W. F. Beekman.........................	5 00
Mrs. Hugh Auchincloss, annual subscription.....	10 00
Mrs. A. T. Sackett	10 00
Mrs. William K. Thorn	20 00
John J. Cisco...............................	25 00
A. V. H. Stuyvesant.........................	40 00
F. Skiddy...................................	50 00
Miss Lizzie Cornell	5 00
Mrs. A. Cotting..............................	5 00
Cash, F. H. C...............................	20 00

Legion Co. 1—One Dollar Each.

Kitty Johnson, Mrs. Olliffe, Lillie Graham, Anna L. Petit, Minnie Somerville, Geo. P. Stringfield, A. V. Williams, Mrs. Stacey, Miss Stacey, Wm. Bleakley, Arthur Davis, Grace Jackson.........	12 00

March.

Mrs. W. P. Furniss	$5,000 00
Mrs. J. P. Kernochan	50 00
Mrs. G. W. Pell	10 00
Jas. A. Raynor	5 00
Miss Mary McKee, support of Jno. Wilson	5 00
William W. Mali	25 00
Mrs. H. D. Wyman	25 00
Fordham Morris	1 00
Miss Emmett	3 00
Mrs. S. Whitlock	5 00

Subscriptions for 1873, through Mrs. H. C. Von Post:

Mrs. Dr. Metcalfe	10 00
Mrs. Jas. J. Phelps	10 00
Mrs. Fitzgerald	10 00
Mrs. Von Post	10 00
S. E. W.	10 00
Mrs. A. B. Morrell	5 00
William Whitlock, Jr.	10 00
Mrs. Gustav Schwab	10 00
S. C. Thompson	10 00
Miss Burr	10 00
Mrs. H. Edgar	5 00
Mrs. F. A. Lane	5 00
Mrs. David Dows	25 00
Mrs. S. P. Nash	10 00
E. L. Perry	10 00
Mrs. L. A. Clarkson	5 00
Mrs. Geo. H. Van Nort	5 00
Mrs. P. M. Lydig	5 00
Mrs. C. S. Little	5 00
Mrs. D. M. Fitch	5 00
Mrs. J. L. Englehart, annual subscription	5 00
W. B. Fletcher	10 00
S. S. St. George's Church, Flushing, support of Chas. Haubeil	10 00
Estate of Thomas C. Moore, legacy	965 83
Cash, C. D.	10 00
Mrs. Martha E. Coles	10 00

G. Banyer	$10 00
Miss C. L. R. White	5 00
Miss M. D. Smith	5 00
Mrs. W. A. Dooley	5 00
Mrs. G. A. Morrison	5 00
Mrs. A. Denison	2 00
J. P. Gerard Foster	20 00
Mrs. N. Chandler	5 00
Mrs. J. J. Petit	5 00
C. B. Curtis	5 00
Mrs. Wm. C. Emmett	5 00
Mrs. Wm. B. Dinsmore	5 00
Mrs. T. G. Thomas	5 00
T. M. Wheeler	5 00
Joseph Larocque	25 00
M. Ulshœffer	5 00
E. A. Duycklnck	5 00
Cash	20 00
American Express Co.	25 00
Isaac L. Kip, M. D.	25 00
Mrs. Dunham Jones Crain	5 00
Mrs. Crocker, annual subscription	5 00
Mrs. Rutherford Stuyvesant, annual subscription	5 00
Mrs. Wm. Remsen	5 00
Mrs. A. N. Lawrence, annual subscription	5 00
The Misses Hadden, annual subscriptions	10 00
Mrs. Samuel Ogden, annual subscription	5 00
Mrs. Jno. B. Church, annual subscription	5 00
Mrs. Azel Graham, annual subscription	10 00
Mrs. Jessie G. Kentor, annual subscription	5 00
Mrs. Jno. C. Hamilton, annual subscription	5 00
Mrs. Edwin Post, annual subscription	5 00
Miss A. P. Slade, annual subscription	5 00
Mrs. George Bell, annual subscription	5 00
Mrs. Chas. Wall, annual subscription	5 00
Miss Bell, annual subscription	24 00
Mrs. Ogden Hoffman, annual subscription	5 00
Miss M. C. Hoffman, annual subscription	3 00
Miss V. S. Hoffman, annual subscription	3 00

Mrs. A. M. Kalbfleisch, annual subscription	$5 00
Chas. W. Cooper, annual subscription	25 00
William Cooper, annual subscription	25 00
Mrs. Stephen Williams, annual subscription	1 00
Mrs. W. H. Wisner, annual subscription	10 00
Mrs. S. Lawrence, annual subscription	5 00
Miss E. M. Cotheal, annual subscription	5 00
Mrs. Poillon	10 00
H. Wagner	5 00
J. A. Hoyt	1 00
Mrs. N. Ludlum	25 00
Mrs. Mesier	10 00
Friend, through Mrs. Munro	5 00
Mrs. Hannah Slade, support of a child during one year	138 00
Mrs. E. Charlier	10 00
Mrs. E. Kearney	10 00
Cash	10 00
R. Soutter	20 00
H. J. Boorchell	5 00
Cash, J. H.	5 00
J. Halsted	10 00
Mrs. N. Lawrence	5 00
Cash	5 00
Cash	2 00
E. Ludlow	10 00
R. J. Livingston	25 00
S. C. Williams	10 00
Mrs. Z. Diedrich	5 00
D. W. C. Ward	5 00
Mrs. G. DeForest	5 00
Valentine G. Hall	25 00
Charles H. Mount	10 00
Mrs. S. W. Quincey	3 00
Mrs. Walter Shriver	10 00
Mrs. J. Q. A.	5 00
B. Aymar	10 00
Wm. Latimer	20 00
Cash, Mrs. H. O. J.	5 00

Cash, W. B.	$5 00
S. T. Skidmore	5 00
Mrs. H. G. Stevens	25 00
J. H. Beekman	5 00
H. W. Nieman	5 00
Jas. Emott	10 00
J. A. Garland	10 00
M. & H. Clarkson	25 00
Wm. C. Rhinelander	50 00
C. Denison	10 00
Fanny J. Searles	5 00
Jas. Moir	5 00
George Chesterman	25 00
Mr. and Mrs. D. LeRoy	10 00
Mrs. J. G. Lightbody	10 00
Mrs. A. Breese	5 00
J. C. Furman	5 00
Mrs. F. T. Dufais	10 00
Harry Holbrook	5 00
F. C. Havemeyer	10 00
J. M	5 00
Mrs. E. Keteltas	10 00
E. S. J., 16 East 43d St.	10 00
J. B. Slawson	10 00
W. L. Chamberlain	10 00
Jas. Stokes	10 00
Richard Irvin	25 00
J. O. Ward	1 00
S. C. Evans	5 00
Cash, W. M.	6 00
Mrs. George Keyes	5 00
Mrs. A. Vanderpoel	50 00
Mrs. B. Williams	5 00
Miss Alice Furman	5 00
D. G. Williams	1 00

April.

Miss Mary McKee, support of Jno. Wilson	5 00
A. Goodrich Fay	20 00
Miss M. E. Lockwood	5 00

J. W. Dominick	$5 00
W. W. Kip	10 00
W. N. Beach	5 00
H. C. Fahnestock	50 00
J. T. Harris	5 00
Miss H. Swords	3 00
W. A. Camp	5 00
Mrs. W. H. Smith	5 00
J. Van Schaick	100 00
C. H. Van Brunt	25 00
Miss. H. D. Fellows	5 00
Cash	10 00
Mrs. F. H. Delano	10 00
E. P. Wheeler	20 00
Floyd Smith	5 00
H. D. Sedgwick	5 00
Mrs. C. L. Spencer	100 00
St. George's Church, Astoria	45 63
D. G. Watt	10 00
S. C. W	5 00
Mrs. Jno. H. Hall	25 00
Miss Hattie T. Bryce	5 00
Gilman S. Moulton	10 00
W. T. Lusk	10 00
C. W. Sandford	5 00
Cornelius Bogert	25 00
Madeline Walter Bogert	5 00
Mrs. G. P. Quackenboss	3 00
Margaret G. Corlies	5 00
Miss McCurdy	10 00
Jno. Benjamin, support of a child during five months	57 50
Calvary Church, from the Easter offering	100 00
Calvary Church, Sunday School	94 80
St. John's Church, Stamford, through Rev. Wm. Tatlock, Rector	40 17
Mrs. C. L. Halsted	5 00
E. Livingston	20 00
United States Express Company	25 00

G. Gordon....................................	$5 00
Cash, F. H....................................	5 00
Cash..	5 00
E. Ellsworth..................................	10 00
H. K. Enos....................................	10 00
Mrs. G. S. Bowdoin...........................	5 00
B. S. Welles..................................	15 00
Mrs. Henry Salisbury..........................	5 00
C. B. Ransom	10 00
Samuel R. Platt...............................	10 00
Alfred Roe....................................	10 00
Miss Nina Haven...............................	10 00
Miss Alice Haven..............................	10 00
Mrs. T. H. Hubbard............................	20 00
Miss S. E. Coleman............................	5 00
M. W. Wall....................................	25 00
J. R. Maurice.................................	50 00
Cash..	5 00
H. C. Ward....................................	5 00
J. Colles.....................................	5 00
Mrs. J. S. Giles..............................	5 00
C. F. Southmayd...............................	10 00
Mrs. W. G. Ray................................	5 00
Mrs. Cash.....................................	3 00
Thomas Barron.................................	25 00
All Angels' Church, N. Y., Easter offering, through R. M. Hayden................................	5 00
Christ Church, Watertown, Conn., Easter offering, through Rev. W. H. Lewis.....................	28 77
S. S. Christ Church, Lonsdale, R. I., Easter offering, through Rev. C. S. Stevenson, Rector..	33 76
St. James Church, New London, Conn., Easter offering of Infant class, through Rev. R. M. Duff, Assistant Rector.............................	2 00
Miss Brinckerhoff.............................	10 00
Jas. F. De Peyster............................	10 00
Mrs. D. B. Allen, annual subscription.........	10 00
Mrs. J. S. Williams, annual subscription......	5 00
Mrs. Sylvanus Reid, annual subscription........	5 00

Mrs. Edwin Stoughton, annual subscription....	$5 00
Mrs. Wm. P. Dixon, annual subscription.......	10 00
F. T. Whiting, annual subscription..	5 00
Wm. P. Lee, annual subscription..	5 00
Jno. Robinson, annual subscription.............	20 00
Miss Catharine Tracy, annual subscription......	5 00
Miss C. E. Boardman, annual subscription......	5 00
Miss M. E. Horner, annual subscription.........	10 00
Jno. Moulton, annual subscription.............	10 00
Mrs. Jno. Pettigrew, support of a child during one year..	138 00
Miss A. A. Tiemann	4 00
Mrs. G. Gurnet...............................	1 00
Montgomery H. Throop	1 00
A. G. Thorp, Jr., proceeds of fair to make Henry H. Thorp a Life Member.....................	130 00
J. B. Varnum................................	2 00
Miss Ida Whittingham.........................	5 00
C. S. Weyman......	5 00
Jas. Baker...................................	5 00
J. C. Chardavoyne............................	5 00
Mrs. W. Richards.............................	5 00
Mrs. W. C. Arthur............................	5 00
Mrs. Thos. J. Hoyt...........................	10 00
W. T. Ryerson...............................	25 00
Mrs. Wm. Campbell...........................	2 00
Mrs. H. Dexter...............................	5 00
Mrs. F. Lockwood............................	5 00
Mrs. P. R. Kearney...........................	5 00
W. N. Seymour..............................	5 00
Julius Catlin, Jr...............................	10 00
J. D. Phillips.................................	5 00
Mrs. Philip G. Weaver........................	5 00
Mrs. Walter H. Lewis.........................	10 00
Mrs. Thomas B. Kerr.........................	5 00
Lewis Curtis..................................	5 00
Cash...	1 00
Cash...	1 00
A. B. Stockwell...............................	10 00

Mrs. C. Braker, Jr.	$5 00
J. A. Cisco	5 00
George H. Reay	10 00
R. A. Brick	25 00
Mrs. R. T. Auchmuty	25 00
Mrs. H. Barclay	5 00
Alms Box	1 50
Lenten Savings of six little girls, St. James' Class, in St. Chrysostom's S. S.	1 73
Mrs. F. Goodridge, support of a child six months.	69 00
Miss Mary McKee, support of Jno. Wilson	5 00

DONATIONS IN CLOTHING, Etc.

May, 1872.

10 Sundowns, Mrs. Edward R. Bell. Rocking Chair, Mrs. T. M. Peters. Large Parcel of Clothing, Mrs. Burgoyne. Plants and Seeds, Gerald Howatt, Mrs. D. F. Tiemann, Miss A. Tiemann. Barrel of Crockery, Mr. D. B. Bedell, through Mrs. Tiemann. Making and Trimming of 50 Caps, L. J. Phillips & Co., through Mrs. R. F. Ware. Parcel of clothing, Mrs. R. F. Ware; 6 Suits Linen Clothes for Boys, Clinton L. Wheeler. Toys for three Cottages and a Parcel of Clothing, the Misses Melville. Box of Papers, Books, etc., Mrs. Scott. 3 pairs Knitted Socks, Mrs. Porter. 3 Night-dresses, 8 Dresses, and 24 Garments for the little ones in the Ladies' Association Cottage, the Misses Locke. Parcel of Clothing, Mrs. McKee Swift. Parcel of Linen, Ladies of St. Michael's Church. Parcel of Clothing, Miss Charlotte Draper. Hammock, Mrs. Aborn. Parcel of Clothing, Mrs. A. S. Hewitt. Strawberries for all the children, Mrs. A. S. Hewitt. Ice-cream for all the children, Messrs. D. F. Tiemann, B. H. Field, W. G. Langdon, W. P. Lee, Rev. Dr. Peters. 42 Garments, 6 Patchwork Spreads, made by Robina McKay (2), Vinnie Ostrander, Julia Kelley, Annie, Roundtree (2), Ella Camp, Maria L. Wolff, Ida Doushea (2) Ida Pool (2), Annie Louritry, Sarah Rider (2), Clara Morris, Emma Blauvelt, Lizzie McCall, Dora Armstrong, Bella Gordon, Agnes Maud Doak (2), Fanny Rockenstyne,

Nettie Withers, Josephine Kruse, Estelle McIntyre, Addie Myers, Mary Slater, Rebecca Smith, Ada Marshall, Jane E. Shields, Charlotte Ely, Georgie Roundtree, Josephine Miller, of Bp. Wainwright Memorial Church. Large hanging Maps for the School-room, Cora L. Bull and Friends, and Wm. P. Lee.

ASSISTANCE IN SEWING. Making of 13 Aprons, Mrs. L. A. Rodenstein.

ASSISTANCE IN WRITING. Miss Peters, Luther Pardee.

RECEIVED BY THE LADIES' ASSOCIATION FOR THE SALE AT THE RECEPTION.

Miss Bell, $10; Mrs. DeRuyter, $5; Mrs. Aborn, $10; Miss Cooper, $5; Miss Grace Wildes, $5; Mrs. L. M. Underhill, $5; Mr. Langdon, $5.

DONATIONS IN REFRESHMENTS, FANCY ARTICLES, FLOWERS, ETC.

Mrs. Hume, Mrs. R. Tweed, Mrs. Keator, Mrs. E. E. Anderson, Mrs. Tiemann, Mrs. E. Wells Sackett, Mrs. R. F. Ware, Mr. J. Sprague, Miss Simpson, Mrs. G. B. Draper, Mr. Squeir, Madame C. Meurs, Madamoiselle See, Mrs. W. P. Lee, Miss Holmes, Mrs. Anthon, Miss Kate Chauncey, Mrs. Schlueter Miss McCurdy, Mrs. Whitlock, Mrs. Whiting, Miss H. Swords, Mr. Walter Reid, Mrs. C. E. Whitehead, Miss Ella Dick, Miss Cooper, Miss E. H. Cotheal, Miss Fanny Cotheal, Mrs. L. A. Rodenstein.

June.

2 Wrappers, 10 Dresses, 9 Aprons, 19 Garments, 8 pairs of Stockings, Scrap Book, the Misses Hadden; Candy for the Montgomery boys, Miss Fanny Wiley; Parcel of Clothing, Mrs. Jarvis Slade; Vegetables and Clothing, Mrs. T. M. Peters; Cherries, Mrs. D. F. Tiemann, Mrs. Brown; Basket of Sandwiches, Mr. John Dalley; Parcel of Clothing, Mrs. Drexel; 3 barrels of Potatoes and 72 bowls of Strawberries, Walter S. Duryea.

FRESH AIR FUND.

Miss Pinckney, $10; Louie Lee's savings, $2.50; Rev. S Cox, D. D., $5; A Friend of the Sheltering Arms, $3.05; Mrs. H. D. Wyman, $5; Horace Williams, Clinton, Iowa, $50.

July.
  Ice Cream for all, Miss Elsie Tiemann; Cakes for all, Mrs. D. F. Tiemann; Parcel of Clothing, Mrs. C. C. Baldwin; Basket of Rolls, Box of Cakes, Mr. R. Prior; 25 Aprons, 18 pairs of Stockings, 5 Pocket Handkerchiefs, young ladies of Mrs. Earle's school, Rye.
  ASSISTANCE IN SEWING. Mrs. Herr.

FRESH AIR FUND.

Mrs. Von Post, $20; Mrs. Dr. Metcalfe, $20; Mr. Stewart Brown, $20; Mr. E. P. Wheeler, $10; Mrs. A. C. Burr, $5; A Friend, $5; Mrs. Williamson Bacon, "fresh air for little girls," $5; Mr. Chas. L. Acker, $3; Miss H. M., $2; M. H. H., $1; W. H. H., $1.

August.
  20 quarts of Milk, Mr. John White; barrel of Apples and Pears, box of Tomatoes, box of Beets, Mr. O. B. Potter; 2 barrels of Apples, Rev. C. E. Phelps; Parcel of Clothing (nearly all new), Anonymous; 3 baskets of Peaches, Mr. G. Howatt; 2 barrels of Apples, Mrs. Tiemann.
  ASSISTANCE IN SEWING. Making of 31 Aprons, Ladies of St. Luke's Church, Matteawan.

FRESH AIR FUND.

Gordon Knox Bell.................................$10 00
FOR PIAZZA. Miss Antoinette Tiemann, $15.
FOR VISIT TO CONEY ISLAND. Mr. B. H. Field, $5.

September.
  3 barrels of Apples, Mrs. Tiemann; basket of Apples, Mrs. Peters; 2 baskets Peaches, Mrs. Archibald Watt; 3 barrels of Apples, Mr. John Talmadge; bag of Lemons, Messrs. Acker, Merrall & Condit; 14 pairs Congress Gaiters, Mrs. Thyler; 21 Aprons, Mrs. L. A. Rodenstein; Trip on the "Sylvan Glen" for 120 children, Harlem Steamboat Company, through Mr. E. Wells Sackett.
  FOR THE WOLFE COTTAGE. Through Mrs. Everett, Droplight and Shade, Mrs. Martin Hoffmann; new Centre Table, Mr. James Pettit; 2 Suits Linen Clothes for Boys, Mrs. John Stephens.

FRESH AIR FUND.

Mrs. Wm. Alex. Smith..............................$10 00

October.

2 pairs Stockings and a large roll of Matting, Mrs. D. F. Tiemann; 9 pairs knitted Socks, Mrs. L. A. Rodenstein; 3 barrels Apples, Hiram Paulding, Jr.; Table-cover for the Wolfe Cottage, Miss O. P. Cleveland; 3 dozen Garments and 11 pairs of knitted Cotton Hose, Mrs. W. H. Swift; Overcoat and 3 Suits for Boys, Mrs. D. S. Jackson; 6 Bartholomew's Drawing-books and a parcel of Clothing, Mrs. John H. Stevens; 3 barrels Apples, Mr. O. B. Potter; Carriage of many parcels at various times, saving a large amount of expressage, Messrs. Acker, Merrall & Condit; Tomato Catchup, Mrs. Treharne; parcel of Clothing, Mrs. Willson; 7 pairs Stockings, Miss A. Tiemann; parcel of Clothing, Mrs. T. M. Peters; Water-filter, Mrs. H. C. Von Post; parcel of Clothing, Mrs. Jarvis Slade; 5 Books for prizes, 3 dozen Reward-Cards, Rev. Dr. Peters.

November.

Parcel of Clothing, Mrs. T. M. Peters; 24 pounds Ham, bag of Lemons, Dried Peaches, Messrs. Acker, Merrall & Condit; 6 barrels Apples, Mr. O. B. Potter; quantity of Rolls, Mr. R. Prior; parcel of Clothing, Mrs. Willson; pair of Blankets, Mrs. Treharne; 1 dozen Toilet Towels, Mrs. Tiemann; parcel of Clothing, Mrs. Richard Vose; 12 dozen Merino Shirts, Mr. W. W. Mali; Hood, Miss Cornelia F. Erving; Candy, and 6 pairs knitted Socks, Miss Rudderow; Drop-light, Miss A. Simpson; 4 Chairs for the Cooper Cottage, Mrs. Keator; parcel of Clothing, and 18 new Garments and 8 pairs knitted Socks, a Lady of S. Paul's, East Chester. Table-cover and Droplight, Mrs. A. S. Hewitt; 8 yards of Flannel, and valuable parcel of remnants of Dress-goods, Lord & Taylor; Table for the Girls' Play-room. Mrs. Pettit; 3 Plush Hats for girls, Messrs. Gunther, 502 Broadway, through Mrs. Tiemann; Bagatelle Board, Anonymous; 2 barrels Turnips, Rev. C. E. Phelps.

ASSISTANCE IN SEWING. Making of 6 pairs pantaloons, Miss Rycroft; making of 6 pairs pantaloons, the Misses Sherrill; 5 White Aprons, Miss A. Simpson.

FOR THANKSGIVING.

Basket of Cakes, Mr. R. Prior; 6 Turkeys, barrel of Apples, Mrs. Isaac P. Martin; bag of Oranges, Mrs. R. W. Howes; 100 Mince Pies, Miss Wolfe; bag of Oranges, box of Raisins, Messrs. Acker, Merrall & Condit; Mr. B. H. Field, $5; Mr. R. Sterling, $5; Mr. & Mrs. W. A. Smith, $10; Gordon Knox Bell, $1; Mr. John Warren, $10.

FOR PIAZZA. Mr. B. H. Field, $25.

December.

Barrel of Oranges, Messrs. Acker, Merrall & Condit; Grapes and Figs, Anonymous; Turkey, Mrs. W. J. Beebe; barrel of Apples, Mr. Charles Borst; barrel of Apples, Mrs. Andrew Bleakley; parcel of Crockery, Mr. D. B. Bedell; Toys for Christmas Tree, Miss Brierly; 2 Hams, 2 bags of Hominy, and a barrel of Apples, Mr. W. S. Corwin, through Mrs. Tiemann; 6 dressed Dolls and Toys for twenty-eight children, Miss Kitty Everdell and Brother; Ham, Mrs. Einstein; half barrel of Apples, half barrel of Sugar, Mrs. Frost; Candy, Mrs. Glover; 14 Flannel Skirts, Miss Hoffman; barrel of Apples, Mr. N. P. Hosack; 2 loads of Evergreens, Mrs. D. S. Jackson; Decorations for the Tree, Miss Keator; 3 large boxes of Vegetables, Mrs. Keator; Turkey, Sausages and Oranges, Mr. R. V. McKim; 2 Turkeys, 4 Chickens, Mrs. R. MacDonald; Six yards of Flannel and a pair of Blankets, Mrs. S. P. Nash; Boots and Flannel for the Ede boys, through Mrs. Vogel; barrel of Apples, Mrs. E. H. O; Christmas Tree, Mrs. T. M. Peters; pair of Stockings, Mrs. Porter; bag of Nuts, Mrs. Thos. J. Powers; load of Greens, Dr. L. A. Rodenstein; load of Greens, St. Michael's Church; 150 cornets of Candy, Miss Ann White Stuyvesant; 6 pairs Scissors, Miss S.; 2 dozen dressed Dolls, and 3 dozen other Toys for the tree, the Misses Stephens; White Aprons, Candles, and Decorations for the Tree, Miss A. Simpson; Boy's Overcoat, Mrs. Lewis A. Sayre; Lamb, Mr. Andrew Smith; pair of Stockings, Miss A. Tiemann; quantity of Nuts and Droplight, Mrs. D. F. Tiemann; box of Clothing, Ornaments and Toys, Mrs. P. C. Tiemann; 6 Dressed Dolls, the Misses Tiemann; 4 pairs Stockings, Mrs. D. H. Turner; barrel of Apples and Oranges,

Mr. Williamson, through Mrs. J. W. Munro; barrel of Sugar, 100 pounds Buckwheat, quarter of Beef, barrel of Flour, 4 Geese, 8 Turkeys, Mr. E. K. Willard; 50 Mince Pies, Miss Wolfe; large parcel of new Books, Mr. F. S. Winston; Toys and Clothing, Dr. Zacharie.

Through Mrs. Ware: 10 pairs Socks, 2 Sacks, Messrs. Vanderlip & Taylor; large Iced Cake and a bag of Mottoes, Mr. Barmor; 8 Caps for Boys, Mr. J. R. Terry; 4 Muffs and Boas, Messrs. L. J. Phillips & Co.; 140 Toy Books, Mr. S. W. Johnston; 10 pair Stockings, half dozen Handkerchief, Le Bouteller Bros.; pair of Blankets, Mrs. Austin Flint.

ASSISTANCE IN SEWING. Making of six pair Pantaloons, Miss Rycroft; making of 85 Aprons, etc., Ladies' Society of St. James' Church, Gt. Barrington, Mass.

——:o:——

CHRISTMAS BAGS.

PROVISIONS, 248 BAGS.

Anonymous, 16 bags; Mrs. C. C. Adams, Mrs. C. F. Alvord, Mrs. E. E. Anderson, Mrs. W. C. Arthur, Mrs. Andrew Bleakley, Mrs. Birdsall, Mrs. A. Boody (2 bags), Mrs. H. J. Barbey, Mrs. Wm. Barton, Mrs. P. R. Bonnet, (3 bags), Mrs. John Brower, Mrs. Williamson Bacon, Mrs. W. B. Clarkson, Mrs. R. L. Cutting, Mrs. Charles Cole, Mrs. N. Chandler, Mrs. A. A. Cleveland, Mrs. Colden, Mrs. H. Cutting, Mrs. John DeRuyter, Mrs. S. Delamater, Mrs. Delano, Mrs. John A. Dix, Mrs. E. Einstein (2 bags), Mrs. H. Everdell, Mrs. E. D. Freeborn, Mrs. D. W. Fitch, Mrs. B. H. Field, Mrs. Furness, Mrs. Wm. B. Fletcher, Mrs. Fosdick, Mrs. George F. Gilman, Mrs. R. Hatch, Mrs. R. Hoffmann, Mrs. Henry S. Hoyt (2 bags), Mrs. W. B. Hoffmann, Mrs. E. S. Higgins, Mrs. W. W. Huntington (2 bags), Mrs. Hinton, Mrs. F. Hendricks, Mrs. Fanny Hitchcock, Mrs. Lewis Johnston, Mrs. Johnston, Mrs. Geo. Jones, Mrs. O. H. Jones, Mrs. C. A. Jones, Mrs. Colford Jones, Mrs. J. P. Kernochan, (4 bags), Mrs. Keator, (3 bags), Mrs. C. B. Lockwood, Mrs. C. S. Little, Mrs. C. Myers, Mrs. R. McDonald (2 bags), Mrs. John T. Metcalfe (4

bags), Mrs. J. W. Munro, Mrs. Mears, (2 bags), Mrs. H.
McKenna, Mrs. Jacob W. Miller, Mrs. Henry W. Miller, Mrs.
T. M. Peters, Mrs. Piotrowsky, Mrs. S. R. Platt, Mrs. Charles
P. Palmer, Mrs. J. Pettigrew, Mrs. C. A. Peabody, Mrs.
Quackenbos, Mrs. Harry Rider, Mrs. W. G. A. Robbins, Mrs.
Gustav Schwab (4 bags), Mrs. N. Sands, Mrs. W. G. Ray
Schieffelln, Mrs. Sistare, Mrs. Shedden, Mrs. R. Stuyvesant,
Mrs. Wm. Alex. Smith, Mrs. E. W. Sackett, Mrs. Stephens,
Mrs. Richard Vose, Mrs. J. Walker, Mrs. D. G. Yuengling (2
bags). Miss F. Cutheal, Miss M. A. Cooper, Miss Glover, Miss
Marion Hall, Miss Mary Hitchcock, Miss Lizzie Holmes (2
bags), Miss Jenkins, Miss E. C. Jay, Miss Mary W. Knox, Miss
M. E. Lockwood (2 bags), Miss Lynch, Miss L. E. Morgan,
Miss Sarah McGunigle, Miss Olcott, Miss Mary Pondir, Miss
Pell, Miss M. G. Pinckney, Miss Nelly Ryerson, Miss A. Simpson, Miss May Townshend (2 bags), Miss Wilkes, Miss Sallie
Whiting, the Misses Furniss (2 bags). Mr. J. W. Alsop, Mr.
Samuel Auchmuty, Mr. Hermann Bachran, Mr. Baldwin, Mr.
W. B. Bishop, Mr. J. H. Beekman, Mr. J. H. Brown, Mr.
George Brooks, Mr. Brill, Mr. Christian Börs, Mr. J. A.
Benedict.

Through W. J. Beebe: Allin & Evans, C. Amman & Co. (2
bags), B. G. Arnold & Co. (2 bags), Beebe Bros., Bucklin,
Crane & Co., S. C. Bendick, Beard & Cummings, Allie L.
Beebe, C. W. Durant, A Friend, Penfold, Chatfield & Co.,
Murdock, Fisher & Co., Stanton, Sheldon & Co., Wm. Scott
& Sons, George S. Scott, C. V. A. Schuyler & Son (2 bags.)

Coleman & Co., J. H. V Cockroft, R. S. Clarke, Bowie Dash, S.
Davidson, C. Dowling, Doyle & Hueston, J. H. Ellis, T. R.
Edson, 2 East 35th Street, J. P. G. Foster, A Friend of Rev.
Dr. Peters (2 bags), Henry Graham, B. W. Griswold, L. R.
Green, Wm. P. Howell, John Higgins, P. H. Holt, Valentin
Kettman, P. V. King & Co., E. H. Ludlow, L. P. Morton,
R. McDonald, Albert McNulty, Henry Morgan, John and Mary
O'Shea, Levi Pawling, A. Polhemus (2 bags), J. A. Prigge, J.
J. Petit, J. W. Quincy, Richardson, Boynton & Co., C. B.
Ransom, Chandler Robbins, R. W. Rodman, Alfred Roe, N.
H. Sabin, Alfred Schermerhorn, B. Schlesinger, R. L.

Schieffelln, W. A. Stevens, John A. Stephens, Maj. Gen. C. W. Sanford, Wm. H. Thompson, R. W. Thompson, M. Ulshoeffer, E. H. Van Buren, J. F. Williams, Edward Wood, Wm. Whitlock (3 bags), Mr. White, Mr. Zimmerman through Mrs. Kentor.

Margie and Bennie, Master Gordon Knox Bell, Master Van Horn Stuyvesant, Paul, Ruth, Elsie and Addie Tiemann, (4 bags), Mr. Thos. Watts' Children (10 bags).

CLOTHING, 51 BAGS.

Anonymous, (2 bags), Mrs. M. Baldwin, Mrs. Bishop, Mrs. Draper, Mrs. S. R. Dorrance, Mrs. Austin Flint, Jr., Mrs. H. H. Garner, Mrs. Gerry, Mrs. D. S. Jackson, Mrs. J. F. Kernochan, Mrs. Leavitt, Mrs. Lamborn, Mrs. A. N. Lawrence, Mrs. Livingston, Mrs. Millbank, Mrs. Morse, Mrs. C. Myers, Mrs. Samuel Pike, Mrs. Frank E. Richmond, Mrs. Slade, Mrs. W. C. Schermerhorn, Mrs. George S. Stringfleld, Mrs. T. G. Thomas, Mrs. Von Post, Mrs. Richard Vose. Miss S. Cammann, Miss L. Clarkson, Miss Alice Crawford, Misses Amy and Edith Draper, Miss Fanny Martin, Miss Murdock, Miss Annie Paulding, Miss Julia Pierrepont, Miss M. J. Somerville, Miss Scott, Miss Nelly Rodenstein, Miss C. L. Wolfe (2 bags), Miss Whittingham, Mr. J. Colles, Mr. A. Dempewolf, Mr. Wm. M. Evarts, Mr. A. Gallatin, Mr. P. S. Halstead, Mr. Lowell Lincoln, Mr. G. H. Talman, Mr. Terhune, Mr. F. A. Thompson, (2 bags), Master John K. French.

TOYS, CANDY, BOOKS, AND MISCELLANEOUS,
56 Bags.

Anonymous (3 bags), Mrs. C. C. Baldwin, Mrs. N. P. Beebe, Mrs. D. C. Blodgett, Mrs. Carey, Mrs. C. A. Cammann, Mrs. J. W. Drexel, Mrs. Dresser's Children, Mrs. E. A. Duyckinck, Mrs. Everdell, Mrs. Embury, Mrs. Rufus Hatch, Mrs. Hartley, Mrs. O. H. Jones, Mrs. N. Lawrence, Mrs. E. L. Ludlow, Mrs. Leroy, (2 bags), Mrs. Parkin, Mrs. Phoenix, Mrs. Chas. Rhinelander, Mrs. Wolcott Richards, Mrs. J. B. Slawson, (2 bags), Mrs. W. P. Talboys, Mrs. C. S. Weyman, Mrs. S. J. Zabriskie, Madame Mears, Miss Belle Ballantyne, Miss S. Cammann, Miss Frost, Miss Mary Hitchcock, Miss M. H. Lawrence, Miss Morgan, Miss Susan

Pell, Miss Eliza de Rham, Miss Slawson, Miss C. E. S. Stuyvesant, the Misses Ripley, the Misses and Master Willard, G. W. Bruce, T. H. Faile, E. L. Molineux, Geo. W. Powers, W. L. Pomeroy, Charles de Rham, F. S. Winston, Bennie and Hannah, J. C. Hull's Sons, Little Madeleine Livingston, Louisa and Jack Morgan, Master Reginald H. Sayre, Lulu and Mabel Van Rensselaer, Freddy Ware.

RECEIVED FOR CHRISTMAS 1872.

Mrs. Jas. R. Boyd, $5; Mrs. D. T. Brown, $5; Mrs. Brown, through Miss Wilkes, $10; Mr. Stewart Brown, $20; Miss Kate Bell, $20; Mrs. Henry Bucking, through Dr. Rodenstein, $10; Mrs. Commodore Eagle, $2; Mrs. Ann R. Edwards, $5; Mr. Wm. M. Evarts, $5; Mrs. Dresser's Children, $2; Miss A. J. Garner, $10; Mr. J. Montgomery Hare, $10; Mrs. Thomas J. Lloyd, $10, Dr. Jenkins, $10; Mr. and Mrs. Daniel Le Roy, $10; Mrs. Eliza Lee, $5; Miss E. Low, $10; Mrs. W. K. Kitchen, $10; Mr. Henry W. Morris, $5; Miss Mary W. Sackett, $4; Mr. and Mrs. Wm. Alex. Smith, $10; Mr. Robert Smith, $5; The Misses Stephens, $10; Children of Seabury Hall; Phil. Rhinelander, $2; Joseph Holley, $0 50; Epinger Children, $0 50; De Forest Bostwick, $0 50; Mrs. C. A. Sherman, $3; Miss Annie Paulding, $2 25; Miss A. Tiemann, $5; Miss Julia A. Tiemann, $5; M. H. Mallory & Co., (advertising bill) $2 40; Horace Porter, $5.

FOR PIAZZA.

Mrs. R. F. Ware, $5; Mr. D. Clarkson, through Mrs. R. F. Ware, $20.

January, 1873.

Basket of New Year Cake, Mrs. D. F. Tiemann; 3 vols. Sermons to Children, Messrs. E. P. Dutton & Co.; bag of Lemons, Messrs. Acker, Merrall & Condit; 6 vols. for the Library, and 3 Photographs, Rev. Dr. Peters; box of Clothing, Miss Harriet White; 18 fancy boxes of Candy for the Sewing-class, Miss Julia A. Tiemann; 12 pounds Gelatine, Mr. William Cooper; half gallon Turpentine, 25 pounds Paris White, 20 pounds French Zinc, 1½ pounds White Glue, ¼ pound Ultra Blue, Messrs. D. F. Tiemann & Co.; Christmas bag of Sugar, Louie Lee; Christmas bag of Clothing, Mrs. H. Spofford; 2 parcels of Clothing, the Misses Baretto, through Mrs. Everett; Appleton's Journal for 1872 and 1873, Mr. P. C. Tiemann; 8 pairs knit Stockings, Mrs. J. W. Livingston; Children's Magazine for 1873, May Peters; Lamb, Mr. J. B. Churchill; 24 yards Canton Flannel, Mrs. A. C. Russell; 6 dozen Prayer Books, N. Y. Bible and Common Prayer Book Society, through Mr. Jas. Pott; 3 vols. for the Library, Mrs. H. C. Von Post; Christmas bag of Cakes and Clothing, Miss Marcia Sherrell; Letter-balance, Messrs. Fairbanks & Co.; Kit of Mackerel and 2 cans Peaches, Miss J. A. Tiemann.

ASSISTANCE IN SEWING. Making of 29 Aprons, Ladies of St. Luke's Church, Matteawan; making of 9 Canton Flannel Skirts, Ladies of St. James' Church, Great Barrington; making of 6 Aprons and 22 Towels, St. Michael's Ant Hill.

ASSISTANCE in WRITING. Miss Peters, Miss M. Tiemann.

FOR NEW YEAR'S DAY.

Mrs. W. B. Bishop, $5; Mr. and Mrs. G. W. Read, $5; Two Old Friends, $4; Miss Julia Baretto, $3; Mr. D. Sanford, $2; Cash, through Mrs. Keator, $1.

February.

20 new Garments, Employment Society of the Church of the Intercession, Carmansville, through Mrs. E. K. Willard; 3 new Bureau-Washstands, Mrs. F. S. Church, 400 Oranges, Mrs. B. H. Field; 14 Dresses, 2 Aprons, 5 White Skirts, all new, Mrs. Phœnix; Cakes for the Nursery, Mrs. Burchard; Atlantic Magazine for 1872 and 1873, Mr. P. C. Tiemann; Children's Friend for 1873, Elsie Tiemann; Infant's Magazine for 1873, Addie Tiemann; Harper's Weekly for 1873, Mrs. Peters.

ASSISTANCE IN SEWING. Making of 6 Dresses, Misses Sherrill; making of 48 Aprons, Ladies of St. Luke's Church, Matteawan; making of 16 Aprons and 10 Towels, St. Michael's Ant Hill.

March.

Parcel of Clothing, Miss Anna D. R. Wood; Oranges and Lemons, Messrs. Acker, Merrall & Condit; Quilt and 5

Garments, Mrs. M. H. Beard; Parcel of Clothing, Mrs. Richard Vose; 1 dozen Question Books, Messrs. E. P. Dutton & Co.

ASSISTANCE IN SEWING. Making of 12 Aprons and 12 Towels, St. Michael's Ant Hill.

April.

Secor Sewing Machine, Mr. E. Miller, through Mrs. R. F. Ware; 6 dozen pocket-handkerchiefs, 2 dozen spools of cotton, 23 yards of calico, a dinner-set, and 10 dozen Easter eggs, Mrs. D. F. Tiemann; Pictures for Easter eggs, Mrs. Newhall; 1,000 Paper napkins, Julius Schlueter; Candy for Easter, Mrs. E. Martin; 12 dresses, 2 under garments, Mrs. Phœnix; Hot cross buns for Good Friday, Mr. R. Prior; 30 trees, Mrs. Archibald Watt; Barrel of flour, Mr. W. G. Langdon; $5 " for the Wolfe boys," Mrs. B. H. Field; Box of blocks, A. W. C; Parcel of clothing, Mrs. E. E. Anderson, 5 dresses, 5 aprons, 4 garments, 3 dolls, scrap-book and several toys, "Cheerful Givers of the Church of the Good Shepherd, West Springfield, Mass.; 27 articles of clothing, Lenten work of Mrs. Hitchcock's Sunday School class, St. Peter's Church, Morristown, N. J.; Shawl, Miss Sarah McGunigle; Oranges, Acker, Merrall & Condit; 18 garments, 14 pictures, 8 horns of candy, Miss C. E. Wolbert and her pupils—Nellie V. C. Phelps, Kitty Wright, Nellie Fowler, Julia Pinckey, Maria Wellmann.

ASSISTANCE IN SEWING.

Making of 21 aprons, Helping Hand Society of St. Ann's Church; Making 3 dozen towels, St. Michael's Ant Hill.

FRESH AIR FUND.

$5—Grace, Ella, Willie and Nettie Whitlock.

PRAYERS

TO BE USED BY THE FRIENDS OF

"The Sheltering Arms."

ALMIGHTY and most merciful Father, whose well beloved Son, our Saviour, did welcome the young children to His arms and bless them, look with pity, we beseech Thee, upon these little ones committed to our care, that, being shielded from temptation and delivered from evil, they may glorify Thy holy name, and finally, by Thy mercy, obtain everlasting life, through Jesus Christ, our Lord. AMEN.

Oh, Lord God and Heavenly Father! infinite in love and full of mercy, send down thine Holy Spirit, as upon all friendless children and orphans, so especially upon these little ones, whom Thou hast given into our keeping. Grant that the old Adam in these children may be so buried, that the new man may be raised up in them.

Grant that all sinful affections may die in them, and that all things belonging to the Spirit may live and grow in them.

Grant that they may have power and strength to have victory, and to triumph against the devil, the world, and the flesh.

Grant that, being dedicated to Thee, they may also be endued with heavenly virtues, and everlastingly rewarded, through Thy mercy, O blessed Lord God, who dost live and govern all things, world without end. AMEN.

www.ingramcontent.com/pod-product-compliance
Lightning Source LLC
Chambersburg PA
CBHW032359230426
43672CB00007B/753